MW01716998

Musical Performance in the Diaspora

This book examines the place of musical performance in diasporic experience and politics. It illustrates how ethnographic investigation of musical performance may contribute to the analysis of diaspora. The essays explore diverse examples: calibration and contradiction in representations of Caribbean diasporic performance, postcolonial perspectives on colonial encounters through readings of a French West Indian folk song, memories of a Kazakh homeland in Western Mongolia, celebrations of Diwali in New Zealand, mourning and cultures of survival amongst Aboriginal and Jewish communities in Australia, and cosmopolitanism in strategic diasporic identity formation in Peru.

Some of the topics discussed in *Musical Performance in the Diaspora* include:

- the expression and shaping of diasporic and postcolonial identities through performance
- musical memory in diasporic contexts
- the gendered dimensions of diasporic performance
- the impact of state policies on diasporic performance
- the politics of 'new' forms of diasporic music-making

Presenting a rich array of theoretical approaches and wide-ranging ethnographic case studies, this book challenges uncritical notions of diasporic 'hybridity', broadens current analyses of performance in the diaspora, and draws attention to the ethical demands and political work of ethnography.

This book was previously published as a special issue of *Ethnomusicology Forum.*

Tina K. Ramnarine is Professor of Music at Royal Holloway University of London. She is the author of *Creating Their Own Space: the Development of an Indian-Caribbean Musical Tradition* (University of West Indies Press, 2001), *Ilmatar's Inspirations: Nationalism, Globalization, and the Changing Soundscapes of Finnish Folk Music* (University of Chicago Press, 2003), and *Beautiful Cosmos: Performance and Belonging in the Caribbean Diaspora* (Pluto Press, 2007).

Musical Performance in the Diaspora

Edited by Tina K. Ramnarine

Routledge
Taylor & Francis Group
LONDON AND NEW YORK

First published 2007 by Routledge

2 Park Square, Milton Park, Abingdon, Oxon OX14 4RN
711 Third Avenue, New York, NY 10017, USA

Routledge is an imprint of the Taylor & Francis Group, an informa business

First issued in paperback 2016

Typeset in Minion by Datapage International Ltd, Dublin, Ireland

British Library Cataloguing in Publication Data
A catalogue record for this book is available from the British Library

ISBN 13: 978-0-415-43972-5 (hbk)
ISBN 13: 978-1-138-99430-0 (pbk)

Contents

Musical Performance in the Diaspora: Introduction

Tina K. Ramnarine

'Is a lie so big even history believe it.' This is a line repeated twice in *Goodbye Columbus*, referring to the lie that 'Columbus could die'. In this rapso, Brother Resistance sings about the continuing effects of the development of plantation economies, importation of labour forces from around the world and modification of insular ecosystems that have characterized the Caribbean since 1492. It is part of a huge song repertoire dealing with themes of diaspora and postcolonial politics and reflecting the Caribbean as a site of diasporic encounter.

Attention to human mobility has expanded traditional frames of reference, which study music in a specific cultural and geographic location. Diaspora has been

---

Tina K. Ramnarine is Reader in Music at Royal Holloway University of London. She is author of *Creating their own space: The development of an Indian-Caribbean musical tradition* (University of West Indies Press, 2001), *Ilmatar's inspirations: Nationalism, globalization, and the changing soundscapes of Finnish folk music* (University of Chicago Press, 2003), and *Beautiful cosmos: Performance and belonging in the Caribbean Diaspora* (Pluto Press, in press).

highlighted in attempts to analyse musical performances in contemporary global processes and human migrations. Diaspora often articulates with historical sensibilities and postcolonial politics, offering perspectives on the legacies of empires, historiographies and modes of cultural representation. Diaspora, then, is something more than simply migration. A classical concern in diaspora studies has been the relationship between diasporic context and a homeland elsewhere, with displacement, transnationalism and nationalism appearing as central analytical tropes. Among the research methods ethnographers have developed to investigate diasporic networks are multi-sited fieldwork and virtual (Internet) searches. Today, conceptual understandings of 'diaspora' are becoming increasingly eclectic, with the term achieving greater applications in ways that risk overlooking memories of violence in the shaping of many diasporic sensibilities.

While diaspora has something to do with 'history' it is also about 'newness'. Ethnographic research has encompassed both modes, from analysis of historical specificity, musical memory and the preservation of tradition to the musical creativities, new performance spaces and new musical sounds of diasporic practices. The former mode reminds us that diasporas are historically specific and that the past shapes a sense of diasporic identity while the latter prompts us to question the rigidities and essentialisms of 'diasporic identity'. The politics of diasporic identities often articulate with the politics of national, postcolonial and/or minority identities, leading to fresh sets of specificity and rigidity in thinking about diaspora. As Eric Williams wrote in his famous formulation at the outset of postcolonial national sovereignty in Trinidad and Tobago, 'There can be no Mother India ... There can be no Mother Africa ... There can be no Mother England ... There can be no Mother China ... There can be no Mother Syria or no Mother Lebanon ... The only Mother we recognise is Mother Trinidad and Tobago' (1964, 279). If the contradictions between asserting specificity and avoiding rigidity make sense to ethnographers, how might we theorize the contradictions themselves?

One way of responding to this question is to plunge into the problematics of otherness. We can begin with diasporic groups becoming settled in new homelands in societies that often come to be described as 'multicultural'. The multicultural society places the diasporic subject in a category of difference. Embedded in the ideology of the 'multi' is the contradiction of all living together, all different. Thus Agawu refers to multiculturalism in his essay, 'Contesting difference', to ask how one might decide (say an ethnomusicologist) if a culture is 'sufficiently different' for study, a judgement which must be made in relation to 'a prior set of analytical acts' since differences are 'not simply there for the perceiving subject' (2003, 232–3). It is instructive to bear in mind the contradiction of the 'multi' and Agawu's point about the presumptions that shape ethnographic research when thinking about diasporic musical practice. In Slobin's (2003) overview of the study of diaspora in ethnomusicology, we see the perpetuation of the model of 'a society with a music' that has been one of the discipline's cornerstones. This model is tenacious, even as it becomes complicated when applied to music in contexts of migration, diasporas, multicultural societies and transnational circulations. Thus Slobin writes about 'diasporic neighbourhoods' (where cultural borders might still be contained within geographically defined parameters in a multicultural society) and cites Averill on Haitians in New York living in diaspora, 'posed between cultures' (1998, 146). More importantly, Slobin alerts the reader to how little has changed in ethnomusicological perception despite the emergence of diaspora discourse in this academic field in the 1990s. 'Traditionally', he notes, 'we talked about immigrants, or minorities, or ethnic groups, and much effort went toward figuring out "acculturation"' (2003, 285). If the more recent discourses on diaspora and diasporic cultural production in terms of 'hybridity' do not seem so far removed from earlier analytical formulations and ethnographic representations, Slobin rightly points out that the subtleties of diaspora discourse as being more than just about demographics have also been embraced by ethnomusicologists. Diasporas have been understood as non-uniform, historical and political formulations. As such, they encourage us to look beyond music and people on the move as merely complicating our cherished conceptual presumptions about music mapped onto geographies and societies. Diaspora as something more than a question of demographics challenges us to rethink some of our paradigms.

Identity, of course, provides a stumbling block to rather more radical reconceptualizations that might be fostered by the diasporic turn within ethnomusicology, for the people we work with also assert, celebrate and maintain 'diasporic identities'. The diasporic subject is thus constructed as different from all sides. For the diasporic subject, questions of identity are inextricable from the past and from his/her relationship to a former homeland, whether or not that home is several times removed through generations. Where the diaspora has formed as the result of violent encounter in which the past has been ruptured, as has been the case in many colonial projects, a sense of diasporic identity has enabled the diasporic subject to feel connected to a precolonial history. Holding onto a sense of 'the loss of not having had that loss to lose' as the character Alford George does in the novel *Salt* (Earl Lovelace 1996, 256) plays a crucial role in adherence to specific identities and resurfaces in postcolonial projects. Music is central to these projects. Hall argues that difference matters and the challenge is to capture a 'sense of difference which is not pure "otherness"' (1996 [1990], 115). He refers to the discovery of 'blackness' and the legacies of 'slavery' in Jamaica of the 1970s, a discovery which:

> could only be made through the impact on popular life of the post-colonial revolution, the civil rights struggles, the culture of Rastafarianism and the music of reggae—the metaphors, the figures or signifiers of a new construction of 'Jamaican-ness'. These signified a 'new' Africa of the New World, grounded in an 'old' Africa:—a spiritual journey of discovery that led, in the Caribbean, to an indigenous cultural revolution; this is Africa, as we might say, necessarily 'deferred'—as a spiritual, cultural and political metaphor. (Hall 1996 [1990], 116)

Deferral alerts us that sometimes the point is not the extent to which the past can be reconstructed in the diaspora, but that its traces are felt at all. As Gilroy writes, 'contemporary musical forms of the African diaspora work within an aesthetic and political framework which demands that they ceaselessly reconstruct their own histories, folding back on themselves time and again to celebrate and validate the simple, unassailable *fact of their survival*' (1993, 37, emphasis added). While the diasporic subject's desire to reclaim a past that extends into the precolonial era reinforces diasporic difference, the relocation of that same subject (often in former colonial Metropolitan centres) has also challenged notions of culture, particularly of national culture, as Gilroy (1987) has theorised extensively. Multicultural discourses (which embrace diasporic communities as a part of multicultural societies) also become implicated in the promotion of revisions to nationalist ones. But how successful are these revisions? Gilroy notes that diaspora 'allows for a complex conception of sameness and for versions of solidarity that do not need to repress the differences within a dispersed group in order to maximize the differences between one 'essential' community and others' (2000, 252). The essentialisms of both diaspora and multiculturalism raise problematic issues about 'ethnicity', a site of difference to which I shall return, but the distinctions between 'difference' articulated above reveal contrasting approaches to the politics of otherness.

Musical 'Calibrations'

Drawing on my own ethnographic research on the Caribbean Diaspora in Britain, I would like to offer a few thoughts on how history, difference, identity and multiculturalism are calibrated in musical performance and cultural display. From a steelband concert given in 1951 in a hall newly constructed in the tide of post-war optimism (the Royal Festival Hall) to contemporary post-Notting Hill Carnival celebrations as part of 'Black History Month' in the institutional setting of the Victoria and Albert Museum, contrasting interpretative moves regarding these performances lead us into different routes through the diasporic and multicultural maze. Previously, I have been exploring Carnival performance events in urban public spaces in thinking through a series of questions about the politics of ethnicity, multiculturalisms, and the ways in which minority and/or diasporic status are embedded in, challenge and transform national life (Ramnarine 2004a, in press). In re-reading some of these performances here I turn to Ato Queyson's literary theory of reading for the social, drawing on the idea of 'calibrations' by way of testing its application to the analysis of musical performance in multicultural contexts and drawing attention to an ongoing ethnomusicological commitment to musical ethnicities.

Queyson relates an anecdote about a reading primer that was used in schools in Nigeria in the 1960s, and which was studied by Anthonia Kalu as a schoolchild. The primer featured the following lines:

> This is a man.
> This is a pan.
> A man.
> A pan.
> A man and a pan.

In Trinidad and Tobago such a reading primer would not have caused any bafflement, for it might have been read as referring to the steelpan, a musical rather than a cooking instrument and, indeed, one dominated by male practitioners in the 1960s. But, for Kalu, the baffling question was why a man and a pan? Eventually Kalu suggested that the man and a pan had nothing to do with African general experience which would have placed women in cooking roles, but referenced the domestic arrangements of colonial households in which cooks were often male. As such, a seemingly 'innocent' reading primer becomes a tool for naturalizing colonial domination in the minds of children and leads them to forms of cultural comparison later on in life. The man and a pan anecdote is a good illustration of what is meant by calibrations as used by Ato Queyson, who calls for calibration as 'a form of close reading of literature with what lies beyond it as a way of understanding structures of transformation, process, and contradiction that inform both literature and society' (2003, xi). While the term is used in engineering to refer to the processes of fine-tuning instruments, Queyson writes that he intends 'calibration' to mean 'that situated procedure of attempting to wrest something from the aesthetic domain for the analysis and better understanding of the social' (2003, xv). In this enterprise, he presents calibrated readings that confront us with issues of comparison, and with the disjunctures between social reality, representation and translation—themes with which ethnomusicologists are all too familiar as they correspond to much debated ethnographic problems highlighted in critiques about the production of ethnographic texts.

Given the profound debates over these issues within the ethnographic disciplines, why turn to this notion of calibration? What insights can it provide into diasporic musical practice, the politics of multiculturalism or questions about the 'administering' of musical ethnicities? One of the themes for the 2006 meeting of the European Seminar in Ethnomusicology was 'administering musical ethnicity—to whom, by whom, with what consequences?' I thought there was something very interesting about the choice of verb in this theme. 'Administering' implies some kind of imposition or at least some process of enabling. Administering involves more than one actor—someone administering to someone else. It highlights agents and agency in the politics and performance of diaspora and in establishing power relations. Administering fits well with anthropological debates about the display of others in museum spaces, with the idea of cultural comparison and with state policies on multiculturalism. Contemporary diaspora discourse can also be understood in terms of 'administering', for 'diaspora' is a term that often seems to be presented as synonymous with 'ethnic group' or is defined in terms of 'ethnicity'. Of course, in the anthropological sense of group construction and relationship (cf. Eriksen 1993) a diasporic group is an ethnic group. But there are confusions over ethnicity, which involve 'race' discourse and minority status (see Eriksen 1993, 4). Analysis of diasporas cannot be limited to these issues, even if they are pressing ones for various diasporas, including the Caribbean Diaspora in Britain. The confusions over diaspora and ethnicity nevertheless provide a good example of the possible applications of calibration, in the sense of conceptual fine-tuning. Is the turn to diaspora within academic debate simply another approach to 'new' ethnicities? More important than terminology and categorization, what appeals to me in the metaphor of calibration is the emphasis on things not fitting, on adjustments in the musical and social worlds, and on the contradictions between discourses. With calibration we do not necessarily reach a resolution. We are left with chipping away at pieces that do not match. In contrast to musical metaphors that highlight processes of flow, accommodation and harmony, calibration grates and therefore seems to reflect the social world (and academic debate) more truthfully. The metaphor of calibration leaves a space for confronting the discomforts of diaspora as it converges with racism, discrimination, violence and inequality.

Calibration is not about homologies between the aesthetic and the social. A significant dimension of a calibrated reading is that it highlights the disjunctures between representations and realities. Queyson notes the problem of this disjuncture as persisting in:

> the difficulty in ascertaining the minimum requirements for a representation to be actually perceived as invoking a reality beyond it. . .we can gauge that what persists unanswered in many theories of [representation] is what it is that allows a spectator or reader to recognize something as representing something else when the representational nexus relies on forms of conceptual translation of phenomena of apparently startling incommensurability. . .in other words how do we psychologically grasp the representation as relevant to anything beyond it? (Queyson 2003, xxiv)

This emphasis on representations being divorced from the realities beyond might be applied to models of the 'multicultural society', for models are representations, tools to make sense of the social world. Two contradictory models of the multicultural society are either to emphasize cultural exchanges resulting in various 'fusions' that characterize global cities like London or to foster a view of various cultural groupings maintaining distinct traditions. The former model contains an aspiration to inclusiveness but can also be linked to ideas about integration, homogeneity and the potential loss of cultural distinctiveness. The second model, by contrast, promotes 'cultural diversity' and a view of culturally separate groups inhabiting the same (usually urban) spaces. Both models rest on assumptions of difference. Both models invite cultural comparisons. In fact, much multicultural discourse favours the second model. As Lundberg, Malm and Ronström note, the concept of multiculturalism stems from discourses in the USA in the 1960s which focused on ethnic groupings that were seen as being part of a 'mosaic'—and therein lies the contradiction of multiculturalism: 'Society and cultural life is seen as divided into clearly defined groups. The ideal is inclusivity at society level and exclusivity at group level. Ethnic activists, purists and the various groups' politicians guard the borders of the mosaic tiles' (2003, 42). Strategies for inclusion and exclusion thus compete with each other, nevertheless having to coexist. Lundberg, Malm and Ronström observe the effects of multicultural ideologies with reference to the Swedish case, but their observations can be usefully applied to other contexts too. There are 'troublesome' consequences to linking multiculturalism with ethnic groups. Diversity becomes both a 'diversity of expression' and a 'diversity of cultures', to the extent that differences between groups are over-emphasized, groups are rendered homogeneous, and the contributions made by members of one group to the cultural expressions of other groups are rendered invisible (see Lundberg, Malm and Ronström 2003, 43). Borders between groups in the multicultural society come into focus together with the emergent creative expressions, often described in terms of 'hybridity', that mark crossings over them. The paradox is that borders come into focus precisely because 'hybridity' blurs their clear demarcations, shifting attention from the multicultural to national and transnational networks, bringing into tension the political urges of ethnic transnationalism and regionalism, and foregrounding creative exchanges in transnational arenas. The border is a metaphoric and literal marker that simultaneously affirms and challenges people's sense of identity and difference.

A purely celebratory approach to multiculturalism or to hybridity that continues to understand cultures as essentially discrete, defining their borders and attaching equal value to them (and we might note that ethnomusicologists have tended towards 'happy hybridity' in these ways: see Lo 2000), obscures everyday interaction that moves beyond borders on one hand and political inequity, racism and social disadvantage on the other. If we change the paradigms how do we understand musical life in a multicultural society? Diasporic music-making should not be understood as merely the result of population movements, the settlements of diasporic groups and cultural contact in the multicultural society. Rather, diasporic music-making can be understood in the ordinariness of creative production, as musicians working as individual agents in their everyday environments, making musical choices that suit them and their audiences. In moving beyond simple understandings of hybridity as musical cultures in contact that result in 'new' musical expressions we move towards politically articulated readings of social relations and creative processes. Blacking, for example, argued not for the multicultural but for the multi-musical in which the aesthetic dimensions of music might transcend its social and cultural ones. Writing about the teaching of music in schools, he suggested that the aim 'must not be to reinforce tribal boundaries or to encourage tokenism... music education should not be used to emphasize culture, because as soon as that happens there arise arguments about cultural hegemony, as well as false notions of what culture is' (1987, 149). Current theorization of musical hybridity might lead us to question where the boundaries of the multi-musical lie in terms similar to the vagaries of the multicultural. Blacking, nevertheless, points to a critique of the culture concept that has gained theoretical ground in the past decade. Music in the diaspora likewise suggests we radically rethink the 'place' of 'culture', and, if we also discard 'ethnicity', we can take another look at knowledge of peoples, places and reified domains of cultures (cf. Ramnarine 2004b).

Museums, however, are spaces in which cultures are made visible. Things are put on display. But how are those things represented in museums and how do spectators understand them? Following the Carnival arts in museum spaces in London gives visibility to the ways in which musical and cultural expressions are forged through interaction, through movements 'between' groups and through shared experiences of musical practice. Such shared experiences compel us to critically assess the contradictions of 'multiculturalism' and rethink the epistemological ideologies—particularly the emphasis on discrete cultures—that underscore the 'multicultural'. As part of 'Black History Month', post-Carnival performances were clearly mapped onto a particular ethnic group and framed by an understanding of the multicultural society that highlights discrete cultures. But, as Queyson emphasizes, there is a disjuncture between the representation (of a particular ethnic group performing Carnival in the museum in Black History Month) and the reality of what we actually observe (which is open participation in the Carnival performances). The visibility and audibility of Carnival museum performances might challenge some of our representations of the multicultural society.

The challenge has been accepted by theorists who have turned to models like interculturalism in exploring, as Bharucha puts it, 'different modes of citizenship across different national contexts, through subjectivities that are less mediated by the agencies of the state' (2001, 42). Yet, interculturalism does not provide ready solutions to the problems of otherness. Bharucha notes that the desire for creative interaction in intercultural encounter 'is fraught with tensions, compulsions, hidden agendas, and funding realities' and that the exchange is 'extremely fragile, based more on intuition and good faith than on any real cognizance of the Other' (2001, 46).

The museum space itself returns us to issues about cultural comparison and dominating powers that were raised in the man and a pan story earlier on. In *Objects and others*, Stocking notes that museums are the 'archives of material culture' involving 'relations of power' in that 'objects thrown in the way of observers in the museums were once those of others'. Market processes also influence museums such that its objects come to be regarded as 'fine art' and thereby undergo 'processes of aestheticization' (1985). Many of the activities offered in the Carnival performances at the Victoria and Albert Museum, such as face painting and costume design, could be read as instructing the spectator in the aesthetic dimensions of Carnival arts. The costumes are objects that can be regarded as examples of material culture and fine arts. To what extent are we viewing the objects of others when viewing Carnival arts in the museum? Reading the museum spaces in terms of the issues that distanced anthropology from museum collections—the repatriation of cultural property, rightful ownership, the circumstances of acquisition, control over the representation of the meaning of objects—conforms to and confirms tropes of cultural diversity and cultural comparison. The post-Carnival performances at the Victoria and Albert Museum could be viewed as a cultural display of an 'Other', of museum space temporarily given to highlighting one of Britain's multicultural groupings, as an institutional facilitation of cultural comparison. This representation is at odds with my earlier observations on performance participation. For a calibrated reading, therefore, a key question might be about the terms of comparison. Who sets them? Goulbourne writes that 'it is hardly necessary to detail the obvious cultural presence of Caribbean people in Britain, but it is important to note that this presence continues to have a significant impact in various areas of British national life' (2001, 16). The 'visibility' and 'audibility' of Carnival arts (to use Goulbourne's descriptors of DJs and loud music in clubs) also transformed the museum space by overturning expectations about objects on display—after all, these were performances not only objects—by questioning the representation of musical ethnicities, and by reversing relations of power invested in museum collections. Entering this institutional space as a Carnival practitioner might be a gesture in harnessing institutional power in the struggles over representation, following Lidchi's comment that the processes of organizing displays 'require both symbolic and institutional power' (1997, 205). Asserting rights to space have been part of establishing Caribbean Carnival performance in Britain and debates about Carnival urban routes remain current. A museum display is only a temporary claim to urban institutional spaces. Thus Riggio describes such a claim as a 'transgressive appropriation' of spaces, which emphasizes that masqueraders are 'cultural intruders in territory not their own' (2004, 25). Such a view is in contrast to one Carnival practitioner's statement that the Victoria and Albert museum with its display of culture was an appropriate place for Carnival also 'rich in culture and heritage' (a comment by Roy McEwen, representative of the Caribbean Music Association). Ownership over spaces, and ownership of culture and heritage reinforce cultural comparison, the mosaics of multicultural understandings of society and diasporic sensibilities. But histories and geographies are much more intertwined than that. Thus, the study of diaspora often requires postcolonial analysis too.

The 1951 steelband performance to which I referred earlier was given by the *Trinidad All Steel Percussion Orchestra* (*TASPO*) at the Festival of Britain celebrations on the South Bank in London. Contemporary steelband projects all over Europe can be traced to this debut performance. The festival was one way of displaying other parts of Britain, through its empire, and thereby also putting the world on display. In the postcolonial present, the debates at the level of local government around Notting Hill Carnival are about how to market what has become Europe's largest street festival as a tourist industry, thereby revealing the extent to which diasporic and postcolonial sensibilities have changed over the past half century. Postcolonial re-readings of cultures performed, histories and otherness together with postcolonial political movements have contributed to changing representations and realities. I hope that what might be indicated by these few ethnographic details on Carnival performance is the scope of ethnographic enquiry once we ask the kinds of questions that take us beyond the comforts of familiar conceptual models. What does non-Caribbean participation in Carnival performance events tell us about the restrictions of multicultural models? How can you tell who is Caribbean and who is not? A belief in musical ethnicity is allied with a commitment to the idea of multicultural society as a mosaic of clearly defined groups, rendering some participants in Carnival performances visible, and others, invisible (see Figure 1). The study of musical performance in diasporic contexts should have the potential to offer more than a variation on familiar models in which musical and social worlds are carved up all too neatly.

But here I must pause. The challenge to invisibility we note in diasporic musical production and identity construction is also met in 'hyphenated identities' (e.g. Black British, Asian American) that highlight multiplicity. Here diaspora becomes a trope that takes on some of the analytical characteristics of hybridity (somewhat ironic given the latter's roots in the obsessions with categorization), similarly obscuring singular sensibilities. Yet the multiplicity, like the 'multi' of the multicultural, is subject to unceasing division. As Radhakrishnan (2003) asks in writing about his children's experiences of life through the frames of hyphenated identity, what are the relations between 'ethnic self' and 'national status'? I do not like the question with its assumed rigidities on the construction of identities even as I reproduce it here. But it is a question that points to some of the dilemmas in hyphenated diasporic sensibilities. Asking questions about hyphenated identities leads to an examination of the very concept of ethnicity:

> If ethnic identity is a strategic response to a shifting sense of time and place, how is it possible to have a theory of ethnic identity posited on the principle of a natural and native self? . . . Is ethnic selfhood an end in itself, or is it a necessary but determinate phase to be left behind when the time is right to inaugurate the 'post-ethnic'? (Radhakrishnan 2003, 121–2)

Will the post-ethnic result in the triumph of the national? Or would the post-ethnic have to be allied with the post-national too? The alliances and/or non-alliances between ethnic sensibility and national status remind us of the terminological slippages between 'ethnicity' in its anthropological sense of group boundary constructions and its popular conflations with 'race' discourse, where the borders of ethnic belonging are mapped onto images of the body.

In reflecting on some of the routes through which the construction of diasporic hyphenated identities might take us, my point is not that diaspora results in binary categorizations (the hyphen) but that we should question the models that might lead us into thinking that it does. The polarities of hyphenated identities reduce the tangle of experiences to the straitjackets of ethnicity and nationalism. The social world is more complex than any of the models through which we seek to understand it. In

Figure 1 Carnival at the Victoria and Albert Museum (photographs taken by Tina K. Ramnarine, 2001).

between the mosaics of the multicultural, the polarities of hyphenated diasporic identities, the questioning of culture and ethnicity, and the incommensurabilities of representations and realities, is it any wonder that we might struggle to conceptualize musical performance in the diaspora such that we may be able to 'identify the complexity but not ... let it overwhelm the account' (Slobin 2003, 290)?

Study of musical performance in the diaspora does not allow us to capitulate to the dangers of 'unchanging difference' (Gilroy 2000, 253). The analytical vocabulary, despite its shortcomings, reveals the attempt to understand diasporic musical production as a process with commonly used terms, including intercultural, collaborations, hybridities and 'in-betweeness'. I have found the notion of calibration useful in asking what it is that we look at when we study musical performance in the diaspora and when we observe cultural displays of the diasporic community and the multicultural society. Calibration points to the disjunctures between representations and realities, between the visible and the invisible. It moves away from bipolar models. Instead of trying to work through the complexities of creative 'mixes', it shifts attention to competing claims, theoretical disagreements, and even social and musical realities that might not have much to do with our conceptual models. It resonates with 'the feeling that the many kinds of borders first proposed by the Renaissance, reinforced by the Enlightenment, and institutionalised in the nineteenth century have become increasingly difficult to reconcile with the reality we perceive' (Trouillot 2003, 4). I have turned to calibration to argue against using the diasporic turn as merely another way of labelling and mapping the musical world even as we take into account the specificities of diaspora. Metaphors change. While I have temporarily replaced the resolutions of musical flow (the metaphor that I have turned to most often in trying to portray the social entanglements evoked by musical sounds) for the frictions of calibration, I remain persuaded that ethnographic work, its problems notwithstanding, provides a method for close scrutiny of both flow and contradiction. Ethnographic work reveals how we position ourselves in the political realms of diaspora, postcolonialism, nationalism, ethnicity or multiculturalism to which the study of music takes us. This is why the representation matters and why Brother Resistance questions the truths of scholarship ('even history believe it'). Brother Resistance also offers a new reading: 'I have a duty to tell the true story', paralleling trends in various disciplines (e.g. history, postcolonial studies and ethnomusicology) in re-reading colonial documents and attending to oral histories to hear other accounts of the past. Similarly, performance takes us into unexpected ways of looking at the disjunctures between representation and reality. Gosden and Knowles, writing about New Guinean colonial culture, suggest that a wide range of performances 'were attempting to make real something no one was sure existed' (2001: 15). Contradictions can be as illuminating as they are frustrating. In their wake, the ethical demands and political work of ethnography are foregrounded. Ato Queyson invites us to 'read for the social'. In the spaces of engaged ethnomusicology and political conscience within the academy, we can also *write* for the social.

The Articles in this Volume

This volume focuses on the insights into diaspora that might be offered by ethnographic approaches to musical performance and postcolonial readings of diasporic musical production. The reflections above, drawing on my own most recent ethnographic work on music and diaspora, have been offered by way of presenting various themes explored in this collection (history, homeland, belonging, creativity, multiculturalism, identity, postcolonial politics). The articles that follow present diverse case studies, theoretical approaches and calibrated analyses resulting from the different historical circumstances of various diasporas. Together they emphasize the specificity of diaspora, reveal different contexts in which the term has been applied or claimed, and respond to questions concerning the expression and shaping of diasporic identities through performance. The volume contributes to a growing literature that includes the study of music in relation to particular diasporas, for example the Caribbean Diaspora (Allen and Wilcken 1998), Jewish Diaspora (Kartomi and Dreyfus 2004) and Indian Diaspora (Chaudhuri and Seeger 2007), as well as other cross-cultural collections (Slobin 1994; Turino and Lea 2004). The idea for this volume was formulated in conjunction with co-organizing a one-day conference for the British Forum for Ethnomusicology on 'Diaspora, Postcolonialism and Performance'. The conference focused on how performance contributes to diaspora studies and postcolonial theorization, and aimed to broaden and challenge current analytic models that focus on cultural interactions. Ideas from that conference, particularly with regard to the politics of identity and the body, have found their way into this volume. Contributors focus on music festivals, individual biographies, song texts, musical instruments, intellectual movements, state processes, and the gendered dimensions of diasporic experiences. From economies of desire in colonial encounters (Hill) and performances of mourning that remember ancestors (Breyley) to intercultural borrowings in African Peruvian theatre (León), or from state interventions in creating wider diasporic groups (Johnson) to the connections between musical instruments, their makers, players and places (Post), all of the articles include discussion on relationality. They provide ethnographic and textual details on the production, maintenance and transformation of social relations. Recurring themes include musical memory, the impact of state policies on diasporic performance, social relations and references to home.

Edwin Hill takes up representations of the 'Other' in French imperial mythologies and unpacks complex narratives around the figure of the *doudou* (the black or *métisse* Creole woman). A close reading of her song, 'Adieu madras', takes us from a standard item in the biguine repertoire to moments of colonial encounter, desire and exchange. Through critical engagement with French Enlightenment thought (referring to Rousseau), 20th-century black liberationist writing (drawing on Fanon) and Josephine Baker's film roles, Hill explores the musical, political and social nuances of 'Adieu madras', the constructs of racial thought that place the burdens of colonial differences and hierarchies on the shoulders of the *doudou*, and the *doudou*'s ability to sing through moral ambivalences and social ruptures. By pointing to their colonial equivalents, Hill shows us that there is nothing new in people living through the labels of hyphenated diasporic identities and that colonial and postcolonial representations of them are mutually informative. The song 'Adieu madras' shows how music illuminates some of the complexities around colonial desire and power that have been highlighted in postcolonial critiques (for example, Young 1995). The analysis is an exercise in postcolonial musicological thinking that focuses on the *doudou*'s lament to emphasize attachments between colonial island and imperial metropolis and that might lead into further debate on social relations and colonial legacies to finally free the *doudou* from her cage of 'geography, culture and colour'.

Jennifer Post explores the classic concept of 'homeland' in diaspora studies and points to ideas gaining greater theoretical ground about the making of homes in diasporic contexts. In resonance with the project of rethinking national belonging as argued in Gilroy's key text *There ain't no black in the Union Jack* (1987), she suggests that the homeland is no longer the geographic locations from which Kazakhs in Mongolia were displaced generations ago, but is now in the places they inhabit. Kazakhs in Mongolia are part of a transnational community, but it is significant that, following repatriation to Kazakhstan from the early 1990s onwards, there has been a pattern of Kazakh populations re-migrating to Mongolia. Drawing on the notion of ethnoscape and pointing to the ancestral histories of Kazakhs in Mongolia, a musical instrument, the *dombra*, provides a way into looking at the maintenance of a sense of Kazakh national identity in the homeland of Mongolia. Though Post refers to 'Kazakhs in Mongolia' for narrative clarity, a crucial theoretical point about the relation between home and diaspora emerged in our virtual discussions. The designation Mongolian-Kazakh is common in the literature and, in fact, the Kazakhs in Mongolia with whom she has interacted in pursuing fieldwork identify themselves as Mongolian.

Henry Johnson explores Diwali as a public festival in New Zealand, charting how state bodies as well as participants have shaped diasporic identities in a multicultural context. In this case, a South Asian homogeneity is promoted through cultural display. Explicitly drawing on Gilroy's 1987 text, Johnson emphasizes the continuing importance of narratives of origin, such that public Diwali festivals can be regarded as occupying a 'space between cultures'. State policies celebrate multiculturalism through such festivals but package them as belonging to 'Others' in a 'contradictory and hegemonic relationship between cultural celebration and ethnic consumption'. His article highlights the relations between ethnoscapes and soundscapes as they are shaped by multicultural policies in New Zealand.

Gay Breyley considers the processes of decolonization and the continuing effect of colonization in 20th-century Australia, bringing into conversation the testimonies of three women to show how experiences of displacement have been refracted through state policies and how cultural knowledge has been reproduced in contexts of loss. The life stories of these women give us insights into cultural memory. They show how biographies and personal narratives illuminate reverberations from the past within dispersed communities. The biographies highlight the geographic and historical complexities of diaspora and lead to unresolved questions about diasporized subjects. So indigenous people are described as 'diasporic' having been dispersed forcibly from homelands by state authorities. Their displacement and identification as diasporic only makes sense in that it raises questions about the modern nation state as "homeland". Similarly, ongoing colonial effects result in the political displacement of indigenous people. By contrast, state narratives of Australian 'whiteness' have absorbed the Jewish Diaspora such that a subsequent migration can be described in terms of joining an 'Australian Diaspora' in the USA. What remains to be seen is whether further migrations like this might result in a reclamation of Jewish identity such that the marker of Australian identity becomes subsumed in another geographic context.

Javier León explores how performers of the *Grupo Teatro del Milenio* have developed strategies for engaging critically with their identities as African Peruvians. He draws on notions of cultural reclamation, cosmopolitanism and intercultural collaboration to show how their theatre practice as a revival movement is in fact a modern project situated in an urban professional environment, which also creates 'a new space for the mass consumption and dissemination of their music among non-Afroperuvian audiences'. In an example of intercultural borrowing, Filipino musical instruments and dances are used 'to create an Afroperuvian reading of an African dance that never existed'. In exploring the relations between theatre representations and Peruvian realities, we are brought back to Ato Queyson's arguments about the transformations, processes and contradictions that inform society. Although 'reading for the social' was not part of my original call for this volume on musical performance in the diaspora, the articles can be read through this frame. They all point to both musical performance and the study of music as mediums through which intertwining, contrapuntal, (dis)connected and startling histories can be represented. In highlighting different kinds of diasporic political agencies (in which ethnomusicologists might be implicated through study of music in the diaspora), we see these histories as being not just about understanding the past but also about shaping the future.

Acknowledgements

I wish to express thanks to Mine Dogantan, co-organizer of the one-day British Forum for Ethnomusicology conference (November 2005) and to Middlesex University for hosting the conference. Thanks are also due to fellow members of the Royal Holloway Postcolonial Research Group with whom I discussed Ato Queyson's book in one of our reading sessions (January 2006), to participants at the European Seminar in Ethnomusicology for allowing me to test the application of calibration at this seminar (September 2006), and to Rachel Harris who kindly read through this volume before publication.

References

Agawu, Kofi. 2003. Contesting difference. In *The cultural study of music: A critical introduction*, edited by Martin Clayton, Trevor Herbert and Richard Middleton. New York and London: Routledge, pp. 225–37.

Allen, Ray and Wilcken, Lois, eds. 1998. *Island sounds: Caribbean popular music and identity in New York*. New York: New York Folklore Society and Institute for Studies in American Music, Brooklyn College.

Averill, Gage. 1998. Moving the Big Apple: Tabou Combo's diasporic dreams. In *Island sounds: Caribbean popular music and identity in New York*, edited by Ray Allen and Lois Wilcken. New York: New York Folklore Society and Institute for Studies in American Music, Brooklyn College.

Bharucha, Rustom. 2001. *The politics of cultural practice: Thinking through theatre in an age of globalisation.* New Delhi: Oxford University Press.

Blacking, John. 1987. *"A commonsense view of all music": Reflections on Percy Grainger's contribution to ethnomusicology and music education.* Cambridge: Cambridge University Press.

Chaudhuri, Shubha and Seeger, Anthony, eds. 2007. *Remembered rhythms: Music and the India Diaspora.* Oxford and New York: Berg.

Eriksen, Thomas Hylland. 1993. *Ethnicity and nationalism: Anthropological perspectives.* London: Pluto Press.

Gilroy, Paul. 1987. *There ain't no black in the Union Jack: The cultural politics of race and nation.* London and New York: Routledge.

———. 1993. *Small acts: Thoughts on the politics of black cultures.* London: Serpent's Tail.

———. 2000. *Between camps: Nations, cultures and the allure of race.* London: Penguin.

Gosden, Chris and Knowles, Chantal. 2001. *Collecting colonialism: Material culture and colonial change.* Oxford and New York: Berg.

Goulbourne, Harry. 2001. The socio-political context of Caribbean families in the Atlantic world. In *Caribbean families in Britain and the trans-Atlantic world,* edited by Harry Goulbourne and Mary Chamberlain. London and Oxford: Macmillan Education, pp. 12–31.

Hall, Stuart. 1996 [1990]. Cultural identity and diaspora. In *Contemporary postcolonial theory: A reader,* edited by Padmini Mongia. London, New York, Sydney and Auckland: Arnold, pp. 110–21.

Kartomi, Margaret and Dreyfus, Kay, eds. 2004. *Silk, spice and shirah.* Special issue of *Ethnomusicology Forum* 13 (1).

Lidchi, Henrietta. 1997. The poetics and the politics of exhibiting other cultures. In *Representation: cultural representations and signifying practices,* edited by Stuart Hall. London, California and New Delhi: Sage, pp. 151–208.

Lo, Jacqueline. 2000. Beyond happy hybridity: Performing Asian-Australian identities. In *Alter/Asian,* edited by Ien Ang, Sharon Chalmers, Lisa Law and Mandy Thomas. London: Pluto Press, pp. 152–68. Available at: <http://dlibrary.acu.edu.au/research/adsa/lo.htm>

Lovelace, Earl. 1996. *Salt.* London: Faber.

Lundberg, Dan, Malm, Krister and Ronström, Owe. 2003. *Music, media multiculture: Changing musicscapes.* Stockholm: Svenskt Visarkiv.

Queyson, Ato. 2003. *Calibrations: Reading for the social.* Minneapolis, MN: University of Minnesota Press.

Radhakrishnan, R. 2003. Ethnicity in an age of diaspora. In *Theorizing Diaspora,* edited by Jana Evans Braziel and Anita Mannur. Oxford: Blackwell, pp. 119–31.

Ramnarine, Tina K. 2004a. Imperial legacies and the politics of musical creativity. *World of Music* 46 (1): 70–82.

———. 2004b. Music in the diasporic imagination and the performance of cultural (dis)placement in Trinidad. In *Island Musics,* edited by K. Dawe. Oxford: Berg, pp. 153–70.

———. In press. *Beautiful cosmos: Performance and belonging in the Caribbean Diaspora.* London: Pluto Press.

Riggio, Milla Cozart, ed. 2004. *Carnival: Culture in action – the Trinidad experience.* New York and London: Routledge.

Slobin, Mark, ed. 1994. Music in diaspora: The view from Euro-America. Special issue of *Diaspora: A Journal of Transnational Studies* 3 (3).

———. 2003. The destiny of "diaspora" in ethnomusicology. In *The cultural study of music: A critical introduction,* edited by Martin Clayton, Trevor Herbert and Richard Middleton. New York and London: Routledge, pp. 284–96.

Stocking, George W. 1985. *Objects and others: Essays on material culture.* Wisconsin: University of Wisconsin Press.

Trouillot, Michel-Rolph. 2003. *Global transformations: Anthropology and the modern world.* New York and Basingstoke: Palgrave Macmillan.

Turino, Thomas and Lea, James, eds. 2004. *Identity and the arts in diaspora communities.* Warren, MI: Harmonie Park Press.

Williams, Eric. 1964. *History of the people of Trinidad and Tobago.* London: Deutsch.

Young, Robert. 1995. *Colonial desire: Hybridity in culture, theory and race.* London and New York: Routledge.

Adieu Madras, Adieu Foulard: Musical Origins and the *Doudou's* Colonial Plaint

Edwin Hill

> *Il part et l'amputation de son être disparaît à mesure que le profil du paquebot se précise. Il lit sa puissance, sa mutation, dans les yeux de ceux qui l'ont accompagné.*
>
> (*Adieu madras, adieu foulard* in Fanon 1952)

Edwin Hill was awarded a Bachelor's degree in music performance (percussion) and a Master's degree in French literature from the University of Iowa. He is currently a PhD candidate in the Department of French and Francophone Studies at University of California, Los Angeles. He is completing an interdisciplinary dissertation, 'Black soundscapes white stages: The meaning of sound in the Francophone Black Atlantic', which views the torn aesthetic and ideological relationships between Antillean music and literature from the 1920s to the 1960s as a colonial struggle over the meaning of Caribbean vernacular culture. This work adopts the methodological approaches of postcolonial theory, literary criticism, ethnomusicological analysis and cultural studies, and includes research in Guadeloupe and continental France.

As a character in the repertoire of French colonial mythology, the *doudou* represents the Creole woman of colour desperately in love with a French man but stranded in her colonial place. Caged in by geography, culture, and colour, she melancholically sings, in the *Doux parler des îles* ('the sweet speech of the islands', Creole), her hopeless plight of seduction, love and abandonment. Josephine Baker, in keeping with this black Atlantic orientation, most famously brought the *doudou*'s voice and body to life. Her signature song '*J'ai deux amours*', often performed as a duet, genders black transatlantic loyalty to France, conflating it with interracial romance and intercultural charm. At the same time, her films' portrayals of the comic or 'light' melancholia constitutive of the *doudou*'s amorous condition imply analogous cultural limits for francophone black Atlantic relations. Despite her character's irresistibly seductive talent, her beloved Frenchmen, after brief flirtation, always return to French wives or families, to Paris, the the *real* France, metropolitan culture, its aesthetic, its 'whole way of life'.

I hear Frantz Fanon's reference to *Adieu madras, adieu foulard*, quoted in the epigraph above, as evocative of the way that singing, like Frantz Fanon's statement on speaking, 'is most of all to assume a culture, to carry the weight of a civilization' (1952, 13). *Adieu* (in)famously sings the inscription of the *doudou* into Antillean folklore and the French imperial imagination. Attributed to Claude François Amour, marquis de Bouillé *c.* 1770, the song testifies to the long history of musically engendering colonial longing. Its Creole text depicts the *doudou* who has rushed in vain to the port to catch her lover, presumably a white French sailor, before he sets sail to return to France for ever.

Refrain	*Refrain*
Adieu madras, adieu foulard,	Farewell madras, farewell scarf
Adieu robe soie, adieu collier choux,	Farewell silk dress, farewell necklace
Doudou en moins li ka pati	My sweetie is leaving
Hélas, hélas! cé pou toujou!	Helas, helas! It's for ever
Doudou en moins li ka pati	My sweetie is leaving
Hélas, hélas! cé pou toujou!	Helas, helas! It's for ever
Verse I	*Verse I*
Bonjou Missié le gouvêneur	Good day Mister Governor
Moin vini fé oune pétition	I came to make a petition
Pou mande ou autoisation	To ask you authorization
Afin laissé doudou moin ici	To leave my sweetie here

Verse II	*Verse II*
Non, non, non, non, déjà top tard	No, no, no, no, it's already too late
Batîment déjà sur la bouée	The ship is already on the buoy
Non, non, non, non, déjà top tard	No, no, no, no, it's already too late
Dans un instant appareiller	In an instant it sets sail
Variant	*Variant*
Non, non, non, non, déjà top tard	No, no, no, no, it's already too late
La consigne est déjà signé	The register is already signed
Non, non, non, non, déjà top tard	No, no, no, no, it's already too late
La navire est sur la bouée	The ship is already on the buoy

Adieu, like the well-known *Lisette quitté la plaine* from Saint-Domingue, lies at the heart of the soundtext tradition in the francophone Antilles that is intimately connected with the circulation of transatlantic ships. Often referred to as *chansons de cocotte* or *chansons galantes*, these written Creole lyrics and European melodies constitute some of the earliest Creole song texts as well as the early texts of literary aspiration in the francophone Antilles. As early as the mid-18th century, French and Creole colonists adopted the perspective *and the voice* of populations of colour when writing these romantic songs. At the same time, masking and satire, as well as the treatment of biological and cultural hybridity, complicates hearing *Adieu* as a duet, in other words as a simple binary structure of opposition providing clean-cut terms of resistance and complicity.

While their satire disguised any serious emotional investment in the subject of black love, these songs gave voice to the anxiety surrounding the power of Antillean women slaves to obtain freedom for themselves and their children through intimate relationships with white men. In this sense too the *doudou*'s presence goes back just as far as does French West Indian textual production—from novels and poetry of the interwar period of the 1920s and 1930s, back to travel narratives and ethnographic accounts of the 19th and 18th centuries, all the way back to the interdiction and punishment of interracial sexual relations in the infamous 1685 *Code noir*, the official code of conduct and punishment for French colonial slavery. The *doudou*'s long transcultural life demonstrates the way French and Antillean texts have historically 'stressed' the proximity of black female sexuality to power, money and politics.

Adieu constitutes an important *lieu de mémoire* of this long and contentious history in francophone Caribbean culture. Its music and lyrics, as Régis Antoine writes, 'in registering a certain psychological truth of old, and by their ability to function ideologically, would have prolonged literary influence' (1998, 145). From the interwar period to the 1960s, many writers staged the *doudou*'s emotional posture and musical drama with French culture.

This paper contributes an interdisciplinary dialogue and cultural analysis of the figure of the *doudou* through a critical listening to *Adieu madras, adieu foulard.* I suggest that this highly symbolic soundtext situates the historic representation of the *doudou* to coincide with mythologies about the origins of French-Antillean imperial relations and the conditions of transnational cultural enjoyment and exchange.

I begin my investigation of the *doudou* mythology with a close reading of Frantz Fanon's quoting of the song. How does Fanon locate *Adieu madras, adieu foulard* in the subjective soundscape of his critical narrative *Black Skin White Masks*? In the second section, I turn towards an analysis of the song itself. What lines of investigation does Fanon's quote suggest for a postcolonial musicology of the *doudou*? How does *Adieu* stretch beyond the level of the subject to become a 'political signifier of the island's attachment to the *métropole*' (Antoine 1998, 145)?

In the closing section I ask how the old regime pathos and pre-revolutionary portrayal of unequal social relations in *Adieu* could find representational life and relevance in Enlightenment and republican discourse. While I interpret the *doudou*'s *Adieu* as singing an apostrophic elegy to the rigid borders of French old regime hierarchy and colonial slave society, I argue that *Adieu* must also resonate with the 'unity of melody' proposed by French Enlightenment thought in order to enter the nostalgic coffers of the Republic's *patrimoine.*

Fanon's Colonial Endings

Fanon's reference to *Adieu* comes in *Le Noir et le langage*, the first chapter in *Black Skin White Masks. Adieu* offers a performance of colonial relations that symbolically crystallizes many of the major themes of Fanon's work: the colonial construction of 'race', the dynamics of language practice in French assimilation discourse, the meaning of movement for the French West Indian colonial subject and the role of desire in the socio-cultural mythologies of 'race'. *Adieu* interrogates the possibility of authentic colonial love by musically plotting a psychic and affective *dénouement*, in other words a 'colonial ending', to the blurring of racial constructs and cultural economies of French imperial power.

Fanon's critical performance places *Adieu* in its most common performance context: in the French West Indies, the song was often sung and played to bid farewell when transatlantic ships left the port. Yet even before departure from the island, the Fanonian subject undergoes alienation, experienced and determined through an intense relationship to language that internalizes the racial subject's distance from assimilation and, in the metropole, marks the exotic other.

> *Le Noir entrant en France va réagir contre le mythe du Martiniquais qui-mange-les-R. Il va s'en saisir, et véritablement entrer en conflit ouvert avec lui. Il s'appliquera non seulement à rouler les R, mais à les ourler. Epiant les moindre réactions des autres, s'écoutant parler, se méfiant de la langue, organe malheureusement paresseux, il s'enfermera dans sa chambre et lira pendant des heures—s'acharnant à se faire* diction. (Fanon 1952, 16, emphasis in original)

Diction, in broadest sense, means a way of speaking. An old usage placed the accent on syntax; for example, 'poetic diction' in this sense referred to the chosen arrangement of words. I read Fanon's scene as using *diction* in its musical sense, i.e. not learning the language as much as learning to perform the language. The demands for social and racial assimilation that frame the dynamics of colonial mimicry produce only subjects that, as Homi Bhabha and others have argued, are always 'almost but not white'. Plainly put, attempts to repeat 'French values' reproduce and reinforce subjective and cultural distance from French society.

Fanon's emphasis above, both in the expression '*s'acharnant*' and in his use of italics, depicts the desire involved in the interpretation and perfection of the subject's French, a desire to subsume the excessive racial body, the lazy tongue, and to make a self of 'pure' language. As much as a question of clear French articulation, my reading of Fanon's *diction* suggests that the hard work of mimicry requires constant *répétitions* in the French sense of 'rehearsal'. Fanon's description of the black Antillean in France who "will lock himself up in his room and read [aloud] for hours" points up the practice involved in the performative interpretation of social texts. In other words, if mimicry is (public) performance, it is even more (private) practice, a determined and desirous *shedding* of speech.

Fanon's description leading up to *Adieu* appropriately harks back to scenes of arrival in early ethnographic accounts and travel narratives where the trope of the appearing/disappearing island stages the slow specular striptease of nature for fantasies of imperial conquest. 'He leaves, and the amputation of his being disappears as the profile of the ocean liner becomes visible' (1952, 18). Fanon's text performs the emergence of the colonial subject by reworking the positions of enunciation and reception such that, rather than identifying with the singing *doudou*, this Fanonian subject identifies with the departing colonial agent, formerly the white French sailor. Fanon posits the black colonial subject's physical movement towards France as generative of and engaged with a cultural and psychical movement (of alienation) there. He describes this movement towards the other as invoking a change in *form*, a '*nouveau mode d'être*' (1952, 19).

While in practice and lyrics *Adieu* bids *farewell*, Fanon's critical listening perspective situates it as a cultural production that also signals an *arrival*. The provocative 'He leaves, and *the amputation* of his being *disappears*' creates something of a mixed metaphor, 'as the *profile* of the ocean liner becomes *visible*'. In one sense, the metaphor suggests that the subject arrives, just as the ship does, and just as lack (amputation) disappears. Here, the disappearance of amputation, the erasure of lack, leaves the false sense of what Fanon calls being 'full of oneself'. Yet, in another sense, the metaphor's subject/amputation relation also reads as the *realization* rather than the absence of lack. In other words, there was something (amputation) that was there that is now gone (disappears), leaving an empty space. In this case, the metaphor of the subject/ship points towards a direct relationship to amputation, since the latter disappears just as the subject/ship too will soon depart. As imminent disappearance the subject/ship arrives, yet that arrival signals the impending 'parting' or separation (amputation) of that same subject.

The juxtaposition of leaving and arriving signals more than the physical movement of the subject. I read Fanon's performance of this scene as suggesting that colonial discourse dictates that its subjects inhabit this inverse relationship, equating the movement of the French West Indian subject to an engagement with the real and symbolic economies of French imperialism. As with negritude poets such as Aimé Césaire, the shock and recognition of alienation comes while abroad. Movement to, and even *within*, the imperial metropolis creates a parallel slippage in the subject, a tear in the process of identification (another type of separation). Fanon's mixed metaphors, his movement between sound and text, speaking and singing, and reading and hearing indicate the slippage involved in the desire to be loved *comme un blanc*, to be loved *the way* in which a white person loves, but also *as* a white person.

I interpret the sonic history of Fanon's colonial performance as a path for investigating the instantiation of a primal scene of desire, thrusting the self into the neither/nor relationships of colonial subjectivity. What is it that Fanon's subject of *Adieu*, the departing subject, will not have been? In other words, what is this voice that Fanon's subject takes as the signal of his disappearance from the mythology of colonial culture into the 'real' (read French) world, and what subjective positions, emotional attitudes, and cultural relations do his processes of identification eschew?

Fanon's subject arrives at the port to disappear. 'He reads his power, his mutation, in the eyes of those who have accompanied him. *Adieu madras, adieu foulard*' (1952, 18).

Colonial Family Romance

The *Marseillaise* instructs us to have no pity in our attack on the reputed author of *Adieu*, a loyal monarchist who helped Louis XVI flee the French Revolution and continued for many years to lobby in his support. Born in Auvergne, François Amour, marquis de Bouillé, arrived in Martinique in 1765 after gaining Louis XVI's attention for his military exploits during the Seven Years' War. De Bouillé was still a young French military officer when Louis XVI appointed him as *gouverneur* of Guadeloupe. Neither the authorship of the *doudou*'s colonial plaint nor the song's proximity to musical genres already familiar to the French prevented *Adieu* from becoming an exotic symbol of French Creole identity and French-Antillean relations. Seen as a 'hybrid' with its European music and Creole complaint, *Adieu* comes to stand for the authentic or true musical expression of Antillean local culture.

Yet if *Adieu* crystallizes the *doudou*, the latter's popularity gives *Adieu* access to musical territories beyond the local boundaries of the Antilles. In addition to occupying a place in the canon of *chanson coloniale*, *Adieu* appears in repertories varying from French marine songs, to French folk albums, to local French Boy Scout choral groups. The popular music of Fanon's generation was no exception to this dynamic. While they clearly needed to master several styles in order to make a living, French Antillean musicians, who performed in France in the famed *Jazz-Age Paris* of the 1920s–50s, made their living playing biguine in *bals nègres*. Some of the most prominent, such as Sam Castendet, the Martinican drummer and clarinettist, came to France in the context of the Guadeloupean stage for the 1931 Colonial Exposition in Paris. Castendet offers perhaps the most standard rendition of the song. The instrumentation and up tempo, in comparison to the other versions, might allow for dance.

While the patient ascending line, made up of the major tonic triad, reproduces the calling out, briefly reaching the major sixth, the height of its determined aspiration, its high musical resting place cannot be maintained. The melody's steady climb up takes the first four bars while the musical fall happens in half the time and is thus repeated once to complete the opening eight-bar phrase. The descending line suggests both the sadness of the fall, through its relation with the relative minor, and a sweetness of the fall, through the interlaced thirds and the regular quarter-note/eighth-note rhythmic frame to soften the landing.

In Henri Salvador's solo guitar and vocal rendition we can hear this movement very clearly. A native of French Guiana whose parents were Guadeloupean, Salvador moved to Paris as a child, and broke onto the French Jazz and cabaret scene with his innovative blend of African-American, Caribbean, and Brazilian musical styles. His version of *Adieu*, exploiting the ambivalence in the narrative voice, transforms *Adieu* into the nostalgic lament of an Antillean expatriate community: '*si aujourd'hui je vis à Paris/C'est pas pour ça que j'oublie le pays*' ('If today I live in Paris/That doesn't mean I've forgotten home). Salvador's cover is a recovery, re-placing the loss back on to the person leaving the island.

If *Adieu* initially became an Antillean trope because of the mythology of the *doudou*, its context of performance—transatlantic ocean liners leaving port—helped transform *Adieu* into a nostalgic complaint of exile and diaspora by the time it became a biguine standard, if a problematic one. Salvador's notably French versed textual re-appropriation of *Adieu* points to the way musicians must deal with the post/colonial cultural politics of Antillean performance in France as well as the consequences of metropolitan success back on the islands. Rather than attesting to the biguine's alleged *doudou*ist posture, a question I take up elsewhere, *Adieu* has become a biguine standard in the sense that it must be dealt with. Artists must cut their teeth on *Adieu* and, by extension, cut their teeth on their ambivalent place in the colonial pleasure industry. By taking on musically its ambivalent history, re-covering *Adieu* forces recognition of the transatlantic, imperial dynamics of Antillean musical culture.

The movement of thirds in the melody suggests hearing the song as a lullaby (Hazael-Massieux 1996). Consideration of *Adieu madras* as a lullaby both places women as important agents of this musical production, and suggests the role musical culture assumes in the pedagogy of colonial sentiment. In traditional French today, '*doudou*' generally refers to a child's comfort blanket, or, figuratively, to any such fetishized object. The term's meaning suggests that the *Adieu*'s fetishization of the fabric—madras, scarf, silk—relates the romantic break up to a more fundamental type of separation anxiety. At the same time, the 'madras' itself represents the hybridity of the Creole woman, evoking both the importance of Indian cultural production in the history of the Antilles and the circulation of cultural material from one colony to the next, especially in the Caribbean.

Colonial family romance 'played a greater role in the Vieilles Colonies than in other parts of the empire because there the battle between the Old Regime and French Revolution continued late into the twentieth century' (Vergès 1999, 6). *Adieu* stages this confrontation between the old and new orders through a (musical) Oedipal *mise-en-scène*, constituting a key precursor to the use of familial metaphors in imperial discourse which Vergès's work situates as emerging in the 19th century. As a figure of the *métis*, the *doudou* appropriately evokes the mutability of social order, the advent of something new. Yet I suggest that the construction of the *doudou* marks French West Indian culture and people as frozen at the temporal cusp of a new age, always almost becoming a new people. While *Adieu* entices the French imperial subject to imagine alternative, 'supplemental' familial relations with the colonial other, its ultimate injunction, which addresses the absent colonial subject around which this world revolves, puts everyone back in their imperial place.

A musico-physiological relation may contribute to viewing *Adieu* as linked to a maternal lullaby: the *mouchoir* waving goodbye and the movement of the boat brings to mind the rocking back and forth of the *da*, the Creole nanny (also referred to as a *nounou*), another major figure for representing French colonial relations in the Antilles as an (extended) family affair. In other words, the subtext and sociocultural history suggest not only that the *doudou* sing *his* child to sleep, but that she carries and cares for *their* child, giving new meaning to her vain race to catch him before he sets sail. The designation of the interlocutor as a captain, lieutenant, etc., depending on the variation, suggests that the *doudou* has fallen in love with a French officer – a common theme in the literary tradition of the *doudou*, such as in the work of Mayotte Capécia that Frantz Fanon critiques and in cinematographic depictions of the *doudou*, for example, Josephine Baker's *Zou zou*, as well as in the musical history of *chanson coloniale* (see Liauzu and Liauzu 2002)—but it also posits this interlocutor as father figure.

Yet in this Oedipal scene the desirous son departs freely and the father addresses his '*non*' to the *doudou*. It is the colonial m/other who must hear the threat and bear the mark of any French imperial cut. She stays on the island, yet she sings to him (for us), even as he leaves earshot of her musical seduction. The *doudou*'s farewell to silk dresses and Creole jewellery signals not only the material and social capital she will now lose, it also situates loss as the very marker of her identity. He will mourn during performance and move on to new *trouvailles*. She will remain. *Adieu* may be considered a waltz, but its historic socio-cultural performance contexts (farewell and lullaby) suggest this was no dance for the *doudou*, stuck on the island. She is always waiting, as Fanon puts it, almost motionless. While the farewell song marked the beginning of the ocean liner's social dances and musical performances, the *doudou* watches the ship's agonizingly long disappearance. Melancholia marks her emotional posture, eternal waiting her colonial place.

The sound of the *doudou*'s farewell, a farewell to her own cultural production, to her self, rings like what Fanon calls the '*raté*', a mechanical backfiring. The prosopopoeiac slippage signals the colonial conditions of *Adieu*'s authorship and its structures allegorize the ambivalent conditions of social performance facing the *doudou. Adieu*'s confusion of the point of narrative focalization points to the way this 'colonial voice' serves as a musical 'black face', constructing a structure of fantasy that resonates best from the position of the absent other, the departing imperial subject or the Fanonian departing subject as described earlier. *Adieu*'s Oedipal scene redirects the trauma of imperial castration, the loss of self and the violent encounter with the symbolic back to the Creole woman.

Significantly, if the song's success has to do with its musico-textual hybridity, its lyrics, on the contrary, stage a conflict between the French text and the Creole voice, the French lover's signature and the *doudou*'s musical petition. Perhaps the musical figure of thirds can then be thought of in a structural light. Here the captain is the third, the judge who hears and denies the *doudou*'s oral petition. The latter constitutes the final word on the separation between the two; its signature guarantees the authenticity of the Frenchman's desire and his duty to leave the colony behind. Writing here invokes the law of the father, of difference, distinction, and separation (in some variants of the governor's verse he says the ship has already set sail). The signed name, never spoken or sung out in the song, also remains off limits (harking to decrees enacted at the end of the century which outlawed the practice of freed slaves adopting their former master's family name). *Jouissance* denied the *doudou*, the text fails to render legal or judicial satisfaction, becoming rather a witness to her lack.

By 'triangulating' the *doudou*'s call—hearing it as the Oedipal movement of desire and the French imperial history of moving African culture and bodies—we locate subject positions in relations of cultural pleasure whose discursive economies make the harsh conditions of sentimental exchange resonate with the economic conditions of the French slave trade and the French colonial pact, or, more precisely, *l'Exclusif.* The expression *pacte colonial* 'was created in an ulterior period to make one believe the colonial regime was the result of a *pact*', Charles André Julien emphasizes, 'that is, an accord freely consented to and implying reciprocal obligations, whereas it was imposed by France on its colonies which protested its application' (1981, 13). The *doudou*'s struggle in *Adieu*, as well as the subsequent use of the song to represent Antillean attachment to France and the French colonial condition, underlines the slippage Julien denounces behind the term *pact.* This fundamental textual move shares much with Antillean literary history as well, for 'the French writer's compromise with the enslaved black', Antoine explains, operates 'by the literary genre of prosopopoeia, a substitution even more artificial since authentic speech was first withdrawn from the slave' (1978, 93).

The figure of power in *Adieu* bears witness to this intimate moment, and intervenes to ensure a certain outcome by guarding the border, invoking the official text—'*l'écriture du registre*', the origin of modern textual production in the French West Indies (Chamoiseau and Confiant 1999)—and, perhaps most importantly, by keeping the time. One of the most striking and consistent aspects of transcolonial sexual relations, as depicted in literature and song, is its ephemeral nature. As Alain Ruscio points out, 'far away loves, in the days of the Colonies, run short most often' (1996, 341); few *chansons coloniales* and so-called erotic texts depict transcolonial couples staying together. 'Love stronger than patriotism, here's something not common in the France of the 1930s' (Ruscio 1996, 329).

Time ensures distance between the writer and its object. *Doudou*ist poetry of the 1920s and beyond, a topic I will return to in closing, typically adopts the time of the imperfect (or past continuous) verb tense in French, rather than that of the past historic (*le passé simple*), to portray the *doudou*'s spiritual *après coup* as a sublime emotional landscape. The imperfect constitutes here a nostalgic and melancholic mode, but also figures a specific type of emotional and Antillean denial of temporal coevalness. Instead of depicting the lived relationship itself, *doudou*ist poetics walls up an empty temporal shell, either situating itself before the relationship, in the excitement of seduction, or after the relationship, as nostalgic look back on what can be no more. A song of seduction *and* farewell, *Adieu* encapsulates this time loop and cultural rhythm, making the *doudou* resonant with its empty temporal shell.

Adieu, as an imperial symbol, seeks to reify these time limits within the French imperial mythology of transatlantic, transcolonial relations. As Ruscio notes, *chansons coloniales* often contradict the reality of French colonial experiences, acting at times 'like a veil . . . between reality and fantasy' (2001, 298). In other words, the myth of ephemeral relations dreamed of by colonial discourse comes up against historical, sociological, and cultural phenomena that prove the contrary by their very existence. Régent's archival research shows that unions between free people of colour and between whites and women of colour have the demographic particularity of living together as couples for long periods before having married. Rather than ephemeral relations, the long history of the *doudou*, and the advent of the *métissage*, proves *Adieu*'s mythology of time and separation often remains just that.

How can we then structurally define the situation of the *doudou* in these performative and poetic economies of desire? Brenda Berrian associates the *doudou* with 'a singing style that originated when mulatto mistresses entertained their French lovers with Creole songs' (2000, 72). The *chanson de cocotte*'s dynamics suggest that, as much as historically constitutive of a musical corpus, made up of a particular musical context, discrete musical form and/or set repertory, we should consider this 'singing style' a form of *diction* in the Fanonian sense elaborated above. And in the case of that style's ability to seduce power for not just material gain but for freedom, we might consider *doudou*ism as a form of sweet talk with stakes in the '*doux*' or 'sweet' product that made the Antilles the most prized colonies of the 18th century: sugar. The *doudou* strives to become diction, but the ear of the other usurps her *jouissance*, making her voice itself the sign, or in performance the act and movement, of her designation. Her song locates a linguistic-symbolic economy of colonial speech as failed diction, as a conversion into colonial musical pleasure.

Adieu stages this lost vocal authority as a beautiful amorous history, a past life of consent and recognition that remains present only in the term of endearment for *him*, '*doudou*', that becomes *her* proper name, for *she* only serves as a sign for the desire of the other. The *doudou* is not a woman; *she* is rather a structural, temporal subject position in the intimate psychosocial microphysics of colonial power, stuck, in other words, in the struggle of power in the minor. Yet lyrically this naming, and name sharing, constitutes a type of outlawed metonymy, an absolute limit for transatlantic imperial relations. It attempts to categorize these key intimate relationships as not political by occluding the flow of desire as a function of colonial culture and its designation of race and gender. The *doudou*'s cry fixes her geographically, but also signals her emotional stuckness and her stuckness in time. The *doudou*'s precarious position at the frontier between the aural and the textual, between action and acting, singing and scripting, evokes the ethical and aesthetic dilemmas posed by transnational relations while simultaneously constituting, for centuries, the dominant legal and emotional structure of social mobility.

*Doudou*ist poetics focus on women not only due to the masculinist imperial gaze; this focus also signals recognition of the power of women's choices in the destiny of French colonial and Antillean society. *Adieu* as a *chanson de cocotte* generates desire by singing in Creole and by naming its *métissage*, yet its Creole *sweetie* remains unthreatening by virtue of her pathetic, beautifully helpless, emotional posture. Desire here functions as a cultural and subjective longing for safe forms of cultural metonymy, for identification and relation through movement, displacement or circulation without disrupting the economies of imperial order. Caught between the law of the master/love and that of the state, between the past and the future, between authenticity and affectation, orality and textuality, the *doudou*'s in-between status, her '*mitoyenneté*', both expands and limits her choices. Her aesthetic beauty expands her social mobility yet stages the limits of its ethical outlook and ideological appearance, positioning her as the intimate antagonism between old and new orders of socialization, cultural production and legitimacy in the francophone black Atlantic.

Rousseau's Musical Origins

The colonial voice in *Adieu* may be heard as an echo of the loss and exclusion of the colonial subject in the primal scene of French Enlightenment thought, a situation of the colonial subject '*chez lui*', as Fanon might put it. While Fanon works to position the *doudou*ist plaint as psychically untenable and socially unethical, Jean-Jacques Rousseau, the musical authority of the *philosophes* and author of most of the articles about music in the *Encyclopédie*, effectively inscribes the primal scene of human sociality as a musical imitation of the other's plaint.

If Radano and Bohlman, confined to a preface, oversimplify when they claim that '[f]or Rousseau it was language and its presence in music that most represented racial difference' (2000, 14), the way Rousseau's work seeks relationships between musical meaning and origins, whether geo-temporal or cultural, certainly builds a conceptual ground for racial thought that was key to French Enlightenment thinkers. 'Music serves as the anthropological "missing link" in the eighteenth-century', Downing Thomas writes, staging an 'attempt to trace semiosis to its origin, to pinpoint the semiotic moment which separates culture from nature, and human beings from animals' (1995, 9). This same mythological musical moment served to pinpoint, hierarchize and naturalize differences and boundaries between cultures as well. Even when music historians in the 18th century consider the origin of music with a certain scientific positivism, their connection of scientific phenomena to human representation relies on ideas about pleasure, for '*[l]'attrait du plaisir donna aux hommes la première idée de Musique*' (Blainville 1972 [1767], v).

In his *Essai sur l'origine des langues où il est parlé de la mélodie et de l'imitation musicale*, Rousseau describes the physical need that dictated the formation of the first human societies in northern climates and produced languages centred on exact communication and articulate reason. In contrast:

> *dans les climats doux, dans les terrain fertiles, il fallut toute la vivacité des passions agréables pour commencer à faire parler les habitants:* les premières langues, filles du plaisir et non du besoin, portèrent longtemps l'enseigne de leur père. (1979, 213, emphasis added)

Rousseau's language recalls the Oedipal dynamics of *Adieu* which mark the *doudou*, putting her under the sign of pleasure, and turning this stigmatic trace of the desire of the other into an emblem for the long and emotionally bonding nature of French-Antillean imperial history.

Rather than physical need, here 'moral needs' brought groups together to form larger communities. '*Ce n'est ni la faim, ni la soif, mais l'amour, la haine, la pitié, la colère, qui leur ont arraché les premières voix*' (1979, 168). Perhaps, Rousseau suggests, we may have been able to find ways to meet physical needs without this musical speech, '*mais pour émouvoir un jeune coeur, pour repousser un agresseur injuste, la nature dicte des accents, des cris, des plaintes*' (1979, 169).

Rousseau ultimately suggests that the emotional posture of the musical moment constitutes the primal affective relationship with representation that forms the basis of the collective. Rousseau has a dynamic, diachronic view of cultural life, yet he imagines the conditions of a group's emergence to be historically determinative in its development. Rousseau almost seems to suggest that the origins of representation fundamentally relate the 'genre' of passion constitutive of a group (or 'genre') of people to the 'genre' of music that captures its 'cultural genius'. Ultimately, attempts to identify the true nature of representational forms and the resultant aesthetic hierarchies that emerge from that identification directly correspond to modes for identifying differences in people and developing hierarchical relationships between them. The juxtaposition between Rousseau's essay on the origin of language and music and his *Essai sur l'inégalité des hommes* makes this implication rather clear.

Music constitutes a 'memorative sign', in Rousseau's words, that circumvents reason to hark back instead to that first affective stage. Musical practice triggers socio-cultural attachment and national solidarity by tapping into structures of feeling that elude the textual jurisdiction of the social contract and the contradictions of its cartographies. According to Rousseau, music should, and originally did in warmer climates, provide representation its force, its possibility of exchange and circulation without loss of *propre*, its fundamental expression of the universal while retaining its deep seating in the particular.

Rousseau famously cites *Rans-des-vaches*, a Swiss folksong, as an example of the power of music to represent social solidarity and cultural sensitivity. Rousseau even gives the song its own entry in his *Dictionnaire de musique*, including it in a select collection of transcriptions found in the appendices. 'Rousseau was acutely aware that theatricality plays a necessary role at all levels of personal, social, and political interaction' (May 1989, 443), and he identifies everyday musical practices, as much as state ceremonies and spectacles, as iterative of an originary social moment of identification. In his entry *Musique*, Rousseau writes that Swiss soldiers were prohibited from singing *Rans-des-Vaches* because it

> *faisait fondre en larmes, déserter ou mourir ceux qui l'entendaient tant il excitait en eux l'ardent désir de revoir leur pays. On chercherait en vain dans cet Air les accents énergiques capables de produire de si étonnants effets. Ces effets, qui n'ont aucun lieu sur les étrangers, ne viennent que de* l'habitude, des souvenirs, de mille circonstances qui, retracées *par cet Air à ceux qui l'entendent, et leur rappelant leur pays, leurs anciens plaisirs, leur jeunesse, et toutes leurs façons de vivre, excite en eux* une douleur amère d'avoir perdu tout cela. *La musique alors n'agit point précisément comme musique, mais comme* signe mémoratif. (1768, 314–15, emphasis added)

The power of music comes from its ability to remain present beyond the time-space limits of its initial performance. Rousseau describes, in his entry *Air*, music's ability to locate and incarnate cultural sensitivities and sensibilities that do not rely on material existence and thus elude containment, observation, and analysis.

> *Après un bel Air, on est satisfait,* l'oreille ne désire plus rien; *il reste dans l'imagination,* on l'emporte avec soi, on le répète à volonté; *sans pouvoir en rendre une seule Note on l'exécute dans son cerveau tel qu'on l'entendit au Spectacle*; on voit la Scène, l'Acteur, le Théâtre; *on entend l'"accompagnement, l'applaudissement. Le véritable Amateur ne perd jamais les beaux Airs qu"il entendit en sa vie;* il fait commencer l'Opéra quand il veut. (1768, 29, emphasis added)

In the context of *Adieu*, Rousseau's work suggests that, as a '*signe mémoratif*' (like Proust's madeleine), music sets off the vision of the colonial landscape, its actors and their beauty. Musical imitation, rather than trying to reproduce nature (as in painting), Rousseau contends, seeks to reproduce the emotions one would experience when facing nature. Here lies an important conceptual nexus for considering the landscape genre and the imperial gaze in relation to what we can now call the *genre of the imperial soundscape.* The latter solicits the body and excites the imagination in a pre-conditional move towards the possibility of emotional solidarity.

In Rousseau's view, modern language, and especially the French language (and this goes back to the '*Querelle*'), lacked the expressive musicality of the Ancients and of other cultures. Rousseau asserts that his contemporaries dismiss the fabulous exploits of music recounted in Ancient mythology, its ability to heal or to set off rage for example, only because contemporary French culture and musical practices cannot access this 'genre' of musicality. '*La musique est déchue aujourd'hui de ce degré de puissance et de majesté, au point de nous fai[re] douter de la vérité des merveilles qu'elle opérait autrefois*' (*Musique* 1768, 312).

The phenomenon of the Swiss soldiers abandoning their units after being moved to homesick tears by *Rans-des-vaches*, and the subsequent interdiction of this Swiss folksong during the war, demonstrates for Rousseau the power of music to intervene emotionally within the individual as well as to intervene in the matters of the state. This musical bond's absence poses a formidable challenge for modern states, for the eloquence of song, its ability to hark back to a primal scene of sociality, grants its bearers a fundamental affective structure whose power of imagination invests the individual in an otherwise abstract notion of unity within a vast republic. Music offers a powerful method of persuasion for 'Rousseau's legislator [to] attend to the cultural affective basis of the state' (Scott 1997, 824).

As a product of culture, music, like language, relies on social conventions. Rousseau frequently refers to the Caribs to establish a temporal trajectory of musical culture, allowing him both to situate cultures in time and to hypothesize about music's relationship to what he considered the first social institution: language. Rousseau's geographic anchoring of musical origins, in combination with his notion that 'to decipher the songs of the passions means to be a member of a musicolinguistic system' (Scott 1997, 817), brings together a key discursive history of the notion of soundscapes. Rousseau's line of questioning constitutes a set of representational problematics key to the formation of ethnomusicological thought, revealing ethnocentrism and colonial history as the latter's foundational, even if denounced or deconstructed, discursive launching point.

Todorov argues that Rousseau, who called for further urgent research concerning Caribbean populations, gets 'carried away by the allegorical usage he makes of ethnographic data' (1993, 282). Yet Rousseau's historical conjecture and allegorical 'listening' specifically point up the limits of musicological positivism, underscoring the historiographic crisis in 18th-century musical discourse. 'With the first pages of eighteenth-century histories of music', Head explains, 'we enter a realm of fiction, conjecture and mysticism, peopled by gods and legendary beings' (1997, 3). Considering Rousseau's critique of empiricist (musical) positivism, recourse to allegory and imagination constitute a crucial epistemological and ethical basis for understanding the nature and function of musical representation. Rather than an analysis carried away by its own lyrical *élan*, 'it is the fictitious nature of this discourse', Head argues, 'that makes it of interest from the standpoints of eighteenth-century historiography and musical aesthetics' (1997, 2). Rousseau uses ethnographic data only to corroborate his own imaginative fantasies whereby a primal musico-social moment in warmer climates has sparked good, true and beautiful relationships of representation that Rousseau finds lacking in French culture.

'*[D]ans les pays chauds, les sources et les rivières, inégalement dispersées, sont d''autres points de réunion*', Rousseau (1979, 207) conjectures:

> Là *se formèrent les premiers liens des familles;* là *furent les premiers rendez-vous des deux sexes. Les jeunes filles venoient chercher de l'eau pour le ménage, les jeunes hommes venoient abreuver leurs troupeaux.* Là *des yeux accoutumés aux mêmes objets dès l'enfance commencèrent d'en voir de plus doux.* Le coeur s'émut à ces nouveaux objets, un attrait inconnu le rendit moins sauvage, il sentit le plaisir de n'être pas seul. *L'eau devint insensiblement plus nécessaire, le bétail eut soif plus souvent: on arrivoit en hâte, et l'on partoit à regret. Dans* cet âge heureux où rien ne marquait les heures, *rien n'obligeait à les compter, le temps n'avait d'autre mesure que l'amusement et l'ennui. Sous de vieux chênes, vainqueurs des ans, une ardente jeunesse oublioit par degrés sa férocité: on s'apprivoisoit peu à peu les uns avec les autres; en s'efforçant de se faire entendre, on apprit à s'expliquer.* Là *se firent les premières fêtes: les pieds bondissoient de joie, le geste empressé ne suffisoit plus, la voix l'accompagnoit d'accents passionnés;* le plaisir et le désir, confondus ensemble, *se faisoient sentir à la fois;* là *fut enfin* le vrai berceau des peuples *et du pur cristal des fontaines sortirent les premiers feux de l'amour.* (1979, 211–12, emphasis added)

The bucolic scene, where the '*pur cristal des fontaines*' spark the '*premiers feux de l'amour*', resembles the common staging of the *doudou* by the water (as a siren, a '*blanchisseuse*', a songbird, or on a ship, at the port, at the river, etc.). The juxtaposition between Rousseau's representative account and the *mise-en-scène* of the *doudou* brings to light relationships between French West Indian musicality and the mythology of the island colony as an Edenic space. Rousseau's anaphoric '*là*' lyrically evokes a lost place in space and time, betraying a nostalgic intellectual and artistic longing for (myths of) unity, order and wholeness. '*Le statut du son chez Rousseau est donc chantant, passionnel et surtout nostalgique, car il rappelle un temps perdu à jamais*' (Bermingham 1988, 184).

The binary oppositions emerging from this initial unity represent water as a source of purity but also as a space of encounters, of difference. While these sparks of love ultimately ground Rousseau's ethics of sociality and the progression of civilization, the resultant irretrievably lost innocence marks this musical moment of encounter as the site of human *déchéance.* 'In so far as Rousseau situates the original passionate cry amidst the stirring of pleasure and desire', as Head notes, 'he implicitly implicates the birth of music in the Fall, of which this fable can be read as a trope' (1997, 6). As Rousseau suggests through his scene of musical origins and the birth of civilization, musicality catalyses the fall from an idealized Edenic 'state' as a falling into the love/desire of the other.

Rousseau's creation of '*[c]ette image de l'homme qui n'est conforme ni à sa condition première ni à celle que lui destine la société*', Bermingham writes, '*semble indicatrice de l'épistémè "romantique". Rousseau déplace la nature pour permettre à l'homme de devenir sujet de sa propre histoire*' (1988, 191). This shift is key here; it suggests *Adieu* constitutes a musical moment defining the (assimilationist) Romantic pathos in the *doudouist* aesthetic and designating the *doudou* as the musical correspondent for this modulation in cultural regime. The transformation of *Adieu* from a simple love-story to a transcolonial epic comes from the way it too ambivalently stages a *Paradise Lost.* Indeed John Milton's epic, in which the Fall is staged as an ambivalent scene of origins as a condition for the possibility of free will and human progress, haunts the cultural production of the Caribbean.

Romantic interpretations depict Lucifer as a pathetic (anti)hero in *Paradise Lost* and read Milton's classic epic as a tale of rebellion against tyranny and of the defining dynamics of rupture between old and new orders. Lucifer's pathos, like that of the *doudou*, comes from his charmed, persuasive discourse. The *doudou*'s temporal ambivalence reflects a prelapsarian positioning that figures the Creole woman as Eve in the garden of Eden, but also as a tragic antihero, a beautiful flower of evil or, more simply put, as Lucifer cast down to hell.

Although it moved to decentre, if not completely replace, the reliance of musical discourse on Christian mythology, the moral ambivalence of musical meaning in Enlightenment thought plots a secular epic of musicality that strongly resonates with the spiritual trajectory of musicality in Christian mythology. The oblique history of music constructed within Christian discourse (oblique because of the absence of a direct and complete account of musical origins within biblical scripture) often stages Lucifer as the master musician, musical director and thereby lead worshipper among the angels. Lucifer's musical beauty was outwardly expressed in his adornment in jewels and precious stones, in some accounts his very body is made up of instruments, and his musicality granted him closer proximity to the throne than any other cherub or seraph. Of course music for any other purpose than to praise God was suspect. If '*[l]'attrait du plaisir donna aux hommes la première idée de Musique*' (Blainville 1972 [1767], v), Rousseau's account of the origins of civilization situates musicality as providing the first ideas concerning pleasure.

Corresponding to the shift Bermingham notes above, if man, rather than God or nature, becomes the source and author of his own history in Rousseau's account, *Adieu* also displaces the spiritual reason for colonial beauty. The song represents the colonizer's presence and absence as the creative force behind the *doudou*'s musicality. The latter's structures of feeling and desire bring the *doudou* to the cusp of time, to an engagement with language and text, and to a position of colonial subjection. Rousseau's description of this structure as a primal scene clarifies *Adieu*'s designation of the colonizer, or Western/French man, as the author of Creole musicality and civilization (rather than God), operating a discursive shift that mirrors an Enlightenment secularization of understanding the origins of music and the meaning of musicality. *Adieu* suggests the importance of a secular, 'enlightened' *mission civilisatrice* for French imperialism.

The emergence of musicality in the '*accents passionnés*' that Rousseau describes above, and in which he located the inaugural moment of sociality and therefore '*le vrai berceau des peuples*' (1979, 212), corresponds to a temporal emergence as well. In this '*âge heureux où rien ne marquait les heures, rien n'obligeait à les compter, le temps n'avait d'autre mesure que l'amusement et l'ennui*' (1979, 212). Musical existence structures the primal scene of the subject's relationship to others as a relationship of time. 'For Rousseau, vocal sounds are not so much expressions of ideas as they are moments of identification and social bonding' (Thomas 1995, 105). The soul of the 'savage man', according to Rousseau, lives in the present with no notion of the future. Yet musicality seems to retain in Rousseau's discourse elements of this prelapsarian state, for '[a]s a negation of eighteenth-century languages, primordial speech is situated outside of time. The origin obeys no chronology: it is, by definition, *u-chronique*' (Thomas 1995, 109).

According to Radano and Bohlman, Rousseau's work suggests that '[t]hrough song, the racial difference immanent in nature was given voice' (2000, 15). I suggest rather that it may prove more useful to consider the ways in which Rousseau's conceptualizations of musical time and pleasure seek precisely to define 'race' in ways that will not rely on nature because they go beyond empirical reality. Rousseau's push against a completely empirical understanding of musicality and his connections between the musical genres and 'genres' of people suggests an alternate discursive route for French racial thought.

> *On pourrait et l'on devrait peut-être encore diviser la* musique *en* naturelle *et* imitative. *La première, bornée au seul physique des Sons et n'agissant que sur le sens, ne porte point ses impressions jusqu'au cœur, et ne peut donner que des sensations plus ou moins agréables. Telle est la Musique des Chansons, des Hymnes, des Cantiques, de tous les Chants qui ne sont que des combinaisons de Sons mélodieux, et en général toute musique qui n'est qu'Harmonieuse.*
>
> *La seconde, par des inflexions vives, accentuées, et, pour ainsi dire, parlantes, exprime toutes les passions, peint tous les tableaux, rend tous les objets,* soumet la Nature entière à ses savantes imitations, *et porte ainsi jusqu'au cœur de l'homme des sentiments propres à l'émouvoir. Cette musique vraiment lyrique et théâtrale était celle des anciens Poèmes, et c'est de nos jours celle qu'on s'efforce d'appliquer aux Drames qu'on exécute en Chant sur nos Théâtres. . . .* Tant qu'on cherchera des effets moraux dans le seul physique des Sons, on ne les y trouvera point. (*Musique* 1768, 308, emphasis added)

Rousseau's passage points to the power he accords musical representation not only to speak to communities but also to speak for them. Rousseau, the enlightened theoretician of social inequality and democracy, has few qualms about expressing the importance of musical persuasion, of passionate rhetoric, to trump or circumvent the challenges reason poses for the social contract. 'The inhabitants of Rousseau's state must be brought into unison by the legislator', Scott writes, whose rhetorical 'arsenal . . . includes the power of melodious speech . . . [to] 'denature' the people and transform them into communal beings' (1997, 824).

The successful legislator cannot only use reason or force to get people to obey laws, he needs recourse to another type of authority. 'Rousseau's emphasis on nonrational "persuasion" instead of rational "conviction" as the key to the legislator's task raises the musical and linguistic aspect of founding' (Scott 1997, 825). Musical performance, rather than giving voice to the racial difference imminent in nature, '*soumet la Nature entière à ses savants imitations*'. The location of '*l'Accent pathétique et oratoire, qui est l'objet le plus immédiat de la Musique imitative du théâtre*' constitutes a crucial site of conversion, for:

> *tous les hommes étant sujets aux mêmes passions doivent en avoir également le langage: car autre chose est l'Accent universel de la Nature qui arrache à tout homme des cris inarticulés, et autre chose l'Accent de la Langue qui engendre la Mélodie particulière à une Nation.* (*Accent* 1768, 2)

This musical modulation from the universal to the particular poses key problems for Enlightenment thinkers, for '[t]he legislator's role is extralegal. He furtively attends to mores, customs, and especially opinions', Scott explains. 'Rousseau's legislator attends to the cultural affective basis of the state' (1997, 824). The love of country versus the love of humanity is another way to understand the conflict of *Adieu*. Rousseau writes in language that again echoes the terms of the *l'Exclusif*, '"The legislator who seeks both [these virtues] will not get either one: this harmony has never been seen, because it is contrary to nature, and because *one cannot give a single passion to two objects*" (*Lettres écrites de la montagne*) [I. p. 706]' (quoted in Todorov 1993, 180, emphasis added). Rousseau thinks this problem through in terms of man vs citizen. Man is concerned with both the human kind and the individual. 'We cannot say that one of these terms is valorized here at the expense of the other; rather', Todorov explains,

> there are two independent value systems at work, and we cannot simply eliminate one of them. If we were to give up citizenship, we could no longer guarantee the application of the law (the universe is not a State); if we were to forget about humanity, Rousseau suggests, we would be denying our own most intimate feeling that tells us, when we see another human being, whoever he or she may be, that we belong to the same species. . . . The success of civism is in inverse proportion to that of 'humanism'. (1993, 179, 180)

Adieu has the ability to speak to Enlightenment musical discourse and ultimately to the imperialism of the Third Republic, despite its Ancien regime origins, 'by making reference back to some originary "moment", [whereby] a kind of temporal continuum is created in which the present rejoins with the past in such a way as to efface the past and the future to create an eternal present' (Simon 2004, 196). *Adieu* captures the affective and temporal skips in Enlightenment thought, foundationally located in the musical discourse of the other, pointing to a tricky conservation of colonial and racial hierarchies despite the social and cultural ruptures of the French revolution.

The situation of this moment as primal retroactively posits the *doudou*'s lament as the true origin of colonialist recognition and desire. Rather than musically identifying colonization as the source of lament, *Adieu*, when heard in the paradigms of the French Enlightenment, posits the longing of the colony as *anté*-colonial, interpellating the French colonizing presence rather than suffering from it. *Adieu* reifies this origin in time as '*le moment suspendu entre la préhistoire sociale et l'histoire des inégalités*' (Schmouchkovitch 2004, 105).

Head's sharp insight in the article mentioned above ultimately concerns the ironic posture in contemporary musicology, which now rather peremptorily dismisses questions which were key to its own formation. Rousseau's imaginative staging of the primal scene of sociality may seem quaint; yet, from a contemporary critical standpoint, does not his notion of 'passion' as the truth of representation hit upon the psychoanalytic notion that language speaks otherwise? As Michel Poizat writes, Rousseau's philosophy rests on '*la mise en place comme origine du langage de ce qui fonde la jouissance même de la voix, à savoir le 'hors-langage', l'affect, ou selon le vocabulaire de l'époque, la passion*' (1986, 93).

As Thomas puts it, '[f]rom a psychoanalytic perspective, Rousseau is describing an inaugural (and final) moment of plenitude . . . made to commemorate both an original communion and its loss' (1995, 120). Yet, while the *doudou*'s *Adieu* captures her at the moment of emotional *déchéance*, at the end of her relation, the song's performativity situates her as always still there. She not only bids farewell, she is eternally there waiting. Fanon hints at this dynamic in his remarks about Antillean women. In the ambivalent fashion that characterizes the *doudou* mythology, this staging of eternal availability represents the *doudou* as alternately lascivious, where waiting signals constant sexual availability, and/or faithfulness, where French Antillean relations emotionally surpass (and erase) the physical, material economies upon which the imperial relation was based. Her expectant position at the port conflates scenes of arrival and departure, positing the eternal availability of desirous colonial encounters.

The *doudou* represents this encounter as idyllic and unforeseen; as a symbol of *métissage*, either as the *métisse* herself or as the latter's maternal dark source, she (pro)creates the 'unexpected'—the blurring of colonial power boundaries due to intimate relationships. But how could this encounter not have been foreseen? In fact the demand from French colonists for more French women has been well documented (Chamoiseau and Confiant 1999). *Adieu*'s resonance with myths of origin and its musical time changes pinpoint the negotiation of a transcultural *refoulement* and squarely put its affective weight on the shoulders of the woman of colour.

Josephine Baker's starring roles in the films *La Sirène des Tropiques* (1927), *Zou zou* (1934, note the proximity between this title and *doudou*) and *Princesse Tam-Tam* (1935) offer perhaps the most famous examples of this logic, demonstrating its influence in dominant popular culture in France as well as in French West Indian literature during the Third Republic. Like *Adieu*, these films stage the Creole woman's musicality as making her a potential border-crossing agent and a key player in transcolonial and transnational encounters. Baker's debonair love interest in *Princesse*

Tam-Tam (played by Albert Préjean), a white French writer facing unmet past deadlines for his latest work, escapes the petty machinations *le Tout-Paris* that block his creativity by retreating to the colonies. He happens to discover Baker's character Alwina, a simple, North African shepherd girl, who 'mischievously' steals food from tables in a café to survive. Alwina's cultural naivety and moral innocence intrigue and amuse the writer whose difficult and spoiled Parisian girlfriend avidly participates in the rumour mills and materialistic lifestyle taxing his (implicitly more pure or redeeming) artistic inspiration.

The story of his new novel becomes the (fictitious) experiment of civilizing Alwina: teaching her to dress, to walk in heels, to eat with silverware, but most importantly to love. Here again transcolonial love and artistic creativity juxtapose the colonizer's writing against the colonial subject's musicality to relate an intimate aesthetic sound/text meeting that becomes rather ostensibly a French civilizing project. At the film's climax, the sound of African drums on stage 'seize' Alwina, the 'tam tam' princess, and violently reveals her true self. The drums' rhythms force her to rip herself free of her dress, not only so the rhythm can completely possess her body but because it demands she reveal her skin.

Representations of the *doudou* consistently involve attempts to 'out' her; music typically serves to disrupt the *doudou*'s attempts to mask her true colonial self. Through the *doudou*'s musical hypersensitivity to drums and rhythm the primitive racial atavism lying under the veneer of French assimilation, or the mask (read possibility) of exotic civility, surges forth. Alwina cannot control herself, and more specifically her body. Having been slipped one drink too many, she cannot help but perform a 'savage' dance that the audience loves, but which reveals her inappropriateness for her love interest, sending him back to the arms of his French girlfriend.

The film tellingly ends with the new novel, entitled *Civilisation*, being slowly eaten by a mule (a longstanding symbol for the mulatto). The film's subtly ominous final scene resonates with Rousseau's positioning of the bucolic musical moment of social encounter as a scene of *déchéance*, a mythology so strong it demonstrates its relevance for analysing francophone Antillean cultural relations with French imperialism even during the Third Republic. Alwina, a destitute yet content shepherdess, discovers romantic or passionate love and its musical representation through her encounter with an (imperial) other. The languorous scene of Alwina singing her solo romantic plaint on the bow of a ship posits music as the channel for her 'civilizing' amorous development. But her fall from innocence will be a specular localization of her distance from and alienation within (French) civilization.

Because she is passionate (loving) and suffering (pitiful), because she loses everything but remains faithful, because male authority is re-established through the identification of the threat of pleasure and its subsequent conversion, its submission (to the discourse of the master), the pity elicited from the *doudou*'s suffering plaint echoes within the contours of the mythological self/other musical positioning in Rousseau's Edenic love-story, one of '*le plaisir et le désir confondus ensemble*' (pleasure and desire confused together, a striking way to encapsulate the action of the *doudou*'s affective situation).

Through his imaginative history of musical origins, his notion of melody as a cultural memorative sign and his discourse on affect, Rousseau operates an important shift whereby music, connected to passion and pleasure, becomes an ethical basis for sociality. But Rousseau also clearly points out all along that this first cry, this plaint, also expresses pain. These protagonists are also just as easily (ant)*agonists*. '*Ce n'est ni la faim, ni la soif, mais l'amour,* la haine, la pitié, la colère, *qui leur ont* arraché *les premières voix*' (1979, 168). Rousseau insists on the violence of these passions that '*arrachèrent* les premières voix' (1979, 167, emphases added), yet he does not offer the other's scene, the subject of pain (whom the listening subject pities). The morality generated in Rousseau's account is reserved for the pitying subject rather than the subject of pity.

Conclusion

David Macey argues that 'Fanon's version of the song can also be read as a farewell to the *doudouiste* literature' (2000, 113). However, following the performative leads in Fanon's staging of *Adieu* and my analysis of that song's construction of the *doudou*, I take *Adieu* as a story of origins. More specifically, *Adieu* narrates important 'new beginnings', an oxymoron translating the retroactive nature of (colonial and racial) subject formation as well as colonial discourse. As a cultural statement about origins, *Adieu* makes claims on the very nature of coloniality and of the Antilles. Despite its position at the cusp of the 1789 French Revolution, and despite its authorship by a staunch representative of Ancien Régime colonial power, *Adieu*, rather than clearly singing the swansong of feudal colonialism and the transition into modern imperialism, claims that essence of French/Antillean colonial relations fundamentally transcends the vagaries of politics and history.

This myth stages a transformation that is not one, an apparent moment of mourning stuck instead to the refrain of melancholic lament. The materially and temporally finite needs of colonialism having been met, *Adieu* stages a relation of mutual desire, where emotional (familial and romantic) attachment continues to resonate beyond the spatio-temporal and textual limits of *l'Exclusif*. In fact, *Adieu* serves to slip into the language of a colonial 'pact' that Julien denounces. The representation of desire therefore becomes a representation of representation, a (fixed) testimony of willing submission, whereby the colonial subject has always already elected the endlessly ambivalent trajectory of difference mapped out by French imperialism.

The surprising absence of the *doudou*'s song in postcolonial criticism, in addition to reflecting the latter's methodological privileging of textual paradigms, results from the way her ethical ambivalence cannot be easily re-appropriated for demands for (masculinist) narratives of heroic subversion. Popular music's ephemeral yet continuous production of socio-cultural structures of feeling, knowing and relating (re)produces an aural past that differs from high culture's politics and retroactive histories of canonization. This ephemeral quality lends it a lively flexibility such that aural culture, fuelled through popular networks of circulation, often offers a more timely and flexible barometer of popular ideas and attitudes towards 'race' and French imperialism than the literary figures of postcolonial criticism. While the stakes of the colonial text negotiate forms of authority backed, for example, by the legal contracts of history that situate the state and the citizen, the stakes of colonizing the soundscape often have to do with generating popular legitimacy for discursive shifts and new understandings of the letter of the law. At the same time, the context of the *doudou*'s production reveals the colonial co-authorship of the victim's discourse, which latter detracting critics commonly cite as the problem with the politically correct agendas of postcolonial and ethnically based studies.

While *doudou* began as a Creole term of endearment, later becoming a blank name for French colonial fantasy, critical discourse has designated *doudou*ism as a poetic performance practice that reproduces colonialist portrayals of Martinique and Guadeloupe (Condé 1978; Toumson 1989). Etienne Léro *et al.* employed the term '*doudouiste*' to denounce the sentimentalist ideology that formed the relationship between colonial discourse and the aesthetic conformity of mainstream Antillean poetry. '*Nous haïssons la pitié. Nous nous foutons des sentiments*'—'We hate pity. We don't give a damn about sentiment' (1979, 1). Fanon's merciless critique of the *doudou* also constitutes a disavowal of *doudou*ist sentimentalism which he hears as psychically untenable and socially unethical. I think the analysis above demonstrates the importance of their firm emotional stance that takes on the *doudou* dialectically, but I suggest that this move is generative of the masculinist dynamic of critique in the genealogy of negritude.

Herein lies an integral part of the *doudou*ist problematic, one certainly not absent in Fanon's work: the analysis of the *doudou* inevitably takes the form of an interrogation where the conflation of the aesthetic and of the ethical resonates with patriarchal paradigms of authority and power. Crudely put, this *bête noire* has been on trial since the days of Père Labat, and negritude contributes to that virulent grilling. The problematic gender dynamics facing the representation of black pain and pleasure make negritude's critique of the *doudou* aesthetic resonant with her colonialist designation, since the *Code noir*, as the site of conflicted ethical decisions concerning the true and the beautiful. The *doudou* pits anti/colonial desire (love) against anti/colonial duty (aggression) and gives birth to the moral ambivalence, if not impossibility, of the *métis*. For the *doudou* often sings her plight as a tragic mulatto and her incarnation of the tortured, pathetic female body of colour ambivalently counterpoints pain and pleasure in the strategies of colonists, abolitionists, reformers and black radicals alike.

At the most basic level, the *doudou*'s ability to sing through these discursive ruptures and social transformations related to the French Revolution comes from the fact that for many the revolution changed rather little in daily colonial life. At the same time, French culture, especially beginning with the 18th century, created a number of archetypal 'natives' used symbolically or allegorically to debate issues taking place at home. Part of the *doudou*'s longevity comes from the way her prime characteristics—her musicality (and lack of textual ownership: literacy, legal legitimacy, social contract, authorship and 'writability'), her melancholia/pity, her temporal and ethical ambivalence, her (other) beauty—resonate with Enlightenment philosophical debate and later with the republican imperial discourse of the French Third Republic.

If the *doudou*'s life is all about beauty, *doudou*ism's hegemonic power play represents a long history of the willing submission of that beauty to the discourse of the master. If the *doudou*'s lament is her seduction, and just as importantly her performance of seduction, her song suggests that the colonizer cannot be heartless, that even relations of overt force must also rely on types of complicity, that macro-level ruptures are often only hearable, rendered meaningful, through micro-level structures of continuity. Just as *Adieu* names 'ethnicity' but not 'race', the limited and elliptic nature of its narrative, which only recounts (what appears as) the penultimate action of love, relies on the listener's imaginative hearing of song and voice to fill in the *doudou*'s narrative *body*. It is then this type of cultural imagining which must metonymically work and allegorically rework the tale of the subject into one of the colony, and, by extension, of the role of colonial origins in the French republic.

While negritude's scream seeks to operate poetic aggression by sounding the psychic distance between the colonial subject and the hexagon, the *doudou*'s demands will be heard only if her condition of pain sounds beautiful and thus resonates beyond the trauma of separation and interrogation. *Adieu*'s portrayal of the *doudou* as an object of pity constitutes, in direct relation with her musicality and her ambivalence, melancholia as a mode of imperial relations. The *doudou*'s beauty is her passion, but her performance of lament, which the colonizer cannot *not* hear, sets the stage for ethical demands. If the *doudou*'s performance elicits 'the desire of the other', it attaches to the latter 'the pity of the other' in order to stage the debate about the consequences and realities of French colonialism.

References

Antoine, Régis. 1978. *Les Écrivains français et les Antilles: Des premiers pères blancs aux surréalistes noirs.* Paris: Maisonneuve & Larose.

———. 1998. *Rayonnants écrivains de la Caraïbe.* Paris: Maisonneuve & Larose.

Bermingham, Ronald. 1988. Le cri de la nature et la nature du cri: Étude d'une coupure épistémologique. In *Études sur les discours de Rousseau,* edited by Jean Terrasse. Ottawa: Association nord-américaine des études Jean-Jacques Rousseau.

Berrian, Brenda F. 2000. More than a doudou: women's subversive songs. In *Awakening spaces: French Caribbean popular song, music, and culture.* Chicago Studies in Ethnomusicology. Chicago, IL: University of Chicago Press.

Blainville, Charles Henri de. 1972 [1767]. *Histoire générale, critique et philologique de la musique.* Geneva: Minkoff Reprints.

Chamoiseau, Patrick and Raphaël Confiant. 1999. *Lettres créoles: Tracées antillaises et continentales de la littérature, Haïti, Guadeloupe, Martinique, Guyane (1635–1975).* Paris: Gallimard.

Condé, Maryse. 1978. Propos sur l'identité culturelle. In *Négritude: Traditions et développement,* edited by Guy Michaud. Paris: PUF.

Fanon, Frantz. 1952. *Peau noire, masques blancs.* Paris: Editions du Seuil.

Hazael-Massieux, Marie-Christine. 1996. *Chansons des Antilles: Comptines, formulettes.* Paris: L'Harmattan.

Head, Matthew. 1997. Birdsong and the origins of music. *Journal of the Royal Musical Association* 122 (1): 1–23.

Julien, Charles-André. 1981. Preface. In *Toussaint Louverture: La Révolution française et le problème colonial,* by Aimé Césaire. Paris: Présence Africaine, pp. 7–19.

Lero, Étienne, René Ménil, Jules-Marcel Monnerot, Maurice-Sabas Quitman and Simone Yoyotte. 1979. *Légitime défense.* Paris: Éditions Jean-Michel Place.

Liauzu, Claude and Josette Liauzu. 2002. *Quand on chantait les colonies: Colonisation et culture populaire de 1830 à nos jours.* Paris: Editions Syllepse.

Macey, David. 2000. *Frantz Fanon: A life.* London: Granta Books.

May, Gita. 1989. Beauty in context. In *A New history of French literature,* edited by Denis Hollier. Cambridge, MA: Harvard University Press.

Poizat, Michel. 1986. *L'Opéra ou le cri de l'ange: Essai sur la jouissance de l'amateur d'opéra.* Paris: Editions A. M. Métailié.

Radano, Ronald Michael and Philip Vilas Bohlman. 2000. *Music and the racial imagination.* Chicago, IL: University of Chicago Press.

Rousseau, Jean-Jacques. 1768. *Dictionnaire de musique.* Paris: Chez la veuve Duchesne. (1975. *A complete dictionary of music,* trans William Waring. 2nd edn. London: AMS Press).

———. 1979. *Écrits sur la musique.* Paris: Editions Stock. (1998. *The collected writings of Rousseau,* edited by Roger Masters and Christopher Kelly, Vol. 7, *Essay on the origin of languages and writings related to music,* trans. John T. Scott. Hanover, NH, and London: University Press of New England.)

Ruscio, Alain. 1996. *Amours coloniales: aventures et fantasmes exotiques de Claire de Duras à Georges Simenon: romans et nouvelles.* Bruxelles: Éditions Complexe.

———. 2001. *Que la France était belle au temps des colonies … Anthologie de chansons coloniales et exotiques.* Paris: Maisonneuve & Larose.

Schmouchkovitch, Michel. 2004. La fonction du désir dans l'origine des langues selon Rousseau. In *Musique et langage chez Rousseau,* edited by Claude Dauphin. Oxford: Voltaire Foundation.

Scott, John. 1997. Rousseau and the melodious language of freedom. *The Journal of Politics* 59 (3): 803–29.

Simon, Julia. 2004. Music and the performance of community in Rousseau. In *Musique et langage chez Rousseau,* edited by Claude Dauphin. Oxford: Voltaire Foundation.

Thomas, Downing. 1995. *Music and the origins of language: Theories from the French Enlightenment.* Cambridge: Cambridge University Press.

Todorov, Tzvetan. 1993. *On human diversity: Nationalism, racism, and exoticism in French thought.* Cambridge, MA: Harvard University Press.

Toumson, Roger. 1989. *La Transgression des couleurs: Littérature et langage des Antilles XVIIIè, XIXè, XXè siècles,* Vol. 2. Paris: Éditions Caribéennes.

Vergès, Françoise. 1999. *Monsters and revolutionaries: Colonial family romance and métissage.* Durham, NC: Duke University Press.

Discography

Baker, Josephine. 1997 [1931]. *J'ai deux amours.* CD. New York: Arkadia Entertainment.

Castendet, Sam. 1950. Les adieu d'une Créole. In *Sam Castendet et son orchestre integral 1950: Festival biguine.* CD. Paris: Frémeaux.

Salvador, Henri. 1946–50. Adieu foulards, adieu madras. *Le Loup, la biche et le chevalier.* CD. Paris: Frémeaux.

Filmography

Princesse TamTam. 1935. Dir. Edmond T. Gréville. Perf. Josephine Baker, Albert Préjean, Robert Arnoux, Germaine Aussey and Georges Péclet. Kino Video.

Zou zou. 1934. Dir. Marc Allégret. Perf. Josephine Baker, Jean Gabin, Yvette Lebon, Illa Meery and Pierre Larquey. Kino Video.

'I Take My *Dombra* and Sing to Remember my Homeland': Identity, Landscape and Music in Kazakh Communities of Western Mongolia

Jennifer C. Post

A densely packed group of Kazakh women, men and children are gathered on the top of a small knoll. The site, outside the small city of Ölgii in Western Mongolia, overlooks the wide expanse of rolling hills and fields that will soon be cloudy with the dust from racers on horseback vying to win the top spot at the annual Mongolian national holiday festival: Naadam. It will be another hour or two before the racers

Jennifer C. Post is an ethnomusicologist on the faculty in the Music Department at Middlebury College in Middlebury, Vermont. In addition to her recent work in Mongolia, she has conducted fieldwork in India and Northern New England. Her recent publications include *Ethnomusicology: A contemporary reader* (Routledge, 2005); *Music in rural New England family and community life, 1890–1940* (University Press of New England, 2004); and *Ethnomusicology: A research and information guide* (Routledge, 2004).

arrive and the crowd are not facing the fields; instead they are gathered around two chairs where another competition is taking place. In the popular Kazakh *aitys* tradition, two *aqyns*[1] (poet-singers) improvise social commentary on local events and issues, witnessed by members of their communities. The musical competitors, some carefully costumed in traditional Kazakh clothing, display their language skills in song which they accompany using a stringed instrument, the *dombra*, to maintain rhythmic continuity and to punctuate their heightened speech. The competition is a round robin, and as the group of performers gets smaller, the musical commentary becomes sharper and the crowd's laughter and their cheers ever louder. It is July and the performers and audience members sit or stand for hours in the hot sun to witness this proud (some might say defiant) display of Kazakh identity,

The Kazakh people in Mongolia, who live primarily in the westernmost provinces (*aimags*) of Bayan Ölgii and Khovd (see Figure 1), use events and performances like these to express social solidarity in the face of recent social and political changes that are impacting on them in their daily lives. While we may not be able to document their actions as highly organized strategic plans, residents are certainly engaged in mobilized efforts to resist change brought by internal and external forces that threaten many of their social and cultural patterns.

Figure 1 Bayan Ölgii.

Kazakh residents in western Mongolia have maintained an attachment to their pastoral nomadic lifestyle in this mountainous terrain for generations. Bordered by the Altai mountains, the wide steppes, with opportunities for livestock grazing at several elevations, are well-suited for the seasonal migration that frames a way of life for nearly 75 per cent of the population in the province.[2] But the Kazakh people today struggle with the instability that accompanies a country and—especially—a region in transition. Their identification with Mongolia as Kazakh-speaking residents during the last 15 years (since the exit of the Soviets) is affected by large-scale nation-building led by Khalka Mongolians centred in Ulaanbaatar nearly 1,700 kilometres away, whose efforts often exclude elements of Kazakh identity. National markers (including language, food, clothing, social patterns, religion, musical instruments and musical expression) reinforced nationally and internationally have few connections to the everyday lives of the Kazakh people. They are also constantly considering and re-considering invitations from the government of Kazakhstan to repatriate after the break-up of the Soviet Union. Dependent upon seasonal access to grazing lands in the spring, summer and autumn, now their rights to land for their livestock are also being challenged by privatization, the establishment and maintenance of protected areas, as well as the activities of international mining companies that have bought rights to land once used by the herders.[3]

In this study I use musical expression to explore a process of place-making that occurs through the discursive construction and reconstruction of space and place within a community context. I argue that local musical production by Kazakhs in Western Mongolia enables expression and demonstration of local distinctiveness that also exhibits patterns of resistance to change (Gupta and Ferguson 1997, 6). Using the *dombra*, a long-necked lute widely considered a symbol of Kazakh identity as my central theme, I explore the common values expressed in instrument building, instrumental pieces and accompanied songs of local residents, primarily in Bayan Ölgii province.[4] Their production and performances demonstrate connections to homeland, a concept typically identified with diaspora: a place of origin to which residents in 'displaced' communities maintain a continuing attachment (Safran 1991, 84–5). I argue here that the homeland referenced by Kazakh residents in their music is seldom the place from which they (or their relatives) may have been displaced (many generations ago), rather it is the site where they have established a local connection (Mongolia) and, while maintaining their 'Kazakhness' in this landscape, have gained a sense of national identity and pride. Kazakh residents of Mongolia remain, though, in unique positions as Mongolian citizens, for they are also part of a transnational community and they are taking part in an ongoing process of claiming and reclaiming national allegiances and identities during this transitional period (Clifford 1994, 307).

The large-scale Kazakh settlement in what is today the westernmost region of Mongolia occurred in the 19th and early 20th centuries. Kazakhs fought for and settled in areas now known as Kazakhstan, Kyrgyzstan and Xinjiang Uighur Autonomous Region (XUAR) in China beginning in the 14th and 15th centuries, but they struggled against Oirats (Kalmyks) in the 16th and 17th centuries and were driven out of the Ili Valley and Zhunggar Basin (now largely in Xinjiang) during the Manchu Qing dynasty in the 17th century. Many ancestral families of Kazakhs in Mongolia originally lived in these regions. Some migrated in 1862 to the Khovd frontier of Mongolia and the Qing court granted them provisional grazing rights to this land in 1882. In 1912 rights to land in what is today known as Bayan Ölgii were extended to a large group of Kazakh families from the Altai region in China, and when Bayan Ölgii was established as a separate province in 1940 they were provided space to share (with the Altai Uriangkhai ethnic group), giving them a degree of autonomy (Atwood 2004, 294–5; Bulag 1998, 98–9; Finke 1999, 109–11). By 1989, before the exit of the Soviet Union, they comprised 91 per cent of the population in the province. Since the early 1990s there has been substantial repatriation of residents to Kazakhstan, followed by a pattern of re-migration, placing the Kazakh population in Mongolia in flux.[5]

Kazakh people in Mongolia have been sheltered from some of the changes that residents in Kazakhstan experienced during the 20th century. Their language[6] remains relatively intact and they have not experienced the degree of cultural assimilation in the form of Russification that has so radically changed the social and cultural landscape for the Kazakhs to their west nor the Sinification that has affected the Kazakhs to their south in Xinjiang, China.[7] Many still actively practise seasonal migration, and their nomadic lifestyle still remains a choice. The economic status, socio-political histories and everyday lives of the Kazakh people in Mongolia, while rooted in and identified with an idyllic pastoral realm, are exceedingly complex, The recent internal and external events and influences have created variously stable and ever-changing social and cultural landscapes for them. Their family histories remain deeply rooted in clan relationships; they identify, almost exclusively, with one of three clans or *zhüz*[8] of the Middle (*Orta*) Horde: Naiman, Kerei or Uaq.[9] Many local residents are socially unified by a common identification more specifically with Kerei history and ideals. Their ethnic, family and other shared community loyalties pull them in multiple geographic and social directions: to Kazakhstan, China, Ulaanbaatar city, and to family and friends in diasporic communities around the world. Economically the Kazakhs and other ethnic minority groups in these rural regions suffer along with all Mongolian residents who experience high poverty levels. In western Mongolia the number of people who live below the national poverty line is substantially higher than the countrywide figure of 36 per cent.[10] The harsh weather in the western provinces, including the destructive *zud* (a long hot summer followed by cold winter with heavy blizzard conditions) is often devastating for the nomadic families, notably causing loss of livestock, a primary source of food and economic gain.

Homeland, Place-Making and Social Action

Homeland and its significance as a basis for group identification and social action, and especially how it is connected to geographic place and a sense of belonging, are key issues for Kazakhs in Mongolia today. Homeland extends beyond the context of an unchanging 'local' as it is constructed and reconstructed within historical, spatial and socio-political spheres. Homeland can thus be identified as an ethnoscape that encompasses the long and complex ancestral histories of Kazakh residents. Furthermore, as Appadurai notes, the reproduction of locality is connected to rituals that are 'socialized and localized through complex deliberative practices of performance, representation and action' (Appadurai 1996, 206), These social and spatial practices occur by choice and as a result of social and political constraints that have occurred (and changed) over time.

For Kazakhs in Mongolia, their connections to native and ancestral places are rooted in shared histories of family and geographic place that are both real and imagined. While the reinforcement and renegotiation of their place-based, ethnic and national identities has been impacted upon by numerous changes that have affected residents' perceptions of place and homeland throughout the western region, possibly the most difficult one for individuals and families has been the repatriation decision that was first available to them in the early 1990s. For many, the repatriation process has been difficult, and even unsuccessful, particularly because of their long-term identification with and attachment to place. While some assume that a dispersed community moved to an 'ancestral homeland' will 'integrate seamlessly into the "co-ethnic" population', as geographer Alexander Diener notes in his research on this topic, diasporic populations do not exist in placeless or 'de-territorialized' realms (2005b, 465)[11] and, while opportunities to repatriate offered by Kazakhstan tease the Kazakh residents in Mongolia, they have also caused them to reconsider the value and meaning of homeland. In Mongolia today, when Kazakhs refer to homeland, they use *tugan jer* to indicate native land and a*tameken* and *atajurt*[12] for ancestral homeland or motherland. Thus *tugan jer* has been used primarily in the context of the Mongolian homeland and *atameken* and *atajurt* to refer to Kazakhstan. For some residents, these terms also indicate an ancestral homeland in what is today Xinjiang, China. Leaving Mongolia (for Kazakhstan or another country such as Turkey or Russia) represents a loss of connection to their native place and, for many, the home of their ancestors; thus, for many Mongolia is their ancestral homeland.

Kazakhs who do choose to repatriate from Mongolia are identified in Kazakhstan as returnees or *oralmandar* where their social and cultural practices do not always match those of their new compatriots.[13] The years of Soviet rule deepened the division among Kazakhs, who today realize, as they reconnect as a nation, that they have lived their lives in quite different countries. In his study on the migration decision of Kazakhs living in Mongolia, Diener offers the expressions of several poets to support, among other topics, ideas connected to difference and to perception of cultural purity. The poets seem effectively to capture the 'mind-set of migrants' who arrived in Kazakhstan from Mongolia in the early 1990s (Diener 2003, 394). This is expressed by Mongolian *oralman* poet Beken Khairatuly in the following verses of his poem 'Why I Came?'[14]

> I came to tell about my soul's grief
> I came to play Kazakh kui
> They say Kazakhstan is becoming Russified
> I came to know whether it is true or not
> ....
>
> Homeland, I came to take the rays of light
> I came to play a song on the *dombra*
> I came here to cry if you are crying in grief
> I came here to be happy if you are happy
> ....
>
> I came to show you traditions and customs
> If you will be able to understand them.

Here the poet identifies the *dombra* and one of its musical forms, *kui,* as tools for healing the ills of a struggling nation (Kazakhstan). He offers to display and to share the cultural depth and purity maintained by Kazakhs in Mongolia where many argue they have a stronger Kazakh identity (Diener 2003, 395).

The *Dombra*

Dombra production and use in Mongolia provides a lens through which we can explore in greater depth how Kazakh residents in Western Mongolia shape and reinforce their strong(er) ethnic and place-based identities. The *dombra* is the Kazakh form of the two-string long-necked plucked lute widely used throughout Central and Inner Asia.[15] Constructed of hard and soft woods, originally with gut—and now with nylon—strings and frets, the overall style and shape of the instrument has varied over time and by region. In general, there are two forms of *dombra* that are historically identified with regional playing: instruments used for *shertpe* style, linked to eastern Kazakhstan, typically use a smaller resonator and have a shorter neck than those used for *tökpe* style that is identified historically with performers and performances in western Kazakhstan (Kendirbaeva 1994, 109; Slobin and Sultanova 2006). The *dombra* resonator is typically pear-shaped for the longer-necked *tökpe* style playing, and spade-shaped or triangular like the Russian balalaika (one of its relatives) for *shertpe* style playing (Kiszko 1995, 138–9), The most widely used *dombra* today has an artfully formed bowl resonator that is carefully constructed with a series of seven ribs or spines made of thin pieces of wood (cedar, pine, maple, birch, walnut). While the instrument is typically described in literature as having 12 to 14 frets, in fact, in its modern form (in contemporary Kazakhstan, Mongolia and other diasporic communities) it has 19 frets. During the last 50 years, the neck of this widely distributed instrument has been lengthened, in part, I was told, to hold the larger number of frets that provide a wider melodic range, and afford opportunities for greater melodic development than was previously possible.[16] This codification in shape, construction and playing style (in the Soviet era) quickly reached the Kazakh communities both inside and outside Kazakhstan, including Mongolia as well as neighbouring China.

The *dombra* plays multiple roles musically and socially in Kazakhstan, among Kazakhs in Xinjiang in China, and in Mongolia. When used for performance, the instrument provides entertainment and helps to retain cultural memory. Many would identify the *dombra* as the national instrument for Kazakhs wherever they are living. We see evidence of this symbolically; it is frequently displayed on the walls of central living (and visiting) spaces. In the Western Mongolian city of Ölgii, a giant wooden *dombra* greets all who enter from the north (see Figure 2), one of many reminders that the regional population is overwhelmingly Kazakh. In the city and the countryside we hear references to the *dombra* and its music in poetry and song. In fact performers frequently identify it as an essential ingredient in their performances: its presence helps singers remember songs and its sound is tied to narrative, social

Figure 2 A giant wooden *dombra* greets all who enter the city of Ölgii from the north.

commentary and lyric expression. The repeated lines of a popular song taught to children in Tsengel school express this well:[17]

> There is no song without *dombra*;
> There is no beauty without *dombra*.

A performer in Ölgii, originally from Sagai, personifies the instrument when he sings:[18]

> My dear friend *dombra*
> Like me you will be abandoned
> When death comes to me
> You will become ownerless.

Dombra Production and Local Identity

The production and promotion of *dombras* in Bayan Ölgii reveal patterns that show concern for local distinctiveness and Kazakh identity that is connected to the Mongolian landscape. This becomes apparent when we consider how the instruments are made and sold and what local consumers value. It is important to recognize that the production process and construction of values over time have been affected by the unique experiences of the Kazakh residents in Mongolia. While some musicians (especially those connected to the theatre) own *dombras* purchased in or imported from Kazakhstan, during the last ten years an industry for *dombra*-making has been established and maintained in Ölgii city with broad public support. In 2005 the city (with a population of approximately 28,000 people) sustained at least eight part- and full-time *dombra* makers[19] who reported that they had produced and sold, in some seasons, at least 40 instruments in adult and children's sizes each week.[20] While the instruments are sold to Kazakh families in other provinces (such as Khovd where there is a significant Kazakh population) and to visiting tourists, makers indicated that most of their sales are to local and regional families, especially to children and young people.

The social, environmental and economic circumstances in Mongolia place considerable restrictions on *dombra* makers. In the first place, there is little evidence of a master-student or apprenticeship tradition of instrument making in this rural region with a low population.[21] While there were a few master craftsmen in Ölgii in the earlier years of the 20th century, during the Soviet era all instruments for the local theatre orchestra were imported from Kazakhstan.[22] In the countryside, instruments were made locally, but typically individuals made one or two *dombras* for a family member or neighbour. After 1991, when the imported instruments were no longer available, and there was a resurgence of Kazakh identity-building, local industries for instrument making began. This took place informally, as men with experience in engineering and carpentry recognized a need, and saw an opportunity for economic gain. They established their practices based on their technical skills and careful inspection of instruments from Kazakhstan.[23]

Another issue for *dombra* makers is the necessity for them to maintain low prices for their instruments in the continuing poor economic Mongolian climate. In order to make a living from their profession, makers must restrict the time they can give to creative development and careful workmanship. While the use of inlay work, carved or carefully painted designs on long-necked lutes is common in many Asian countries, in Mongolia this practice has been all but abandoned due to local economic need and limited opportunity for custom work. Thus *dombras* made in Mongolia are decorated quite simply—using paper cut-outs or photocopies of designs that are then quickly lacquered onto the instrument.[24]

Access to wood for *dombras* is also a continuing problem for instrument makers. With weak environmental controls, the quality and diversity of woods has declined in recent years. The added expense makes it nearly impossible for makers to consider importing woods from other countries. Because of the time pressure connected to economic need, makers also struggle with woods that they do not have time to dry. During one period, it was reported that new instrument makers attempted to make *dombras* without drying the wood in advance and experienced serious warping, especially of the long necks. Now many use salvaged woods for necks and pegs; their sources include furniture and older homes in Ölgii which were built with woods that now are relatively scarce. One maker I interviewed has been dismantling his house during the last few years in order to complete *dombras* to sell at the local bazaar. While we laughed as we discussed the potential long-term impact on his family, and envisioned his home and workshop with gaping holes in the walls and roof, when I asked him—as I had other makers—what he planned to do when there is no more dry wood to use, he shrugged. The *dombra* makers' plans are not long-term; they need to provide for their families day to day.

Despite the restrictions, the local industry has created an economic, aesthetic and social environment for *dombras* that are uniquely Mongolian. Makers model the basic size and shape of their instruments on those imported from Kazakhstan; at the same time, the active and growing industry has helped makers establish and maintain characteristics for their instruments that demonstrate and reinforce connections to the local landscape as well. They have adjusted design and construction techniques (in some cases using their experience in carpentry and engineering—not instrument making). The sound and appearance of the instruments distinguishes them from other *dombras*, especially because they are made using local woods.

Dombras are designed in Mongolia not only to identify them with specific makers, but the craftsmen make sure their instruments are connected with place, They decorate their instrument with locally created Kazakh patterns or symbols, such as an emblem that represents the Ölgii city seal. I found few contemporary makers who painted designs on their instruments, but those that did included paintings of landscapes that connect makers, along with performers and their communities, to specific places, In Khovd sum, a Kazakh community in nearby Khovd *aimag* (province), I inspected a spade-shaped *dombra* made many years ago by a local man; it was decorated with paintings of the Altai mountains and an *argali* (mountain sheep). In Tsengel sum in Bayan Ölgii a local maker I spoke with decorates his instruments with paintings of the Altai mountains, swans, a heart (to bind the presenter of the instrument to the recipient) and, variously, a local flower or an eagle. That their images are identified very specifically with place was immediately clear to me: the Khovd *dombra* maker lives with the Altai mountains surrounding his village and the rare *argali* is found primarily in his region. I met with the Tsengel maker in his yurt at his summer place (see Figure 3), in an exquisitely beautiful valley surrounded by the Altai mountains, fields of flowers, and with eagles flying overhead.

The practice of keeping (and protecting) cultural traditions (including performance practices in music as well as instrument-building style and technique) in a controlled family or community environment has impacted on the transmission of culture in many Central, South and West Asian communities for generations.[25] If a musical line framed by long-standing tradition is broken, a new generation of committed individuals would need to begin anew, renewing older practices but also giving birth to new traditions. The instrument making I observed in Bayan Ölgii is comprised largely of first-generation makers who are in the process of establishing family-based master-student relationships or apprenticeships that will contribute to establishing even stronger cultural ties to identity and landscape. Among the makers I interviewed, four have established practices that involve members of the next generation in their families. Their children are actively involved in the construction process, acting as apprentices in their workshops. In one family a son in his twenties has just begun to make *dombras* independently, working in conjunction with his father. His son-in-law, once a carpenter, began full-time *dombra*-making after his marriage. In another family, three teenage children work long hours in the workshop with their father. The wives and children in each of these families are also sometimes

Figure 3 The *dombra* maker Chelektai at his summer place in Tsengel sum.

expected to take instruments to the bazaar and sell them while their husbands (or fathers) are at home working, Working together to keep the instrument-making practices local, these makers are well aware that the instruments they make will play an important role in the cultural lives of many in their communities.

Dombra Performance and the Local Landscape

As Kazakh people in Mongolia produce and play the *dombra* today, the instrument and its music carry historical, geographic and social memories that encompass their local landscape. They mark their place in Mongolia with tunes and songs that reinforce these links to locality, using repertoires, playing styles and stories associated with their tunes and lyrics connected to their songs. This situates musicians and audience members—helping them to make imagined connections—providing 'geographic referents' related to the instrument and its music (Dawe 2002, 4). When we examine musical genres and performances popular in the region, performed at weddings and other social gatherings and at cultural centres including the local theatre in Ölgii, we see that location remains a significant element.[26] Local instrumental pieces, especially the popular form *kui*, clearly show the importance of this geographic referencing.

Instrumental Pieces

Musicians throughout Bayan Ölgii province continue to support a solo instrumental genre called *kui* in public and private, formal and informal, performance contexts.[27] Known throughout Kazakhstan—indeed in a related form in many Central Asian countries—*kui* are partly characterized by their accompanying programmatic story-lines that contain allusions to local life, its nature and social circumstances. *Kui* performances in Mongolia provide nostalgic references to specific places, descriptions of the character and behaviour of beloved horses and of common birds, and they describe the complex relationships between humans and their world.[28] The *kui* played in nomadic yurts and the Ölgii city theatre include historical material as well as contemporary pieces. In the countryside the genre is typically performed by a solo musician, while in the theatre, the tradition is maintained by folk orchestras established during Soviet times that offer arrangements of popular *kui* (as well as performances of European art music arranged for the folk ensembles).[29] Older compositions in repertoires of countryside and theatre-based musicians in Mongolia are maintained in ongoing performance traditions and have been documented in historical recordings and at least one notated collection.[30] The *kui* in Mongolia are locally characterized as unique for their tuning, texture and melodic style. The two strings of the Kazakh *dombra* are typically tuned either a fifth or a fourth apart. It is interesting to note that, in Mongolia, local *kui* are associated with—and thus characterized by—fifth tuning, while tuning in fourths is identified with *kui* from Kazakhstan. Thus some musicians refer to fifth tuning as a local custom for Kazakhs in Mongolia, and identify the practice exclusively with this location. While this is not accurate, the dominance in Mongolia of fifth tuning (and its related playing style) does contrast with tuning and performance practice in Kazakhstan where many more *kui* are played with a fourth tuning.[31] This is significant because of the sound of pieces identified as Mongolian products. When the instrument is tuned in fourths, the performer uses the two strings to create a series of harmonic relationships, using both thumb and fingers on the frets.[32] Tuned in fifths, the bass string typically serves as a drone and the melody is played on only one string.[33] Some performers in Bayan Ölgii portrayed their melodies as 'simple' compared to those of Kazakhstan, Yet this characterization is expressed with some pride. One local composer and performer, commenting on the differences between repertoires and playing styles in Kazakhstan and Mongolia, said to me, 'our lives are simpler—and our melodies are straightforward'.[34]

When I asked the Ölgii *dombra* player Seit to play local *kui*, the first piece he chose was his own composition that he called 'Atameken' or 'Homeland'. He made it clear in his discussion that the homeland he was referring to in his piece was Bayan Ölgii and that locality was in the mind of both performers and listeners during its performance when he said: 'This *kui* pictures the landscape in Ölgii, the river in Ölgii and the horse's gallop'. He then described the calls of local birds, the familiar horses' gaits and the movement of waves on a provincial lake that the *kui* demonstrates. Performances of such pieces in Kazakhstan and Mongolia, especially by musicians who have performed in theatre traditions, typically include mimetic hand and arm movements that indicate the beating wings of a bird, the smooth waves on a lake, or demonstrate a rider striking the rump of a horse. The practice, while most likely tied to folkloric theatre, has now become part of the everyday performance culture in Mongolia, especially in Ölgii and nearby sums. Thus Seit illustrated highly stylized playing techniques he identified specifically with local *dombra* players, and stated that this reminded the listeners/viewers of the skills and pride of Bayan Ölgii musicians. 'Atameken' was first performed by a group of children at an Ölgii anniversary event in the year 2000, and Seit described how their performance was enhanced with owl feathers[35] worn on the wrists of the performers. The downy feathers of the young owl are displayed by Kazakh people as a sign of honour, and the message during an important local event, expressed by Seit in his choreographed piece, was enhanced by the visual reinforcement of their movements as they moved their hands to strike the strings of the *dombra*—at the base, face and fretboard.

In the nearby village of Ullankos, Suyenish chose to play 'Tasty Bulakh' ('Stream with stones'), a piece by a local composer. He said that the *kui* represents a body of water located on the Dayan mountainside (along the Chinese border in the southern part of the province). This is a popular place for summer livestock grazing. He said, 'It is a fine tradition to sing about the wonders of nature', and he described the scene: 'There is always beautiful nature on both sides of the stream which flows between the rocks. It is flowing from one stone to another, fast and powerful, Tastulakh'.[36] Indeed, the fast-paced piece provides an 'aestheticized imitation' of the sound of water bubbling through the rocks. The pacing and imitative quality reminded me also of another piece he had played during an earlier visit called 'Khur Oinak'[37]—in a duet with another *dombra* player—in which the musicians drew an acoustic picture of the movements of a particular bird that is often seen flitting and diving through the tall grasses in the steppe.

Similarly, '*Sari ala khas*',[38] a tune attributed to composer A. Kabykei, remains widely in the popular memory. Whenever I mentioned Delüün sum, the region where the lake locally known as Sari ala khas is located, invariably I elicited a version of the story and tune from *dombra* or *sybyzgy* (the Kazakh end-blown flute)[39] players. The stories and memories exist on several levels, for when they are expressed we are reminded that the lake region is a summer place for local people, and that the lake itself is often populated with the ruddy shelduck (or *sara ala khas*, translated locally as 'yellow goose'). Memory and place are connected with a story. One version was recited by one of my translators who had grown up in Delüün:

> Once there was a 'yellow and black goose' that had a group of goslings. They were very happy until a hunter came along and shot the mother. Her wing was broken and, since she was unable to fly, she was left alone when her flock flew south in the fall. The *kui* is about how the goose feels, swimming in the lake, flapping its wings, alone.[40]

Performers construct scenes with their music—and in telling and retelling their stories, they emplace themselves and their community of listeners in the Mongolian landscape. They engage and re-engage in a relationship with place, inscribing their identities through family and community memories and shared practices. Summer place represents the freedom to move (to travel) and to maintain a way of life that is characterized first by the common practice of pastoral nomadism. In addition it also connects families and places; those who have identified a region—a lakeside, mountain or valley as their ancestral territory. Those now settled in the city, who visit their ancestral homes only occasionally, reconnect with place and the Mongolian natural world they all share when they play or hear pieces like these.[41]

Vocal Forms

I found examples of similar practices in older and recently written lyric and narrative songs that were invariably accompanied on the *dombra*. Performers embed historical, geographic and social memories in their lyrics and instrumental styles. Scholars classify traditional Kazakh vocal practices into three broad categories: fixed lyric song (*änshilik*), improvised composition (*aqyndyq*) and oral epic (*zhyraulyq*) (Kunanbaeva 2002, 950–6). In Mongolia, singers typically exhibit repertoires that include pieces from each of these categories. For example, Suyenish (who also played several *kui* for me) is widely known as a respected *aqyn*, yet he sang a series of lyric songs, some that he wrote himself, some performed widely in the region at local festivals and celebrations (*toi*) and spread also through the airwaves on CDs and television programmes from Kazakhstan and Kazakh communities in China. In addition, Suyenish sang *aitys* which are classified as *aqyndyq* pieces providing social commentary. His performances of *aitys* included fixed compositions as well as improvised pieces in competition (where he has been rewarded with numerous prizes for his skill). He also sang examples of musical forms associated with *zhyraulyq* practices, including the narrative song genres, *terme* and *tolgaus.*

One song Suyenish sang, 'Boz Kereyim',[42] he had composed in 1996, when the repatriation programme in Kazakhstan was just a few years old. His song includes references to the travels of Kazakh people who (he imagines) came to Mongolia over the Besbogda Mountains,[43] yet now are 'turning their horses to the native land' (Kazakhstan). His song identifies the clan (*zhüz*) of his people—who are Kerei—and the 15th-century heroic khan Janibek who is linked to the establishment of the first Kazakh khanate in Kazakhstan during the 15th century, He also references a Kazakh 'hero' in China and Mongolia he calls Ospan (*Оспан*) who is actually Osman Batur, known by many as a bandit, who led efforts in Xinjiang in the mid-20th century to resist Soviet and Chinese domination in the Altai region.[44] He sings:[45]

> Like a female white camel who has lost her calf
> Like the back of a grey-black colt
> Oh my Besbogda Mountain, one of Altai's humps
> And Bayan Olgii sands, another true Kazakh place.
>
> *Aqyns* express the grief of the Kereits with their songs
> All my people who turned their horses to the native land, don't cry (like a camel) now
> Those who didn't drink from the water of Aksu[46]
> My people are holding the flag of Janevik and Ospan tightly
>
> Embrace this treasure and keep it in your heart
> And always remember the cherished songs (of my people)
> Oh my Besbogda Mountain, one of Altai's humps
> And Bayan Olgii sands, another true Kazakh place.

Suyenish sings to those who stayed behind (those who chose not to repatriate), using images of place to engage in nostalgic discourse—and to remind his local listeners of their histories and connection to Mongolia, He uses evocative images: the mother camel that has lost her calf, the much loved mountainous terrain of the Altai Mountains that they know so well (and cite so often in song), the earth (the sands) of Bayan Ölgii and the tight hold on a flag that signifies a nation whose heroes freed their ancestors in Kazakhstan, Mongolia and China.

Similarly, in a lyric song originally from Kazakhstan, sung in the Delüün-Tolbo region of Mongolia by Tilekbergen, we learn about the significance of *aul* (residential community),[47] of faith, place, family, movement and musical expression when he offers these images in the song:[48]

My *aul* is moving across the wide steppes
And it connects the earth and the clouds
My *aul* is going far, so let's wake up early
I need to see you before we go.

Refrain
Girl with owl's feather hat, black eyebrows and hair
Sweet and calm is your nature.

If you ask for our *aul*, it is in Amali
Allah gives us everything we need.
When my *aul* moves, I ask for only one thing
Please give good health to everyone who was left behind.

My horse is a strong black stallion
And it is chewing its bit, my elegant black horse
When you are young and healthy, be happy and joyful
For soon the black earth will chew us.

Who will take off the halter from a frisky horse?
Will my family meet father when he comes back safely with the livestock?
One who doesn't sing when he is alive, what will he do?
After death we will just be bones.

My *dombra* will be ready for *kuis* when I turn the pegs
And simple words will be suitable for my song
Today I sing that way
Because my sister asked me to.

It is not surprising that Tilekbergen would choose to maintain a song for his community that reinforces themes connected to everyday life in Mongolia. The unwavering support for immediate and extended family members—and their generosity with visitors regardless of their origin—is apparent in daily events in homes and herding spaces. In the countryside the relationships established and maintained in the *aul* and especially the role the *aul* community plays in providing social and work-related support in difficult geographic and economic circumstances are daily concerns of the herders. In addition, Kazakh families in the countryside maintain their connection to Islam[49] through daily prayer at meals and iconographically through prominent displays in yurts and winter homes of images of architecture and prayers (in Arabic script that most cannot read) that link them to their religion. They are also constantly attending to their livestock which provide them daily meat and milk, wool for warmth, and also demonstrate their wealth and independence (Olcott 1987, 248).

The *terme* performances I witnessed in Mongolia are locally identified by style of delivery and lyrics that, while expressing personal views, represent collective values and concerns. Although it was once largely an improvised genre, the performers I recorded presented composed pieces and nearly all preserved their lyrics in manuscript form. Their melodies range from a recitative style to tunes closely related to melodies found in local lyric songs. For all of these songs, the contemporary local practice included the *dombra* to provide harmonic and rhythmic accompaniment. In *terme*, this was characterized especially by a range of rhythmic patterns—not unlike those used also to punctuate some epic and *aitys* performances. I noted that the instrumental accompaniment plays an important role especially during interludes when the performer plays a repeated accented rhythmic pattern on the *dombra*, such as a series of eighth notes followed by one or more accented quarter notes. The lyrics of the songs, the style of delivery, along with rhythmic punctuation provided by the *dombra*, compel the audience to listen,

Japar and his family spend their summers in an ancestral place—their homeland—a lush and beautiful valley just a few kilometres from the Chinese border. He told me that his family has shared this territory for generations, Inside his family yurt, he took his *dombra* down from its place on the wall, quickly tuned the strings, and offered a *terme* he called 'Tugan Jer' or 'Homeland'. In its 29 verses he names a series of places that are all in the valley that is his ancestral home (in this excerpt noted in italics).[50]

I take my *dombra* in my hand and reflect on my place
My brothers I give my message to your generation
By remembering my ancestors who have died.
Homeland, where my blood was dropped from my navel

Before, there were Dunkir—Khalka people
Then Kerei people settled there
So its history is more than a century
It is my homeland also where my 'cord was cut'

Many *aqyns* praise their homeland
The swaying leaves and feather grass
Even though I can't describe my homeland as they do
I will try to send you my simple, heartfelt words

My *Kongirjal*, *Tishke sai* and *Kizil tas*
Please never take away my good luck
Which was given by *Kudai* [God]
You housed some livestock of my grandfather's *aul*

My great grandfather Mukhamedali spent the winter there
And had five kinds of livestock
They had only a few horses and brought them in *Chintak*
And *Moinakhora* was their autumn place

This name *Metagang jeldisai* was passed from generation to generation
And they had a summer place in *Jeldisai*
Where they had a herd of horses
And there was a well he dug and his children played there.

As Japar continued, his song described in detail the valley where we were staying. Witnessing this process of 'singing the landscape' by naming places connected to the ancestral history of his family, and to the Kazakh presence in this place, was his supporting community: his father, wife and children, other family members and visitors. They all listened intently and when Japar was finished, the group spoke with excitement about the *terme* he had offered to us. In this social landscape, filled with the tension of political change and economic strain, the production was a collective expression of community solidarity focused on maintaining continuity with ancestral history, landscape, and the cultural expression that ties it together.

Conclusion: Performing *Kazakhshylik* (Kazakhness) in Mongolia

In a recent article on historic narratives and Kazakh ethnic identity in post-Soviet Central Asia, Saulesh Yessenova (Esenova) suggests that Kazakh people have strategically worked to reaffirm ethnic boundaries during a particularly troubling time in their history (from the late 19th to the late 20th centuries). She suggests that Kazakh ethnic identity today emerges from a complex process comprised of 'political pressure and resistance, culture and social adjustment' (2002, 14). Using identity narratives in the form of genealogical constructions called *Shezhyre* (a genealogical register of Kazakh tribes and lineages that was compiled in the early 20th century) the once largely pastoral Kazakh people of Central Asia have been able consistently to maintain 'a remarkable sense of ethnic belonging and historic continuity as a nation' (2002, 13).[51]

In contrast to the now dominant settled lifestyle in Central Asia, in Mongolia ongoing pastoral practices—including unique relationships among social, economic and ecological concerns embodied and embedded in the daily lives of pastoral nomads—continue into the 21st century. Yet, for Kazakhs in Mongolia, social and

Figure 4 Singer and *dombra* player, Duan (sitting with his herding companion), provides an impromptu performance in the Sirgal region along the Chinese border.

political pressure (within Mongolia and from Kazakhstan, as well as China) encourages residents to use similarly strategic means to draw boundaries around their ethnicity—to (re)establish and maintain a Kazakh nation—in Mongolia. Using real and imagined images of place and ancestry, they simultaneously connect to their land, the landscape and their shared histories. Faced with a responsibility to their communities that is tied to Kazakh emphasis on 'moral rigor, community spirit and solidarity, and family/kin group obligations' (Yessenova 2003) musicians and instrument makers narrate histories that define Kazakhness (*Kazakhshylik*) in Mongolia. Thus they are not isolated from Kazakhs in Kazakhstan or Kazakhs in other diasporic communities, such as China, but they are carefully protective of their local distinctiveness. In 2006, one young singer from Sagsai sum provided clear evidence of the ongoing interest in maintaining these values. Seventeen-year old Akherke offered her own *terme*, accompanying it using a *dombra* to play the signature rhythmic punctuation. In the piece she systematically—and strategically—cites her family genealogy: the *zhety ata* (seven generations in her Kazakh lineage), and connects herself and her family, their life experience as pastoral nomads, quite clearly to the Mongolian soil as she names Sagsai and Suiksai as her ancestral places.[52]

> I wish you success on your work, all you people
> Let your riches increase each day
> Let me help you understand my history
> And introduce myself and my relatives.
>
> Our tribe is from Khojabirgen, a heroic ancestor
> It is a shame not to know seven generations
> So I'll recite my genealogy
> You people pay attention to me.
>
> I breathe the soft and warm wind from Sagsai steppe
> And I was educated in this good town
> I am Gagarin's daughter; my name is Akherke
> We are descendants of Khoshkharbai's children.
>
> My father's father's name is Kabi
> We pass the summer in a large white yurt in Suiksai
> My third grandfather's name is Saindolda
> My ancestor Khidir, support his soul and spirit.
>
> My fourth grandfather's name is Mamarjan
> His generations were raised and took root
> If you ask me, my fifth grandfather is Imantai
> I know my origin quite well
>
> My sixth ancestor is Mingbay
> Those who didn't know seven generations, listened
> So they continued it and strengthened their knowledge
> Khoshkharbai is my seventh grandfather.

So we are descended from these seven generations
We could keep the character of seven generations
And pass this from generation to generation
That is my origin.

I carry the responsibility in this generation
Some know me, some do not
Let me be known
Akherke is my name, given by my grandfather.

I am also one of the seven generations
I will also help to my parents when I grow up
My clan is Shibaraigir,
I was born as a singer, child [*jien*] of Tölek
My clan is Shibaraigir,
I was born as a singer, child of Tölek

The frequent use of the *dombra* in Western Mongolia for musical expression and as a marker of Kazakh identity helps communities maintain connections to cultural practices and ancestral places. While residents reinforce links to multiple homelands through musical repertoires and instruments, in amateur and professional performances, their music often references the Mongolian landscape, with locally constructed melodies, song lyrics with quite specific and local significance, and instruments that support a locally maintained industry for instrument production. Their actions contribute to community solidarity in response to nationalization efforts of Khalka Mongolians that often exclude Kazakh interests; and they also help residents navigate the struggles over decisions regarding repatriation and the daily impact that globalization plays on their lives.

It is most interesting to me that the community mobilization involves hundreds of children and youth who are encouraged by their families to learn traditional songs and to play local *kui* on *dombra*—in *dombra* clubs and private homes, in rural and urban schools, There is no overarching cultural organization that ensures the children and youth will perform particular repertoires or play *dombras* with specific characteristics. Instead, there are dozens of small and large communities regrouping, reinstating and maintaining a common Kazakh national identity in their Mongolian homeland.

Acknowledgements

Earlier versions of this paper were read at 'Diaspora, Postcolonialism and Performance', British Forum for Ethnomusicology one-day conference, London, 26 November 2005, and on the Faculty Lecture Series at Middlebury College, Middlebury, Vermont, on 27 March 2006. I would especially like to thank my primary translator during 2005 and 2006, Almagul Soltan of Ölgii, for her help with onsite translation as well as translation of song lyrics and narrative information. Unless otherwise noted, songs in this study were translated by Almagul Soltan.

Notes

[1] *Aqyn* (*Ақын*), sometimes *akhyn*, *akyn* or *akin*, is a poet and/or singer who improvises, typically using *dombra* for accompaniment. *Aqyns* are highly regarded for their epic poetry and sung social commentary in *aitys* performances. Many *aqyns* also sing *terme* and *tolgau* and other narrative forms.

[2] The *Mongolian Statistical Yearbook 2002* (National Statistical Office of Mongolia, 2003) lists 74.7 per cent of the employed population in Bayan Ölgii as herder.

[3] In his recently published book on contemporary Mongolia, Morris Rossabi says about the Kazakh people in Bayan Olgii, while they have not faced blatant discrimination nor have they been forced to abandon their language, 'however, Bayan Olgii aimag, where most of the Kazakhs reside, is one of the poorest areas of the country. As of 2003, few resources have been devoted to the economic development of the region, and the Kazakhs have had little representation in the government' (2005, 195).

[4] My research in Mongolia began in 2004 with a relatively brief, two–three-week trip to the western region in the summer of 2004. This was followed by two-and-a-half months of fieldwork in Khovd and Bayan Ölgii in the spring and summer of 2005 and two months of fieldwork in the summer of 2006.

[5] In 1989 there were at least 123,000 Kazakhs living in Mongolia (82,750 in Bayan Ölgii and 12,814 in Hovd and 9000 in the city of Ulaanbaatar) (Finke 1999, 111–12). While the population numbers have changed in Bayan Ölgii due to repatriation and remigration, Kazakhs still comprised a high percentage of the *aimag* population (87–90 per cent). In 1989 Kazakhs comprised 17 per cent of the population in Khovd *aimag* (Finke 1999, 112).

[6] Kazakh is a member of the Turkic language family (subfamily of Altaic languages).

[7] Russification as a unifying and strengthening strategy in Russia and the former Soviet Union affected individuals and communities representing national groups beginning in the 19th century. Residents of all Central Asian countries continue to feel the effects of this assimilation in their everyday lives. In China, Sinification or Sinicization also emerged as part of a political strategy to assimilate diverse residents of this vast country to embrace Han values. Most recent struggles by Kazakh, Uyghur and Kyrgyz Muslim minorities in Western China (since the mid-1990s) and the opening of borders to Kazakhstan and Kyrgyzstan provide opportunities for these ethnic groups to embrace goods and modern values from their kin rather than from China. See Gladney (1994) for a discussion of these issues in China.

[8] In Cyrillic: *жүз*.

[9] In Cyrillic the clans are: *найман*, *Керей* and *уақ*. I was given information on the clans orally by a number of local residents in Bayan Ölgii. Bulag states: 'The Kazakhs in Mongolia are mostly Abak-Kerei and Naiman Kazakhs who settled in the Altai of Hovd regions of Mongolia after the 1864 Tarbagatai Protocol between Russia and the Qing Dynasty' (1998, 98).

[10] This figure represents the population living below the national poverty line on 1990–2002 (World Bank 2005).

[11] Furthermore, Diener says: 'Not only can dispersed ethnic communities possess intense feelings of place attachment for regions outside of the "ancestral homeland," but they may display cultural practices and attitudes hybridized with those of their "host" society' (Diener 2005b, 465). Diener also provides useful discussions on territorial identity in his article 'Mongols, Kazakhs, and Mongolian territorial identity: Competing trajectories of nationalization' (2005a, 19–24).

[12] In Cyrillic these terms are *туған жер* (*tugan jer*), *атамекен* (*atameken*), *атажұрт* (*atajurt*).

[13] The *oralman* or returnee is a Kazakh ethnic immigrant. Many *oralmandar* have been given this special status by Kazakhstan in order to encourage their return to Kazakhstan from countries such as the former Soviet Republics, along with Afghanistan, Turkey and Mongolia. The *oralman* family receives free housing and social assistance, including help finding employment, along with aid in gaining permanent Kazakh citizenship. The repatriation process proved to be problematic for the government in Kazakhstan who were left to manage social services, employment and housing, and to deal with difficulties related to diversity (King and Melvin 1999–2000, 22). Dave reports that there was a strict quota for Kazakhs from Mongolia that diminished steadily between 1993 and 1999: 10,000 families in 1993; 7,000 in 1994; 5,000 in 1995; 4,000 in 1996; and 500 in 1999. Among the more than 60,000 who may have repatriated from Mongolia, 10–15 per cent have gone back to Mongolia (Dave 2004, 23).

[14] This poem was published in '*Hege Mening Otangha Keldym?*' in the magazine *Egemen Kazakhstan* (21 March 1992, 4: 68–69), translated into English by A. Diener. For the full text of this poem see Diener (2003, 394). Used by permission of A. Diener.

[15] The *dombra* is historically tied to the *tanbur* class of instruments that have been documented in West and Central Asian countries and cultures from the Akkadian era (3rd millennium BCE). Two strains were identified by al Farabi writing in the 10th century: one attached to Baghdad (and found in the southern regions of West Asia) and the other, the *Khorasan tunbur*, found in Persia and many Central Asian countries. There is clear linguistic, structural, performative and other historical evidence of the links among instruments of this type over many centuries. Today variations on the *tanbur* (or *tambur*) are found from Turkey to Western China (see Hassan *et al.* 2006).

[16] Several older musicians in Mongolia who performed for me using a 19-fret modern style instrument that I carried with me as I travelled spoke about the difficulties of playing with the longer neck and additional frets. Several implied that they felt the instrument had become unnecessarily complex (in relation to the repertoires that they chose to maintain).

[17] Recorded in Tsengel sum centre, 22 June 2005.

[18] Erkinbek of Ölgii, originally of Sagsai sum recorded this piece on 8 June 2005.

[19] In fact, among the widely known and respected instrument makers in Ölgii and surrounding regions, just two or three truly work full-time as *dombra* makers. Others combine their work with seasonal carpentry jobs in Ölgii and in Kazakhstan in order to make a living.

[20] Local *dombras* typically sell for 6000T to 10000T ($5–9).

[21] In contrast, in Kazakhstan—and other Central Asian countries—a long-standing tradition of instrument making has been supported especially in urban centers. These traditions are being renewed in the new independent countries with individual and organizational initiatives. For example, the Aga Khan Music Initiative in Central Asia (AKMICA) supports tradition bearers through an apprenticeship programme that provides funding and organizational sponsorship for the *ustad-shagird* (or master student) process. See <http://www.akdn.org/Music/Musicin.htm> for more information on this programme.

[22] This was reported to me by several older musicians who are either current or former members of the local theatre in Ölgii.

[23] Some makers indicated that the process of completing repairs on some of the older *dombras* from Kazakhstan provided the opportunity for them to inspect the instruments in detail, including their internal structure and apparent building techniques used during their original construction. One maker told me that he learned to make *dombras* from a 'how to' article published in a magazine from Kazakhstan during the late 1980s or early 1990s.

[24] The frets are made of fishing line, today imported from China (and sometimes from Russia); and the dots typically inlaid on the fingerboard are marked by the most popular *dombra* maker with coloured-paper dots that in America are purchased as office supplies for temporary identification of boxes or books.

[25] In Mongolia it is difficult at this time to trace any of the instrument-making practices to any formal *ustaz–shakirt* (master-student) tradition from Kazakhstan.

[26] Examples in this section are drawn from live performances recorded throughout Bayan Ölgii. The instrumental and vocal repertoires and styles performed in yurts and homes in sum centres represent one segment of the living traditions in the region. There is limited access to technology for musical production in Western Mongolia, so, while there is certainly an active interest in popular musical forms, they are drawn largely from Xinjiang and Kazakhstan,

[27] In Cyrillic: *күй*. The primary instruments used for *kui* in Kazakhstan are *dombra*, *kobyz* (a two- or four-stringed bowed lute) and *sybyzgy* (an end-blown flute).

[28] While countryside musicians (and instrument makers) are literally describing the world around them, in Ölgii city many residential musicians no longer participate in a pastoral nomadic way of life that provides access to the naturescape they sing about so often. Thus their references are often imagined.

[29] Built in the 1950s with funding from Russia and Mongolia, the local theatre visibly supports music of Mongolia and Kazakhstan as well as Russia (and other European countries). On the wall of their rehearsal room in Olgii are pictures of great composers that include Mongolian men and European men and three icons from Kazakhstan. Originally established and supported during Soviet times, in contemporary life it has become a space for sharing musical styles and practices: from *dombra* players to Russian-inspired orchestras; from conservatory-trained singers to local rap/hip-hop groups.

[30] *Bayan Ölgii Kazakmarynyn dombyra zhane sybyzgy kuileri* (1976).

[31] A primary stylistic division in Kazakhstan is found in the two regional traditions: *tokpe* and *shertpe*. *Tokpe*, as noted earlier, is identified historically with the western region. *Kui* played in *tokpe* style is characterized by Kendirbaeva as 'distinguished by their breadth, rapid tempo, symphonic scope, and monumental nature', while *kui* in *shertpe* style (originally from the eastern region) are characterized 'by their subtlety of nuance, natural performance, and particular lyricism' (Kendirbaeva 1994, 109).

[32] While this tuning and playing practice was represented by many Kazakh musicians in Mongolia as a local practice, in fact it is found both in pieces performed in Mongolia and Kazakhstan.

[33] In the same way the *sybyzgy* player consistently provides a vocal drone a fifth below the melody; this also makes *sybyzgy* pieces easily adaptable for *dombra* players.

[34] Kuangon, interview in Bayan Ölgii, 11 July 2005.

[35] The Eurasian eagle owl (*Bubo bubo*) is highly valued throughout the region. The downy feathers of the young owl are attached to the *dombra* as a symbol of honour.

[36] Suyenish referred to this piece as 'Tastulakh', although the piece and location is more widely known as 'Tasty Bulakh' (*тасты бұлақ*). I believe the composer is A. Kabyikei, but I have been unable to confirm this.

[37] In Cyrillic: *Құр ойнақ*.

[38] In Cyrillic: *Сары ала қаз*. A version of the piece, attributed to A. Kabykei, is found in *Bayan Ölgii Kazakmarynyn dombyra zhane sybyzgy kuileri* (1976, 174–6).

[39] The *sybyzgy* is an end-blown flute that in Mongolia is played using a vocal drone.

[40] This version of the story remembered by Zoya, one of my translators, is in fact a variation on another *kui*, '*Aksak khas*' (Limping goose). The story, as notated in *Bayan Ölgii Kazakmarynyn dombyra zhane sybyzgy kuileri*, is as follows (translation from Kazakh by Almagul Soltan): 'On a beautiful part of a river near a summer place there was a goose with white goslings following it. A man who was a marksman was visiting and had nothing to do. He saw the group of geese and planned to shoot the mother goose (he was especially interested in her because she was enjoying her goslings). When he finally shot her, she tried to fly, recognized that she could not, and started to swim along with her goslings who flew to an island. The man was satisfied that he had shot the goose and was not interested in

retrieving his catch. The mother goose walked with a limp. When it was autumn the birds were ready to migrate, but the mother goose could not fly and her flock left without her. The *kui* player saw her grief and created this *kui*' (1976, 10).

[41] Indeed, Zoya, my translator who is today an English teacher in the city of Ölgii, spoke with pride about her ancestral sum, Delüün. She chose to elaborate on the story told in just a few words by the *dombra* player from another sum. She said that, since she is from that place, she would naturally know the story in more detail.

[42] In Cyrillic: *Боз керейім*

[43] In Cyrillic: *Бесбогда*

[44] Yessenova states: 'The history of the Kazakhs has been traced back to the mid-fifteenth century, when the two outstanding tribal chiefs, Giyet and Janibek, moved their people away from the territory of the Uzbek Khanate to the steppe of Desht-i-Kipchal where they founded an independent political unit known as the Kazakh Khanate' (Yessenova 2002,14). While this is sometimes disputed, official Soviet sources identify Janibek as the first Kazakh khan (Olcott 1987, 8). Osman Batur (Bator), the mid-20th century Kazakh warrior who led efforts to resist Soviet and Chinese domination in the Altai region, was known widely and variously as a bandit and (for some Kazakhs) a hero. See Benson (1988) for more information.

[45] Recorded in Ullankos on 19 July 2005 and again on 17 July 2006.

[46] The Besbogda Mountains are five peaks in the far western region of Bayan Ölgii, on the border between Mongolia, Russia and China. More widely known by the Mongolian name: Tavan Bogd (Five Saints), the naming of Besbodga by local Kazakh using a Kazakh name is one of many examples of how they have claimed connections to specific landmarks using Kazakh instead of the 'official' Mongolian names. *Aksu* is a mineral spring near the base of the Besbogda Mountains, in Mongolia.

[47] The *aul* is a social and residential unit comprised typically of several households that work cooperatively together. Finke says of *aul* in Mongolia, 'Next to the family the nomadic camp, called awil, is the most important social unit in the Kazak society' (1999, 133). *Aul* communities in nomadic camps share work and social life and therefore establish a reciprocity that is can last throughout the year, though it may also be bound only by the season, since some families move their camps more other than others.

[48] Recorded in Delüün sum on 29 June 2005 and again on 2 August 2006.

[49] Kazakhs in Mongolia—both before and after the Soviet presence in the country—have been Sunni Muslims, although their religious education and practices have been affected, and even curtailed, by their nomadic traditions that prevent them from establishing *madrassas* and attending mosques for religious training. Some of their Islamic beliefs are also mixed with traditional Shamanism. Their religious systems were suppressed during the Soviet period and they have enjoyed the greater freedom of expression since 1991. Easier access to Kazakhstan, Turkey and the Middle East has also provided opportunities for travel to these regions for religious training (Kimball 2002, 703–4).

[50] Recorded in Shigertei valley on 29 June 2005 and again on 1 August 2006.

[51] See also Schatz (2004) and Svanberg (1999) on lineage and ethnicity in Kazakhstan and Gladney and Jianmin (2003) for a discussion of nostalgia and the power of genealogy among Kazakhs in China.

[52] Recorded at Suiksai, Dayan Lake on 9 July 2006.

References

Appadurai, Arjun. 1996. The production of locality. In *Counterwork: Managing the diversity of Knowledge*, edited by R. Fardon. London: Routledge, pp. 204–25.

Atwood, Christopher P. 2004. *Encyclopedia of Mongolia and the Mongolian Empire*. New York: Facts on File.

Bayan Ölgii Kazakmarynyn dombyra zhane sybyzgy kuileri. 1976. Ölgii.

Benson, Linda. 1988. Osman Batur: The Kazak's golden legend. In *The Kazaks of China*, edited by L. Benson and I. Svanberg. Uppsala: Uppsala University, pp. 141–89.

Bulag, Uradyn E. 1998. *Nationalism and hybridity in Mongolia.* Oxford: Oxford University Press.

Clifford, James. 1994. Diasporas. *Cultural Anthropology* 9 (3): 302–38.

Dave, Bhavna. 2004. Minorities and participation in public life: Kazakhstan. Unpublished paper. Sub-regional Seminar on Minority Rights: Cultural Diversity and Development in Central Asia, Bishkek, Kyrgyzstan, 27 to 30 October 2004. United Nations Office of the High Commissioner for Human Rights. Available at: <www.ohchr.org/english/issues/minorities/docs/wp5.doc >.

Dawe, Kevin. 2002. The cultural study of musical instruments. In *The cultural study of music: A critical introduction*, edited by T. Herbert, M. Clayton and R. Middleton. London and New York: Routledge.

Diener, Alexander. 2003. One homeland or two? Territorialization of identity and the migration decision of the Mongolian-Kazakh Diaspora. Ph.D. diss. University of Wisconsin-Madison.

———. 2005a. Mongols, Kazakhs, and Mongolian territorial identity: Competing trajectories of nationalization. *CESR: Central Eurasian Studies Review* 4 (1): 19–24.

———. 2005b. Problematic integration of Mongolian-Kazakh return migrants in Kazakhstan. *Eurasian Geography and Economics* 46 (6): 465–78.

Finke, Peter. 1999. The Kazaks of Western Mongolia. In *Contemporary Kazakhs: cultural and social perspectives*, edited by I. Svanberg. New York: St. Martins Press, pp. 103–39.

Gladney, Dru C. 1994, Ethnic identity in China: The new politics of difference. In *China briefing, 1994*, edited by W. A. Joseph. Boulder, CO, San Francisco, CA, and Oxford: Westview Press, pp. 171–92.

Gladney, Dru C. and Wang Jianmin. 2003. Relational identity: Constructing Kazakh identifications in China. CRN Network Meeting, American Council of Learned Societies (ACLS). Available at: <http://www.acls.org/crn/network/meetings_nyc_gladney.htm>.

Gupta, Akhil and James Ferguson, eds. 1997. *Culture, power, place: Explorations in critical anthropology.* Durham, NC: Duke University Press.

Hassan, Scheherazade Qassim, R. Conway Morris, John Baily and Jean During. Tanbūr. In *Grove Music Online.* Available at: <www.grovemusic.com > (accessed 21 March 2006).

Kendirbaeva, Gulnar. 1994. Folklore and folklorisms in Kazakhstan. *Asian Folklore Studies* 53 (1): 7–123.

Kimball, Jeannine D. 2002. The nomadic Kazakhs of Western Mongolia. In *The Turks*, Vol. 6, edited by H. C. Güzel, C. C. Oguz and O. Karatay. Ankara: Yeni Türkiye, pp. 697–706.

King, Charles and Neil J. Melvin. 1999–2000. Diaspora politics: Ethnic linkages, foreign policy, and security in Eurasia. *International Security* 24 (3): 108–38.

Kiszko, Martin. 1995. The balalaika: A reappraisal. *The Galpin Society Journal* 48: 130–55.

Kunanbaeva, Alma. 2002. Kazakh music. In *Garland encyclopedia of world music: The Middle East*, edited by V. Danielson, S. Marcus and D. Reynolds. New York: Garland, pp. 949–64.

National Statistical Office of Mongolia. 2003. *Mongolian statistical yearbook 2002.* Ulaanbaatar.

Olcott, Martha Brill. 1987. *The Kazakhs.* Stanford, CA: Hoover Institution Press, Stanford University.

Rossabi, Morris. 2005. *Modern Mongolia: From khans to commissars to capitalists.* Berkeley University of California.

Safran, William. 1991. Diasporas in modern societies: Myths of homeland and return. *Diaspora* 1 (1): 83–99.

Schatz, Edward. 2004. *Modern clan politics: The power of blood in Kazakhstan and beyond.* Seattle, WA: University of Washington Press.

Slobin, Mark and Razia Sultanova. Dömbra. In *Grove Music Online.* Available at: <www.grovemusic.com > (accessed 21 March 2006).

Svanberg, Ingvar. 1999. The Kazakh nation. In *Contemporary Kazakhs: Cultural and social perspectives.* New York: St. Martins Press, pp. 1–16.

World Bank. 2005. *World Development Indicators.* CD-ROM. Washington, DC: World Bank.

Yessenova (Esenova), Saulesh. 2002. Soviet nationality, identity, and ethnicity in Central Asia: Historic narratives and Kazakh ethnic identity. *Journal of Muslim Minority Affairs* 22 (1): 11–38.

———. 2003. "Knowing the road that leads you home": Family, genealogy, and migration in post-socialist Kazakhstan. *The Silkroad Foundation Newsletter* 1 (2). Available at: <http://www.silk-road.com/newsletter/december/genealogy.htm> (accessed 15 January 2007).

'Happy Diwali!' Performance, Multicultural Soundscapes and Intervention in Aotearoa/New Zealand

Henry Johnson

Henry Johnson is Associate Professor at the University of Otago, New Zealand, where he teaches and undertakes research in ethnomusicology, Asian studies and performing arts studies. He lectures and performs on a number of Asian instruments, including the Japanese *koto* and *shamisen, gamelan* from Java and Bali and Indian sitar. His book, *The Koto: A traditional instrument in contemporary Japan*, was published by Hotei in 2004.

Introduction

Watching the dynamic and highly energetic movements of dancers on stage outside the Town Hall on 24 October 2005 in central Wellington, New Zealand, as part of the annual Diwali celebrations (Hindu New Year; known as the 'Festival of Lights'—also celebrated by Jains and Sikhs), I was particularly moved, first, by the public visibility of this celebration of a religious festival and, second, by the diversity of its soundscape. Attracting an estimated 35,000 people in and around several performance sites, it was clearly a celebration that had dance, music and food as its main focus.[1] The performers on the main open-air stage were simulating to pre-recorded music the popular movements of Bollywood (India's dominant film industry).[2] Several rooms and corridors in the Town Hall were full of local stall-holders selling their brand of cuisine from South Asia; the general public, who seemed particularly representative of the contemporary multicultural make-up of New Zealand (i.e. South Asians and non-South Asians alike), flocked to the stalls in the late afternoon to early evening to purchase a take-out meal; and the entire event was underpinned by a variety of performances from local and international artists performing traditional and contemporary South Asian musics.[3] The main stage in the Town Hall presented performances by local community groups; a smaller hall in the same building focused entirely on India's classical traditions; and the outside stage in Civic Square was reserved for Bollywood dancing and other more popular styles of music and dance. It was an event that had, it seemed, transformed tradition and had public display and performance (broadly defined) at its core.

While meandering through the soundscape in and around the Town Hall, the huge variety of local musicians and dancers were particularly noticeable through juxtapositions of sight and sound, and the invited Indian puppeteers and music and dance performers from Rajasthan stood out as major attractions as part of the local celebrations. The Bollywood dancing was especially visible, dynamic and extremely popular among the audience. It showcased the finalists of the previous day's competition and included a range of acts. While the performers mostly comprised New Zealand's South Asian diaspora, some non-South Asians participated in the event too by taking part in several of the dance groups. The Bollywood dancing was indeed a hub of the celebration. It was compered by well-known Auckland-based Indian radio hosts and provided a dynamic outdoor display of extremely lively sound and movement.

Branded as 'Asia:NZ Diwali Festival of Lights', and 'Wellington Diwali Festival of Lights' and 'Auckland Diwali Festival of Lights' in its respective cities, events such as these provide challenging contexts for ethnomusicological research.[4] They are sites, or contact zones (Pratt 1991), where cultures meet, and where identity display is at the nucleus of performance—cultural and social (cf. Schechner 1985; Turner 1982; Turner and Schechner 1986). These events occupy spaces where cultures meet, 'the space of colonial encounters', as Clifford (1997, 6) might describe them.[5] New Zealand's two main public Diwali festivals can certainly be considered with such a trope. They are contact zones that bring different cultures together (from South Asia and elsewhere); they display a plethora of music and dance styles (traditional and modern), which are performed for insiders and outsiders alike; and they exhibit cultures, musics and identities to an audience that celebrates not only the festival, but also what it means to be a contemporary (Indian/South Asian) New Zealander.

In this paper I argue that Diwali in New Zealand is specifically a New Zealand construct; it constructs a site where diaspora identity is expressed through cultural performance; and it is something that comments through music, dance and cultural display on the experiences of those for whom Diwali has found new meaning (cf. Ramnarine 1996, 135). Such contexts are rich with meanings that are foregrounded through cultural display and emblems of identity, and, along with the underlying processes of intervention in terms of event organisation, provide sites where performance in diaspora studies might be better understood (cf. Braziel and Mannur 2003; Ramnarine 1996, 1998, 2001). Focusing on the 2005 Diwali celebration in Wellington (the capital city of New Zealand), this paper is a critical study of Diwali performance sites and their soundscapes, rather than a study of music sound *per se.*[6] Indeed, it is the very nature of the sites and the way music is organized within them that demands a study that is centred on social traits that allow the music to be performed in the first place. It is from this perspective along a sound analysis/cultural analysis continuum that the article approaches performance.

Labels defining cultural identity are often complex, and a term such as 'Asian' has different meanings in different contexts. Referring to a geographic region on the one hand, it is also used to refer to ethnicity on the other. But 'Asian' refers to different people in different contexts (Um 2005a). In New Zealand, the notion of 'Asian' has made its mark on the new face of a multicultural nation. Not only does the census use this category as a way of identifying the nation's Asian population, but the term has found its way into everyday and official discourses on national identity. Furthermore, partly state-funded institutions such as the Asia New Zealand Foundation (hereafter ANZF; formerly known as Asia 2000 Foundation of New Zealand) do much to promote New Zealand in Asia, and Asia in New Zealand.[7]

New Zealand is a nation of immigrants: some have been in the country for several generations and some are more recent (Roscoe 1999; see also Greif 1995; Larner 1998; McKinnon 1996; Palat 1996; Vasil and Yoon 1996). Among New Zealand's immigrants is a population with a growing Asian presence. While New Zealand's South Asian diaspora dates from the early 19th century (Leckie 1998, 163), it was mainly after 1987 that this immigrant community's numbers increased considerably (see further, for example, Leckie 1981; McLeod and Guru Nanak Dev University 1986; Tiwari 1980; Wilson 1990; cf. Rukmani 2001). According to the census figures of 2001, the Asian population in New Zealand was about 6.6 per cent (or 237,459 people) of the national whole, and within this broad category about 26 per cent (or 61,803) identified with the Indian community (Statistics New Zealand 2002), which was second in population size after the Chinese community.[8] For the Indian community these figures were around double the 1991 figure, and 17,550 were born in New Zealand, which reflected the increase in immigration after 1987 when immigration regulations were relaxed so that it was easier for Asians to enter New Zealand.

New Zealand's South Asian communities have diverse backgrounds, with many coming from Asia, but some arriving from elsewhere, for example, India, Pakistan, Bangladesh, Fiji, Indonesia, and Sri Lanka. (I use the term 'South Asian' broadly.) While most cultural insiders in this study identify with the wider Indian community, there are several complexities to this generalization. Some Indians do not come from India; some other South Asians celebrate Diwali; and some other South Asians do not come from South Asia. In this context it is important to note that different migrants have different histories. One of the facts about Diwali is that it brings diverse peoples together. In this sense, while Gilroy (1987) is partly correct in noting that identity construction is often based on where you are at, not where you are from, the opposite is equally true for such festivals among diverse diaspora communities when where you are from is an important narrative in diaspora identity construction in outward self-identification, especially in New Zealand. It will suffice to say that the label 'South Asian' in this article intends to generalize about a vast range of peoples from many cultures. What many have in common are religious (i.e. Hindu) beliefs and cultural traits.[9] It is also worth noting that Diwali in New Zealand in its public gaze is also celebrated, or at least attended, by many non-South Asians and non-Hindus, but the festival has Hinduism and India, whatever one's religious beliefs, at its core.[10]

The study of music festivals in ethnomusicological research has received considerable scholarly attention, whether in the form of ritual celebrations or of contemporary showcasing of the arts (e.g. folk, world, jazz or international festivals) (e.g. Cooley 2005; Harnish 2006; Hosokawa 2005; Lau 2004; Lindsey 2004; cf. Kirshenblatt-Gimblett 1998).[11] Of importance to Diwali is the idea of performing cultural identity through music and dance, or displaying diaspora, something Appadurai (1996, 13) refers to in connection with cultural performance as 'the mobilization of group identities'. Several ethnomusicological studies over the last decade or so have particularly helped foreground the place of music and its link to ethnicity, especially among diaspora and minority peoples, and in multicultural and transnational contexts (e.g. Averill 1994; Béhague 1994; Lau 2001; Lornell and Rasmussen 1997; Manuel 2000; Radano and Bohlman 2000; Slobin 1993, 1994; Um 2005a). The investigation of festivals in diaspora contexts is an area of research that is especially significant in a modern-day world of cultural flows and travel, and thus deserves to be re-thought in light of linking music to identity construction and expressions of self or collective identity. Lau (2004), for example, writes on the Chinese Qingming festival in Honolulu, USA, and argues that it 'is more than an ethnic festivity; it is a story that the local Chinese tell about themselves through music, public ritual, and performance' (Lau 2004, 129). In another study in diaspora ethnomusicology, Lau (2005) looks at morphing Chineseness in Singapore's multi-cultural context. 'Realizing the importance of racial harmony in securing social stability, the government instituted stringent social and cultural policies to ensure all ethnic groups would coexist peacefully' (Lau 2005, 31). What is relevant to my own work is the way Lau's study incorporates an element that mentions state intervention (i.e. cultural policy) in the performing arts.

In the context of multicultural New Zealand, the public celebration of important cultural festivals is hardly surprising. With Chinese, Indian and Pacific immigrants making up a growing percentage of the population, significant festivals of each community are increasingly part of the contemporary festive calendar. While there are indeed many other communities in New Zealand, the public visibility of Chinese, Indian and Pacific peoples has attracted support for the performance and visual arts of these communities. In Auckland alone, three of the largest cultural celebrations of multicultural New Zealand are the Lantern Festival, Diwali and Pasifika, which represent the Chinese, Indian and Pacific communities respectively (the first two are organized by ANZF).

The type of festival under study in this article is one that has distinctive significance for New Zealand's South Asian diaspora, old and new. This diaspora confronts other New Zealanders at such an event in terms of juxtaposing culture through ethnicity. Diwali in New Zealand brings different South Asian cultural groups, organizations, societies, clubs, individuals, etc., together, and, while striving to avoid essentialist notions in this discussion, South Asians are collectively put on display in a cultural celebration of difference on a borderland, 'inbetweenness' within New Zealand's contemporary multicultural make-up. This trope of difference relates to Clifford's (1997, 250) idea of re-thinking diaspora in terms of focusing on its 'borders, on what it defines itself against' (cf. Anzaldúa 1987; Bhabha 1992, 1996; Pratt 1991; Um 2005b). But what makes the public events in New Zealand especially interesting is that they are organized mainly by ANZF and two city councils. Unlike many festivals of diasporic interest, and unlike some smaller Diwali celebrations elsewhere in New Zealand, or even other festivals celebrated by other South Asians, the public Diwali festivals occupy a space between cultures and are structured around top-down organization. In other words, ANZF and two city councils intervene in the coordination of some diaspora community celebrations.

Lindsay's (2004) ethnomusicological study of festivals looks at the phenomenon of the international arts festival, particularly in Singapore. She argues that, while in Europe and the US its development was in part from colonial sites of cultural display, in Asia it was mainly part of nation-building. Lindsay maintains that 'rather than viewing the International Festival as a site that takes performances "out of context", we should see that the festival *is* the context. It is a global contact zone' (Lindsay 2004; cf. Lindsay 2002; Clifford 1997; Pratt 1991). Diwali in New Zealand is not an international festival like this nor is it a national festival like Brazil's São Paulo carnival that showcases ideas of miscegenation and racial democracy (see Hosokawa 2005), but it does have state and local government support and sponsorship, something that proves useful in understanding its place and relevance in the contemporary New Zealand political milieu. The idea of place and the politics of identity links New Zealand's public Diwali festivals to the idea of localization, where

Diwali is transformed in, and as a result of, a unique local context. Diwali is traditionally a religious celebration, but, while Harnish (2006, 4) notes that 'religious festivals are highly charged environments; expressive elements like music and dance that represent or unify a congregation attain a special status in such settings', the public Diwali festival occupies a space of dual ambivalence. It is simultaneously a religious festival and an event that espouses secular consumption. As one informant mentioned, 'it has started to become more social and less religious' (Bengali informant 2004).

Presenting Diwali as a public event links identity construction to political discourse (Keith and Pile 1993). Indeed, in New Zealand the politics linked to the notion 'Asia' or 'Asian' has been highly charged on many occasions in the nation's relatively short history, but has been especially visible in political debate over the last two decades or so. It will suffice to note the political context in which Asia is understood in New Zealand. The remarks made by Winston Peters in 1996 when he first outlined his newly formed New Zealand First political party's policies, which included much rhetoric against Asian immigration to New Zealand, have haunted the current multicultural make-up of the nation. Even though his policies were labelled racist by many New Zealanders, Peters today somewhat paradoxically, though outside cabinet, holds the position of Foreign Minister in the country's labour-led government (Speden 1996). All this in a political context that saw then Prime Minister Jim Bolger in 1993 describe himself to be pleased at being the leader of an Asian nation.[12]

Contextualizing Diwali in modern-day New Zealand, and relating the festival to the nation's contemporary identity, led to the main title of this paper, 'Happy Diwali!' While one meaning of this title is straightforward in that it refers to the greeting on the occasion of Diwali, the second implies the way the festival is presented in the New Zealand imagination as a community event that brings many local communities together through intervention for a public display of celebration. After all, it was only just over a decade ago that New Zealand anthropologist Jacqui Leckie noted: 'South Asian communities in New Zealand rarely attract much attention from the media' (1995, 133). But the 'Happy Diwali!' trope is one that is underpinned by intervention; a top-down state-driven policy that strives to celebrate multiculturalism, yet packages events such as Diwali as an 'other' in a somewhat contradictory and hegemonic relationship between cultural celebration and ethnic consumption, where the very notion of multiculturalism is never truly realized.

Ethnographic field research at Diwali events over the last three years, especially at Wellington in 2003 and 2005, has led me to focus on public Diwali celebrations in New Zealand in terms of cultural intervention and public display (see further Johnson 2005). That is, the public events in Auckland and Wellington are organized by respective city councils and the part-government-funded ANZF, and, in New Zealand, Diwali has been transformed through a complexity of negotiations by South Asians and non-South Asians alike.[13] (In the discussion I use the term 'Diwali' with reference mainly to the Wellington event.)

Diwali in its diasporic New Zealand context relates to the study of a spatial aspect of performance. In this respect, the public Diwali events held in Auckland and Wellington provide performance spaces that are challenging and raise many questions regarding multicultural music politics. Why are various musics being performed in the same event? Why are there simultaneous performances? What types of music are being played? What might the performances tell us about the South Asian diaspora in the New Zealand context? There are, of course, many other questions, but these are some of those that underpin this study.

Diwali is now examined in terms of tradition and transformation. What is Diwali? What is Diwali in New Zealand? How has it been transformed in the New Zealand context? Focusing on the public Diwali events in Wellington in 2003 and 2005, and as a way of attempting to understand the festival as a site of meaning, the last two main sections examine Diwali soundscapes and community and intervention respectively. It is argued that these core notions underpin the presentation of public Diwali events in New Zealand today, and that their study can help in understanding some of the ways that multiculturalism and transnationalism are played out in the contemporary New Zealand political environment.

Tradition and Transformation

Diwali is one of many Hindu festivals, but it is particularly visible and important in the annual cycle as it marks the beginning of the Hindu New Year. It is primarily an Indian festival, but is celebrated elsewhere in some other South Asian cultures and globally among the South Asian diaspora. In New Zealand, it is with the South Asian communities—particularly Indians and Indo-Fijians—that Diwali has its main traditional meaning as a religious and celebratory event. Reflecting the geographic expanse of the Indian subcontinent, there are several different versions of Diwali, which reflect its multicultural and multi-regional 'home' setting. Likewise, among the South Asian diaspora there are many Diwali celebrations that often have their own distinct local characteristics, which might be the result of the ethnic make-up of the diaspora in question or stem from influences in the new setting.[14]

Diwali, according to Hinduism, is the time when the god Rama returns home to the kingdom of Ayodhya after 14 years in exile. The Hindu goddess of wealth, Laxmi, visits homes on Diwali and blesses people with prosperity. While there are several different versions of the Diwali narrative among the range of communities who celebrate the festival, for this discussion it is important to understand how the festival is portrayed in the New Zealand context, especially by the main sponsor of the two public events. In its advertising for the Auckland and Wellington Diwali events, ANZF publicizes the festival as follows:

> Diwali (also known as Deepavali [and Divali, Dewali]) is one of the most important and colourful of the Indian festivals and is celebrated enthusiastically by Indians all over the world. It marks the beginning of the Hindu New Year and is seen as a brand new beginning for all. Traditionally Diwali is celebrated for five

> days, each day having its own significance, rituals and myths. Light, in the form of candles and lamps, is a crucial part of Diwali, representing the triumph of light over darkness, goodness over evil and hope for the future. During Diwali people light small oil lamps (called diyas) and place them around the home to pray for health, wealth, knowledge, peace and fame. Fireworks are an essential and exciting part of Diwali. The celebration of the festival is also customarily accompanied by exchanging sweets. Diwali is organised by Asia:NZ in partnership with Auckland City in Auckland and with Wellington City Council in Wellington. (Asia New Zealand Foundation, see <www.asianz.org.nz>)

The exact time of Diwali depends on the locale in which it is being celebrated. While it traditionally falls on the 15th day of the Hindu lunar month of Ashwayuja or Kartikka, which many Indians in New Zealand might follow, the events promoted by ANZF are celebrated at a convenient time either in October or November. For local communities and ANZF the celebrations might be held on a weekend close to the lunar event, but ANZF has over the past four years held the Auckland and Wellington events on separate weekends. The reason for this is to allow some performers to attend both celebrations, especially if they have been invited to New Zealand from overseas. ANZF never times the public event so that it falls on the same day as Diwali proper, the reason being that those who would most likely take part in the public celebration would want to reserve the actual day of Diwali for their own personal festivities with family and friends.

In the lead up to Diwali, homes are usually cleaned thoroughly and decorated, debts are repaid and, generally, it is a time to spend money. One overview (there are several versions) of the five days of a traditional Diwali celebration is summarized as follows:

> *Day 1. Dhanteras.* Two days before Diwali. *Diyas* (clay lamps) are lit to drive away evil spirits. Buildings are decorated. Laxmi-Puja (worship of the goddess of wealth) is performed. *Bhajans* (devotional songs) are sung in praise of the Goddess Laxmi.
>
> *Day 2. Narak Chaturdasi.* Day before Diwali. Small Diwali. In Hindu households there is a *puja* (worship) to Laxmi and Rama; songs are sung; *aarti* (offering of light to a deity) is performed.
>
> *Day 3.* Devoted to Laxmi. Bells and drums from temples; chanting of Vedic hymns.
>
> Day 4. *Padwa.* Prayers.
>
> Day 5. *Bhayiduj.* Second day after the new moon.

While the above summary focuses on the Hindu celebration, it should be remembered that other religions also celebrate Diwali. For example, Sikhs celebrate Diwali (also known as Bandi Chhorh Divas) to honour the laying of the foundation stone for the Golden Temple in 1577. Also, in Jainism, the chief disciple of Mahavira, Ganadhar Gautam Swami, attained complete knowledge on this day, making Diwali a special event for Jains.

In New Zealand, ANZF stresses the following description of the Diwali festival, one that is used in publicity and promotion:

> Originally a Hindu festival, Diwali has now crossed the bounds of religion and signifies many different things in different areas of India. For example, in Gujarat, the original home of many Indian New Zealanders, the festival honours Laxmi, the goddess of wealth. In north India, it celebrates the god Rama's homecoming to the kingdom of Ayodhya after a 14-year exile. To light his way and rejoice at his return, the people of Ayodhya illuminate the kingdom with earthen *diyas* and fireworks. (Asia New Zealand Foundation, see <www.asianz.org.nz>)

In October and November, Diwali is celebrated in New Zealand at various times in a variety of spaces, from private to public, and from small to large. While individuals and families might celebrate the festival in their own way in a private or near-private setting (see Kasanji 1980), there are several public events that are openly advertised to the wider general public. The Auckland and Wellington public celebrations sponsored by ANZF are the largest of these, but there are some smaller events that should be mentioned.[15] While ANZF organizes events in collaboration with the city councils of Auckland and Wellington, other events are sometimes held at some smaller centres, some specifically for the local Indian community, and others providing a multicultural celebration for the wider local community. To mention just a few of the more recent events (there are many), in 2004, for example, the Waitakere Indian Association celebrated a public Diwali event at the Henderson's Trusts stadium with cultural performances, stalls and a range of Indian food. Also, the New Plymouth Indian community celebrated Diwali at Puke Ariki on 6 November 2005 with a one-hour cultural performance with music, song, dance and children's posters and wall hangings (Roseman 2005). About half the 2004 number turned out for their local celebrations (Winder 2005). One informant noted: 'probably about 10–15 years ago we used to celebrate in a big way . . . invite a lot of European people' (member of a Christchurch Indian association). In Hamilton in 2002, the local Fijian Indian community had over 1200 people attending their Diwali celebration. The importance of the event for the diaspora community is summarized by the comments of one attendee: 'Celebrating Diwali reminds us of our culture and traditions, and sharing our experiences is an important part of developing understanding amongst our community' (Suresh Kumar, in Bradley 2002). Historically, too, Diwali has been important for Indians in New Zealand, with one event in Wellington being celebrated in 1995 with over 1000 visitors (Ots 1995). What is significant to note here is that Diwali has been an important part of the diaspora Indian community in New Zealand for a long time, and distinct local community organizations have played an important role in festivities and in bringing people and communities together. However, the large-scale Diwali events seem to have captured the public imagination and transformed the event from the (near) private to the (distinctly) public.

The immediate image of the large-scale public Diwali festivals in New Zealand is that they are mostly far removed from any identifiable religious influence (Figure 1 shows the time and place of the prayer event in relation to the other entertainment open to the wider public.) However, as well as having an opening prayer ceremony, at the Wellington event in 2005 the final dance performance was choreographed specifically with the aim of asking the god Ganesha for a Diwali blessing. Nevertheless, the traditional festival has clearly undergone a transformation. This transformation does, of course, take many guises: for example, moving from the sacred to the secular; the inclusion of contemporary music and dance forms; and the recontextualization of the event (cf. *The Indian* 2003). The title of a review of the event in Wellington by one newspaper, *The Dominion Post* (5 November 2005, edition 2, p. 15), seems to summarise the purpose of the event: 'Celebrating India'. It is interesting to note the national emphasis—South Asian, not New Zealand and not the diaspora. That said, there are other Diwali events around the country, for families and communities alike, that sometimes adhere to more traditional ways of celebrating the festival.

Diwali Soundscapes

In the New Zealand context of public Diwali display, as in many other places, performance is at Diwali's core. An underlying aspect of Diwali is that "as a festival of light and beauty it encourages artistic expressions" (<www.diwalifestival.org>). Indeed, not only are music and dance central to the event, but Diwali itself is a performative spectacle that displays constructions of ethnicity and identity in various forms (cf. Schechner 1985). For the purposes of this study, however, the performative aspects of Diwali under investigation are music and dance as expressed through stage performance.

Festivals can often provide spaces that juxtapose or even superimpose different sound worlds. In other words, different performance sites might simultaneously have music performances that are not always totally separated physically or acoustically. With performances across several distinct spaces at Diwali, a Diwali soundscape is constructed where the public is able to pass freely between several physically separate, but sometimes acoustically overlapping, contexts. The notion of soundscape as used by Murray Schafer (e.g. 1977) is useful in studying the Diwali festival context as it helps highlight the transient and permeable nature of performance that underpins the event. That is, performance is restricted mainly to a maximum of ten-minute slots so the audience could hear a vast array of sounds, something that reflects the multicultural, multi-regional and multinational event.

Most, if not all, the performers at Diwali might normally showcase their own style of South Asian performing arts in performance contexts outside Diwali, where a show could well focus on, for example, a specific performer, music genre or dance style. But with Diwali there is a distinct emphasis on the brevity of performance in terms of individual items presented to the public. But brevity in this instance is linked with the notion of inclusivity, which is especially relevant when attempting to understand how performance is structured at the Diwali events. Local community groups are invited

	Town Hall Stage	Civic Square Stage	Illot Theatre	Capital E	Town Hall Foyer	Council Chamber Foyer
3:00		Wellington Tamil Society & Albeli				Massey Art and Design Exhibition
3:15	Preetha and Hema	Bechu				
3:30	Cairo and Tallulah	Wellington Hindi School	New Zealand Indian Fine Arts Society	International Puppet Show		
3:45		Mudra Dance Company			Prayer Ceremony	
4:00		Gala Opening				
4:15		Mudra Dance Company				
4:30		Rajasthani Dancers		Storytelling		
4:45	Wellington Hindi School	Natraj School of Dance	Indian Classical Music			
5:00		Sakhi		International Puppet Show		
5:15	Wellington Telegu Association	Preetha and Hema				
5:30	Hare Krishna	Folk N Funky				
5:45	Natraj School of Dance	Juggler				
6:00	International Rajasthani Dancers	Mastana	New Zealand Indian Fine Arts Society	Storytelling		
6:15		Wellington Telegu Association				
6:30		Indian 21st Century Performing Arts	Indian Classical Music	International Puppet Show		
6:45	Yoga Presentation	Upper Hutt College				
7:00	Jarrod Wood	Nritya-Kala				
7:15		Hare Krishna				
7:30	Shagufta Zia	Sitara				
7:45	Upper Hutt College	Sargam & Akansha		International Puppet Show		
8:00	Vaishnavi	Dhamaka	Bridal Show			
8:15	Gnanasampanthan	Juggler				
8:30	International Rajasthani Dancers	Shagufta Zia		End of Children's Programme		
8:45		Bollywood Finalists	Indian Wedding on Stage			End of Display
9:00						
9:15	End of Town Hall Programme	Sub-Continent Artists Guild				
9:30						
9:45						
10:00		Natraj School of Dance				

Figure 1 Diwali: Wellington 2005, performance sites.

by the organizers to showcase their cultural activities through music and dance. In 2005, for example, the organizers (i.e. ANZF and the city councils) allowed each group to perform twice (if requested), but controlled the length of each performance (the only exception was the classical music stage). While community groups were given the chance to perform, their actual performance could be viewed as a 'snapshot' (or 'sound-byte') of what they do. As shown in Figure 1, the performances were juxtaposed one after the other in a potpourri soundscape of sonic tourism. This relates to what Mitchell describes as a 'synthetic sonic experience of surface impacts' (1996, 85), in that the array of juxtapositions is little more than a token offering that does not truly represent a culture or community group, let alone a type of music or dance. That said, even though ten minutes might seem a short time when compared to the extended performance of, for example, Indian classical music, even ten minutes for an amateur musician/dancer might be a long time.

The performance events at Diwali in Wellington, for instance, were held across six separate, but closely connected, spaces (Figure 1). The Council Chamber Foyer was reserved for an art exhibition of local art students studying at Massey University in Wellington and provided a visual backdrop to the food, dance and music that was predominant through the event. Another context, Capital E, was an indoor space that hosted storytelling and puppet shows, which were primarily for children.

The Town Hall foyer was used exclusively for the formal prayer ceremony that was held in mid-afternoon near the start of the various events. It was the main context that emphasized the religious nature of Diwali, yet most people attending the celebrations at other sites in Wellington would not have been part of the religious activities. Of particular importance was the *puja* (prayer) ceremony, which was conducted in Sanskrit by a local Hindu priest. The main dance/music performance at the opening ceremony in 2005 was choreographed by local dancer Vivek Kinra, who established the Mudra Dance Company and New Zealand Academy of Bharata-Natyam in Wellington in 1992.[16] While research was not undertaken at this event due to its official status where only invited people could attend, some interviewees noted that usually four to six young female dancers perform at the occasion to a pre-recorded backing track.[17] Their dance pays homage to the Hindu god, Ganesha, the lord of all obstacles.

The Illot Theatre was used exclusively by Indian classical musicians and dancers, who were mainly of South Indian origin. In this context, the performers were allowed slightly longer per group in which to perform. What was interesting at this site was the relative lack of audience numbers, and the lack of coming and going of audience members during performances.[18]

The Town Hall stage is a very large hall and included literally hundreds of seats towards the stage, but the rear of the hall allowed enough space for people to walk around freely, as well as for some food-stalls to be situated there. The soundscape in this context included the sounds of music, dancing and talking by the audience who would freely come and go and eat food purchased from the nearby stalls. The performers mainly had ten-minute time slots, except for the Rajasthani dancers who were allowed slightly longer, presumably due to their international status as professional performers. With the exception of the Rajasthani group, each of the acts on this stage, as with the outdoor stage, was accompanied by pre-recorded music, mostly in a popular Bollywood style.

One of several local acts to perform on the Town Hall stage was the Natraj School of Dance. This school of Indian classical Bharata-Natyam dance was established in Lower Hutt (Wellington) in 2002 by Prabhavathi Ravi, a dancer with an international reputation. Diwali provides an ideal context at which to showcase the school's performers from diverse ethnic backgrounds and age, and helps emphasize the importance of community involvement in the event.

In contrast, and adding to the multicultural mix of performances, the group of two dancers, Cairo and Tallulah, performed a very modern dance wearing Pharonic wings that looked more like a cross between a Rio carnival and Middle Eastern belly dancing (one of the dancers gives workshops in Middle Eastern dance, especially belly dancing). The two dancers are Pākehā (European) New Zealanders, one of whom owns a store that sells Indian merchandise. They also include a Pacific Island man in their routine during a sword dance. Cairo and Tallulah perform a fusion dance with matching musical backing. At their performance they danced to the track 'From Rusholme with Love' by the UK group Mint Royale. This piece, with its sitar-driven melody, provided a typical example of what the duo are about—mixing sounds and movements from a range of cultures. During an interview with one of the dancers, it was noted that the Indian community seemed to enjoy their performances and possibly related them to some of the contemporary Indian dance styles that are popular today (pers. comm. 27 April 2006).

By far the most popular, colourful, dynamic and loud performance site was the Civic Square stage. This was the only open-air site. It had the loudest amplification and seemed to attract the most people. One style of music and dance that was especially popular was Bollywood dancing. In recent years, the Bollywood film industry has started to captivate an international audience.[19] Moreover, this industry, which inherently includes substantial music and dance as a primary part of the genre, is often consumed among the South Asian diaspora as a way of celebrating an important aspect of their contemporary culture (see further Kaur and Sinha 2005; Mishra 2002; Ray 2001, 2003). In 2005, the event that dominated the Civic Square stage was the showcasing of the finalists of the Bollywood dance competition. In recent years, Bollywood dancing (as seen in Figure 2) has dominated both the Auckland and Wellington Diwali festivals and it looks as though it will again in 2006. In 2005, for instance, the Wellington Bollywood dance competition was held the day before the main Diwali celebration, with the finalists performing again on the main day (in previous years the competition was held on the day of the Diwali celebration). In Auckland, both the festival and the Bollywood dance competition were held on 30 October.[20]

The eclecticism and multiculturalism of the outdoor stage came to a climax with the performance of the Subcontinent Artists Guild. A poster of a recent perfor-

Figure 2 Bollywood dance group performing at the Wellington diwali festival. Photograph courtesy: Robert Catto <www.catto.co.nz>.

mance of the group describes them as having a 'brand of Bollywood and South Asian music and dance polished with influences of funk, jazz and pop' (see further <www.scagnz.org>). This performance was in aid of Oxfam's earthquake reconstruction work in Pakistan and India.[21]

The extent to which the visual and sonic juxtapositions were merely token offerings is extremely difficult to judge for this study, but some key-informant interviewees did comment on the mixture and commercialization of the event. 'To be honest it's just a collection of many cultural items . . . it is not focused on Diwali at all' (member of Fijian Women's Society). The same informant mentioned that 'in India it's become very commercialized; you go and buy a package of sweets, whereas in Fiji it's still very traditional and you make it in the home and then share it with your neighbour'.

This type of festival setting is an important kind of cultural event that demands study, especially in connection with understanding the reasons for these musical snap-shots. It is from this standpoint that the following section explores some of the underpinning social and cultural reasons for Diwali's eclectic mix of sounds and sights.

Community and Intervention

The recontextualization and transformation of Diwali in the New Zealand context is built around two distinct spheres of local action. The first is community based (among the diaspora), where it is primarily members of local South Asian community groups who stage the public Diwali events in various ways. The second sphere of action is through intervention, where ANZF and the city councils of Auckland and Wellington each sponsors and helps organize the events with a top-down structure. In other words, ANZF and the councils claim ownership of the festival through their organization of the event.[22]

The support from local South Asian community groups is pivotal for the success of the Diwali events. In Wellington, for example, over 50 local community groups are invited to take part and there are more than 200 performers (mostly amateurs from Wellington, with some others from elsewhere in New Zealand and several international invitees). One of the key roles that the organizers have is bringing communities together. The fragmented make-up of the community groups reflects the desire to express a unique diaspora identity, but, while there is perhaps a sense of rivalry between some groups, the Diwali event helps break down cultural barriers. As a way of trying to avoid inter-community rivalry, the organizers choose the order of the performances by drawing names out of a hat. Local communities are essential for many activities, including the setting up of food and craft stalls, the staging of music and dance performances, and as audience members. It is clear from this that the idea of bringing communities together underpins many aspects of the festival. As the perceptions of one informant make clear, 'the objective is to bring the people together . . . that main intention is a get together' (Bengali informant 2004).

The importance of the participation of local communities in the events is evident in the run-up to the festival. In 2005 in Wellington, for instance, a call for performers was posted by Wellington City Council on the ANZF website:

> Calling all performers! Classical or contemporary . . . dance, music, theatre, puppetry, masks, comedy, film . . . young or old . . . individuals or groups . . .!! This year there will be four performance stages, including a children and young person's stage in Capital E! Performances will run from 3pm to 10.30pm. Each group or individual will be given a 10-minute time slot.

While the brevity of each performance has been noted above, one might extrapolate from this that the underlying theme seems to be a desire to bring as many communities as possible together, allowing an equal amount of time for each performance (obviously attempting not to favour one group over another). Members of the South Asia diaspora are brought together, whatever their backgrounds might be, and non-South Asians are attracted to the vibrancy of the event and the sharing of cultures.[23]

While non-South Asian visitors to the events might be seen as cultural tourists (cf. Gibson and Connell 2005), an interesting question arises regarding who is an insider, who an outsider, and whether this has importance to the event at all. Because the events are multicultural in their own right in terms of intra-South Asian and pan-South Asian diaspora cultural display, the unifying theme of the festival itself, which spans communities, cultures, countries and continents, is to celebrate the Hindu New

Year through cultural celebration. Moreover, the public face of the festival in New Zealand's contemporary multicultural setting, especially with its recently increasing Asian diaspora, makes the Diwali events particularly political. The fact that non-Asians/non-South Asians/non-Indians were part of the event in one way or another, whether performing, being a stall holder or simply watching the event, points to the notion of a wider multicultural trope underlying the festival.[24]

More specifically, one of the interesting yet poignant sights at the event in 2005 were the Red Cross donation boxes and collectors for the victims of the Kashmir earthquake, which struck earlier in October. Many members of the Pakistani community were present at the event:

> Pakistan is one of the left out countries. For so many reasons they didn't want to come forward, but we extended the hand of friendship and started interacting with their community and they reciprocated and on the 14th they are performing on the Independence Day function they have the same day. (Member of pan-Indian community group)

Indeed, Pakistani community groups are invited to the event, although to date none has participated except for individuals. In 2005, for instance, one well-known member of the Pakistani diaspora community, singer Shagufta Zia, was seen on the Town Hall stage and the outdoor stage performing devotional (*qawwali*) and other songs.[25] The idea of inclusivity is also present in terms of other intra-South Asian links. One informant noted: 'We too are including the Bangladeshi in this event' (member of pan-Indian community group).

In its publicity, ANZF describes the event as follows:

> The Asia:NZ Diwali Festival of Lights gives Wellington and Auckland Indian communities the opportunity to share this much-loved cultural tradition with other New Zealanders and their families. This event not only celebrates the traditions of Diwali, but is also a celebration of Indian culture. (Asia New Zealand Foundation, see <www.asianz.org.nz>)

The way the festival is described by the main organizer provides clear evidence of the importance of the notion of intervention. The festival's very construction and celebration in the New Zealand context as a wide-scale public event is dependent on ANZF and two city councils. It is clear from this description that ANZF claims ownership of the festival's organization. It is branded as 'the *Asia:NZ* Diwali Festival of Lights', and the promotional material for the festival notes: 'the opportunity to *share* this much-loved cultural tradition with *other* New Zealanders'; 'a celebration of *Indian* culture'; and 'Gujarat, the original *home* of many Indian New Zealanders' (emphasis added). While the writing style of one description of the festival is hardly evidence of more widespread views of it in New Zealand, this example does help illustrate the main organizer's underlying message. The festival is portrayed as the Foundation's, and it wants the local Indian community to share its own culture(s). Even on the main Civic Square outdoor stage, the webpage of ANZF was displayed directly below the stage and right across it on a large banner. Elsewhere, the festival is marketed as 'Wellington Diwali Festival of Lights' or 'Auckland Diwali Festival of Lights', reflecting the local city councils who help stage the event. It is held in partnership with Wellington City Council and Auckland City, but has corporate sponsorship from Telecom, Patak's (an Auckland-based Indian food manufacturer), Radio Tarana (an Auckland-based Indian radio station), Western Union, SkyCity Auckland, More FM Auckland and Wellington, TV3, Lion Foundation, The Edge, Indian Council of Cultural Relations and Cosco.[26] All advertising has many logos from these sponsors. It is in this context that the involvement of higher-level organizations is brought to the foreground.[27]

While ANZF and the two city councils might be criticized for their hegemonic role in organizing the festival, the Diwali events have, nevertheless, captured the national imagination; they dominate the community activities of many South Asians during October or November each year; and there is much funding and sponsorship behind the extremely influential organization that somewhat controls the events. As one informant mentioned:

> We used to do Diwali before until this Asia 2000 took over . . . they started doing this in a big way because they had money from the Auckland city and lots of resources, so instead of competing with that we supported it because they had more resources so we thought why not. (Member of pan-Indian community group)

It is important to reflect on insiders' perceptions of Diwali in New Zealand. What does this cultural soundscape and visual display mean to New Zealand's South Asian diaspora? Most importantly, the ANZF public Diwali events intersect the modern-day fabric of New Zealand's changing ethnoscape. For all New Zealanders the events represent a developing multicultural society, one that exists within a bicultural frame of reference (Māori/Pākehā); for the South Asian diaspora, the events are an emblem of identity, where they came from and where they are at.

Many informants mentioned the importance of Diwali as something that reminded them of their heritage: 'for people who in the process of settling down it means a lot to them because they miss their homeland and they miss so many things related to their culture and heritage' (member of pan-Indian community group). This theme of indexing home was further expressed with the idea of bringing together people who are themselves from multicultural backgrounds to experience Indian culture that has been transmitted to New Zealand. Here, migrants share a wider commonality that is somehow obfuscated in the new context:

> When we have common functions like Diwali and . . . Independence day . . . all the ethnic Indians they come together and we celebrate together, there are some functions where we have to use our language only and then we have a separate function. (Member of a Kannada association)

> The coming together of the younger people experiencing the culture . . . is lost in a way for them because they live far away from the main country. To keep it alive that

> gives me the greatest joy; doing a performance is more of an entertainment and being part of and having that communal feeling; being part of a celebration basically. (Member of Fijian Women's Society)

The idea of continuing tradition was expressed with comments such as 'culture is our daily life and it's very important to carry on and pass it on to the next generation' (member of Hamilton Indian community association).

During field research interviews, several informants noted the different ways that Diwali is celebrated in India and New Zealand. Opinions differed considerably, but the one thing that stands out, it seems, is that things were celebrated differently. For instance:

> Well, in India the celebrations last a long time. It's celebrated more openly and socially. Over here it's a very private thing and you meet friends and family. It could be by yourself. There might be just one Indian living in your street. . . . Over there, everyone celebrates. (Member of a Hamilton Indian community association 2004)

The sponsorship of large-scale Diwali celebrations does much, it seems, to contribute to the well-being of the South Asian diaspora community and is well received as a way of bringing together not only New Zealanders but also disparate migrants in their new home.

Diwali in New Zealand helps in maintaining, constructing and negotiating cultural identity in an age of transnationalism (cf. Castles and Davidson 2000). It helps the diaspora community to connect to home within a transnational environment. As one informant said, 'I will be very honest, I have never felt that I'm too far away from home' (Bengali informant 2004).[28] The contemporary world of diaspora and cultural flows provides a framework in which people can live hyphenated lives: living in one nation-state, but identifying and participating in the culture of another. Diwali is nowadays celebrated in many parts of the world. While it indexes India, the Indian diaspora the world over is celebrating the event. Many of these events take place in multicultural settings, and many gain increased visibility and public support because of this.

Conclusion

This paper has shown how music and dance are pivotal to public Diwali events in New Zealand through performance and cultural display. Festival soundscapes provide unique settings through which to understand the socio-cultural reasons that underpin performance among diaspora communities, and new contexts for performance can be comprehended further only when the local political dynamics of multiculturalism and intervention have been taken into consideration. The public Diwali event in Wellington, as examined in this discussion, has established its own hybrid tradition that is unique to the local and national context, and it reflects underpinning social, cultural and political factors that have helped shape its existence in its contemporary diaspora setting in the first place.

The Wellington Diwali event in 2005 produced a soundscape that might be seen to stand for a new South Asian diaspora identity in New Zealand. The beginning of the 21st century is a time in New Zealand's multicultural history that is increasingly acknowledging, through public display, performance events and public mediation, the identity of some of the country's diaspora communities. Important cultural celebrations such as Diwali are supported by state-sponsored organizations, and help stress the multicultural contemporary make-up of the country, as well as celebrating an important time of the year with the country's second largest Asian community.

Diwali at the Wellington event has intervention at its core. A powerful organization and a city council are essentially responsible for its occurrence, and have financial and political weight that ensures the event is successful. While, in such a context, Diwali has undergone a degree of transformation and recontextualization, it does nevertheless represent uniquely a new spatiality in New Zealand's contemporary ethnoscape. Identity is shaped and constructed in this site as a direct result of performance; performers showcase locally produced acts; and the audience consumes the diversity of South Asian diaspora performance.

Even though it was commented during interviews with festival organizers that the politics of bringing so many diverse community groups together was by far the most difficult thing to do for the festival to be a success, there was, nevertheless, a growing sense of ownership by the community groups who regularly participate. Some now see the public Diwali as their own, which has gradually come about since about the second or third year of the event. The process of 'othering' the South Asian community and its collective musics and dances through the Diwali event shows that New Zealand actually helps construct diaspora identity through its imagining of South Asian homogeneity through Diwali.

The top-down/bottom-up dynamics of festival ownership at Diwali may help show how intervention can help create wider communities, but there are surely questions to be raised regarding the level of intervention into the festivities of other diaspora groups. While ANZF supports the Chinese New Year and Diwali, reflecting the two largest Asian communities in New Zealand, what about all the other Asian peoples who now call New Zealand home? And of non-Asians too? Should their festivals not be celebrated equally within the new multicultural political milieu? I do not intend to discuss these questions here, but they should be considered when looking at diaspora communities in multicultural nation states. After all, it seems that any notion of multiculturalism or form of celebration that foregrounds ethnicity is one that creates a paradox in its own existence. To celebrate multiculturalism, or multiculturally, is a process that helps break down cultural boundaries on the one hand, but on the other its very existence helps reinforce notions of difference. That is, Diwali is a musical event in a multicultural context (in terms of South Asian and New Zealand identities) where people from diverse backgrounds are brought together in ways that interrogate cultural borders built around and enmeshed in tropes of identity politics. Such modes of celebration reflect the contemporary cultural tapestry that helps locate New Zealand in transnational and diaspora discourse. Yet at the same time the very process of coming together points to frames of reference that help reinforce the very boundaries that state sponsorship of the Diwali event is seemingly attempting to break down.

Acknowledgements

I am particularly grateful to the interviewees, who have remained anonymous, from a range of organizations and community groups who have volunteered invaluable information that has made this study possible.

Notes

[1] See further the review of the event in the local newspaper, entitled 'Thousands revel in exotic display of culture and cuisine' (Nichols 2005).

[2] Bollywood dance is derived from the Mumbai film industry, and includes influences from such styles as classical Indian dance, hip hop, jazz and ballet.

[3] For an Indian perspective on New Zealand's multiculturalism see *The Global Indian.* See <www.theglobalindian.co.nz>.

[4] I will use the term 'Diwali', which derives from the Sanskrit word meaning 'row of lights', to refer to these public events collectively, particularly the Wellington celebration. When other Diwali events are referred to, they will be described according to where they are held.

[5] Clifford (1997) borrows the idea of contact zones from Pratt (1991) in his study of museum display in connection with 'the space in which peoples geographically and historically separated come into contact with each other and establish ongoing relations, usually involving conditions of coercion, radical inequality, and intractable conflict' (Clifford 1997, 6–7).

[6] This first public Diwali sponsored by ANZF was held in 2002. It has been held each year since that time.

[7] The Asia New Zealand Foundation was established in 1994 as Asia 2000 Foundation of New Zealand. It is a non-profit, apolitical organization that receives funding from corporate sponsors, including industry and government agencies and ministries.

[8] The latest census was taken in March 2006, the results of which will be released later in the year.

[9] While Hinduism is a worldwide religion, it is predominantly located in the Indian subcontinent, primarily in India (about 94 per cent).

[10] In this context it should be noted that New Zealand is a popular location for shooting Indian films (see, for example, Vasil 1999).

[11] Mention should also be made of the international conference held in Sheffield, UK, in 2004 on the theme 'Festivals and Communities: Realising the Potential'. Such events highlight the important link between peoples and the ways of celebrating identity.

[12] New Zealand is a dialogue partner of ASEAN (Association of Southeast Asian Nations).

[13] ANZF are responsible for the defining what the festival is about and how to brand it; the two city councils are responsible for the logistics of organizing the events.

[14] See further, for example, <www.diwalifestival.org>.

[15] In connection with the funding of the event, in Wellington in 2005 the Asia New Zealand Foundation received the largest amount ($20,000) in a round of grants from the City Council. 'Grants subcommittee chairman Alick Shaw said this year's Diwali festival would be the fourth to be held in Wellington and gave the city's growing Indian community the opportunity to enjoy their culture and share it with others' (*The Dominion Post* 2005, 20).

[16] Bharata-Natyam is a well-known Indian dance form. An important Wellington-based dancer who is involved in the opening ceremony, as well as other performances throughout the event, Kinra migrated to New Zealand in 1990. On Kinra, see further <www.mudra.co.nz>.

[17] The field research for this article was undertaken with permission from the University of Otago Ethics Committee, a requirement of the study being that interviewees would remain anonymous.

[18] On Indian music in New Zealand, see Maurice (2004).

[19] Bollywood dancing has become very popular among many of New Zealand's Polynesian community, something that is sometimes referred to as 'Polywood' (see Stokes 2004). On Bollywood and transnationalism, see Kaur and Sinha (2005).

[20] In 2005, two Bollywood stars were present at the Auckland event, brought to New Zealand by Radio Tarana: Jimmy Shergill and Aiysha. While this added to the transnationalism of the event, it should be noted that Aiysha, who has been 'dubbed the Indian pop queen of the Pacific' (*New Zealand Herald* 2005), was actually born in Australia to Indo-Fijian parents. She sings in English, Hindi and Punjabi and moved to Bombay in 2004. She is well known in South Asia and the Middle East and has two albums and a film debut forthcoming (*New Zealand Herald* 2005). A transcultural element of the Bollywood dance competition was especially visible in 2005. The winner of the Auckland competition, Sonia Rath, who had been in the country for only three months, learned most of her routine from her sister in Rajasthan through two months of telephone conversations and emails (Lynch 2005).

[21] On 8 October 2005, a major earthquake hit the Pakistan-administered region of Kashmir.

[22] On ANZF's involvement in previous Diwali see, for example, Asia 2000 Foundation of New Zealand (2002, 2003) and Barton (2002).

[23] The 2004 Diwali celebrations in Auckland and Waitakere (Henderson) were reported as attracting 'a high number of non-Indian visitors' (*The Global Indian* 2004).

[24] The New Plymouth Diwali event in 2005 was held in the local Assembly of God Church; Santa Claus, too, was present, bearing gifts and sweets (Winder 2005). Indeed, many people identify with a culture or ethnicity when it suits them (cf. Spivak 1987).

[25] Shagufta Zia now lives in Wellington, but is well known in Pakistan and Fiji. Originally from Pakistan, she lived in Fiji for six years. A brief profile of Zia featuring her latest album is found in *Arts Access Aotearoa Newsletter*, August 2005.

[26] The Indian Council for Cultural Relations sponsored the international performers' visit to New Zealand.

[27] The idea of community, and sometimes an imagined community (cf. Anderson 1991 [1983]), is extended to education when considering some of ANZF's objectives in organizing the events. ANZF also has a website for teachers with unit plans, etc.; 'Hindu Festival – Let's Celebrate Diwali' is a social studies resource written by Marg Wright of Christchurch College of Education (see <asianz.org.nz/education/unit_plans/diwali/index.php>). ANZF organizers also arrange various workshops, such as ones in Indian classical music, as well as exhibitions to coincide with the event.

[28] This is something Schiller and Fouron (2001) have called long-distance nationalism. See also Baymeh (1993).

References

Anderson, Benedict. 1991 [1983]. *Imagined communities: Reflections on the origin and spread of nationalism.* Revd edn. London: Verso.

Anzaldúa, Gloria. 1987. *Borderlands: La frontera, the new mestiza.* San Francisco, CA: Aunt Lute Books.

Appadurai, Arjun. 1996. *Modernity at large: Cultural dimensions of globalization.* Minneapolis, MN: University of Minnesota Press.

Asia 2000 Foundation of New Zealand. 2002. Festivals and light. *Spring Review*: 12.

———. 2003. *Diwali Festival of Lights: Sponsor report – 2003.* Wellington: Asia 2000 Foundation of New Zealand.

Averill, Gage. 1994. "Mezanmi, kouman nou ye? My friends, how are you?" Musical construction of the Haitian transnation. *Diaspora* 3 (3): 253–71.

Barton, Pamela. 2002. Asia 2000's first Diwali Festival of Lights. *NZASIA Newsletter* 12.

Baymeh, Mohammed A. 1993. *Transnationalism.* London: Sage.

Béhague, Gerard, ed. 1994. *Music and black ethnicity: The Caribbean and South America.* New Brunswick, NJ: Transaction Publishers.

Bhabha, Homi. 1992. Postcolonial authority and postmodern guilt. In *Cultural studies,* edited by L. Grossberg, C. Nelson and P. Treichler. London: Routledge, pp. 55–66.

———. 1996. Culture's in-between. In *Questions of cultural identity,* edited by S. Hall and P. du Gay. London: Sage, pp. 53–60.

Bradley, Anusha. 2002. Into the light. *Waikato Times* 30 October, edition 2: 17.

Braziel, Jana Evans and Anita Mannur. 2003. *Theorizing diaspora: A reader.* Oxford: Blackwell.

Castles, Stephen and Alastair Davidson. 2000. *Citizenship and migration: Globalization and the politics of belonging.* New York: Routledge.

Clifford, James. 1997. *Routes: Travel and translation in the late twentieth century.* Cambridge, MA: Harvard University Press.

Cooley, Timothy J. 2005. *Making music in the Polish Tatras: Tourists, ethnographers, and mountain musicians.* Bloomington, IN: Indiana University Press.

The Dominion Post. 2005. 11 June.

Gibson, Chris and John Connell. 2005. *Music and tourism: On the road again.* Clevedon: Channel View Publications.

Gilroy, Paul. 1987. "It ain't where you're from it's where you're at": The dialectics of diasporic identification. *Third Text* 13: 3–16.

The Global Indian. 2004. Issue 2, November.

Greif, Stuart William. 1995. *Immigration and national identity in New Zealand: One people, two peoples, many peoples?* Palmerston North: Dunmore Press.

Harnish, David D. 2006. *Bridges to the ancestors: Music, myth, & cultural politics at an Indonesian festival.* Honolulu: Hawaii University Press.

Hosokawa, Shuhei. 2005. Dancing in the tomb of samba: Japanese-Brazilian presence/absence in the São Paulo carnival. In *Diasporas and interculturalism in Asian performing arts: Translating traditions,* edited by H-k. Um. London: RoutledgeCurzon, pp. 61–74.

The Indian. 2003. Alteration in Diwali celebration. Available at: <www.theindian.co.nz>.

Johnson, Henry with Guil Figgins. 2005. Diwali down under: Transforming and performing Indian tradition in Aotearoa/New Zealand. *New Zealand Journal of Media Studies* 9 (1): 25–35.

Kasanji, L. 1980. Food, marriage, and festivals: A comparative study of Indians in Gujarat and Indians in New Zealand. In *Indians in New Zealand: Studies in a sub-culture,* edited by K. N. Tiwari. Wellington: Price Milburn for the Indian Central Association, pp. 221–35.

Kaur, Raminder and Ajay J. Sinha, eds. 2005. *Bollyworld: Popular Indian cinema through a transnational lens.* Thousand Oaks, CA: Sage.

Keith, Michael and Steve Pile, eds. 1993. *Place and the politics of identity.* London: Routledge.

Kirshenblatt-Gimblett, Barbara. 1998. *Destination culture: Tourism, museums, and heritage.* Berkeley, CA: University of California Press.

Larner, Wendy. 1998. Hitching a ride on the tiger's back: Globalisation and spatial imaginaries in New Zealand. *Environment and Planning D: Society and Space* 16: 599–614.

Lau, Frederick. 2001. Performing identity: Musical expression of Thai-Chinese in contemporary Bangkok. *Sojourn* 16 (1): 37–69.

———. 2004. Serenading the ancestors: Chinese Qingming festival in Honolulu. *Yearbook for Traditional Music* 36: 128–43.

——. 2005. Morphing Chineseness: The changing images of Chinese music clubs in Singapore. In *Diasporas and interculturalism in Asian performing arts: Translating traditions*, edited by H-k. Um. London: RoutledgeCurzon, pp. 30–42.

Leckie, Jacqueline V. 1981. They sleep standing up: Gujaratis in New Zealand to 1945. PhD dissertation, University of Otago.

——. 1995. South Asians: Old and new migrations. In *Immigration and national identity in New Zealand*, edited by S. Greif. Palmerston North: Dunmore Press, pp. 133–60.

——. 1998. The southernmost Indian diaspora: From Gujarat to Aotearoa. *South Asia* 21: 161–80.

Lindsay, Jennifer. 2002. A drama of change: Cultural policy and the performing arts in Southeast Asia. In *Global culture: Media, arts, policy and globalization*, edited by Diana Crane, Nobuko Kawashima and Ken'ichi Kawasaki. New York: Routledge, pp. 63–77.

——. 2004. Locality of performance at international arts festivals. *Music and Locality: Towards a Local Discourse in Music*, Proceedings of the Combined Conference of the Australia and New Zealand Musicological Societies, Wellington 2003, edited by Richard Hardie. Music Books New Zealand.

Lornell, Kip and Anne K. Rasmussen, eds. 1997. *Musics of multicultural America: A study of twelve musical communities*. New York: Schirmer/Prentice Hall International.

Lynch, Haley. 2005. *North Shore Times* 21 November.

Manuel, Peter. 2000. *East Indian music in the West Indies: Tān-singing, chutney, and the making of Indo-Caribbean culture*. Philadelphia, PA: Temple University Press.

Maurice, Donald. 2004. The status of Indian classical music in New Zealand society. *Kiwi India Seminar Series*. Victoria University of Wellington, 20 October.

McKinnon, Malcolm. 1996. *Immigrants and citizens: New Zealanders and Asian immigration in historical context*. Wellington: Institute of Policy Studies.

McLeod, W. Hew and Guru Nanak Dev University. 1986. *Punjabis in New Zealand: A history of Punjabi Migration 1890–1940*. Amritsar: Guru Nanak Dev University.

Mishra, Vijay. 2002. *Bollywood cinema: Temples of desire*. New York: Routledge.

Mitchell, Tony. 1996. *Popular music and local identity: Rock, pop, and rap in Europe and Oceania*. London: Leicester University Press.

New Zealand Herald. 2005. 31 October.

Nichols, Lane. 2005. Thousands revel in exotic display of culture and cuisine. *The Dominion Post* 24 October: 3.

Ots, Angela. 1995. Indians celebrate Diwali festival. *The Evening Post* 24 October, edition 3: 3.

Palat, Ravi Arvind. 1996. Curries, chopsticks, and Kiwis: Asian migration to Aotearoa/New Zealand in world-historical perspective. In *Nga patai: Racism and ethnicity in Aotearoa/New Zealand*, edited by P. Spoonley, C. Macpherson and D. Pearson. Palmerston North: Dunmore Press, pp. 35–54.

Pratt, Mary Louise. 1991. Arts of the contact zone. *Profession* 91: 33–40.

Radano, Ronald Michael and Philip V. Bohlman. 2000. *Music and the racial imagination*. Chicago, IL: University of Chicago Press.

Ramnarine, Tina K. 1996. "Indian" music in the diaspora: Case studies of "chutney" in Trinidad and in London. *British Journal of Ethnomusicology* 5: 133–53.

——. 1998. "Brotherhood of the boat": Musical dialogues in a Caribbean context. *British Journal of Ethnomusicology* 7: 1–22.

——. 2001. *Creating their own space: The development of an Indian-Caribbean musical tradition*. Barbados: University of West Indies Press.

Ray, Manas. 2001. Bollywood down under: Fiji Indian cultural history and popular assertion. In *Floating lives: The media and Asian diaspora*, edited by S. Cunningham and J. Sinclair. New York: Rowman & Littlefield, pp. 136–84.

———. 2003. Nation, nostalgia and Bollywood. In *The media of diaspora*, edited by K. H. Karim. London: Routledge, pp. 21–35.

Roscoe, Jane. 1999. *Documentary in New Zealand: An immigrant nation.* Palmerston North: Dunmore Press.

Roseman, Jane. 2005. Community arts diary. *Taranaki Daily News* 2 November, edition 1: 23.

Rukmani, T. S., ed. 2001. *Hindu diaspora: Global perspective.* New Delhi: Munshiram Manoharlal Publishers.

Schafer, R. Murray. 1977. *The tuning of the world.* New York: Knopf.

Schechner, Richard. 1985. *Between theater and anthropology.* Foreword by Victor Turner. Philadelphia, PA: University of Pennsylvania Press.

Schiller, Nina Glick and Georges Eugene Fouron. 2001. *Georges woke up laughing: Long-distance nationalism and the search for home.* Durham, NC: Duke University Press.

Slobin, Mark. 1993. *Subcultural sounds: Micromusics of the West.* Hanover, NH: University Press of New England.

———. 1994. Music in diaspora: The view from Euro-America. *Diaspora* 3 (3): 243–51.

Speden, Graeme. 1996. Peters shrugs off hail of abuse. *The Dominion* 15 February: 2.

Spivak, Gayatri Chakravorty. 1987. *In other worlds: Essays in cultural politics.* New York: Methuen.

Statistics New Zealand. 2002. *2001 census of population and dwellings: Ethnic groups.* Wellington: Statistics New Zealand, Te Tari Tatau.

Stokes, Jon. 2004. Polywood treat blows Bollywood away. *New Zealand Herald* 28 June.

Tiwari, Kapil N., ed. 1980. *Indians in New Zealand: Studies in a subculture.* Wellington: Price Milburn for the New Zealand Indian Central Association.

Turner, Victor W. 1982. *From ritual to theatre: The human seriousness of play.* New York: Performing Arts Journal Publications.

Turner, Victor W. and R. Schechner. 1986. *The anthropology of performance.* New York: PAJ Publications.

Um, Hae-kyung, ed. 2005a. *Diasporas and interculturalism in Asian performing arts: Translating traditions.* London: RoutledgeCurzon.

———. 2005b. Introduction. In *Diasporas and interculturalism in Asian performing arts: Translating traditions*, edited by H-k. Um. London: RoutledgeCurzon, pp. 1–13.

Vasil, Anamika. 1999. Indian film-makers shoot Wellington scenes. *The Dominion* 29 January, edition 2: 3.

Vasil, Raj and Hong-key Yoon. 1996. *New Zealanders of Asian origin.* Wellington: Institute of Policy Studies.

Wilson, Jim. 1990. Hindusim. In *Religions of New Zealanders*, edited by P. Donovan. Palmerston North: Dunmore Press, pp. 157–72.

Winder, Virginia. 2005. Diwali a spot of light at dark time. *Taranaki Daily News* 31 October, edition 1: 1.

Diasporic Transpositions: Indigenous and Jewish Performances of Mourning in 20th-Century Australia

Gay Breyley

Gay Breyley is Faculty of Arts Postdoctoral Fellow in the School of Music – Conservatorium at Monash University, Australia. Her current project is a study of selected musical and poetic texts of Persian-speakers in Australia. Recent publications include articles in the *Journal of Australian Studies, Borderlands* and *Altitude*, and chapters in Cynthia Huff, ed. *Women's life writing and imagined communities* (London and New York, 2005) and Sue Williams *et al.*, eds, *The regenerative spirit: Australian post-colonial reflections* (Adelaide, 2004).

In recent years, ethnomusicologists have shown increasing interest in the complex relations between musical performance and commemoration (for example, Reily 2006), personal and collective memory (Muller 2006; Shelemay 2006), loss (Reyes 1999) and forms of mourning (Magowan 1994; Randhofer 2004, 36–41). Regina Randhofer suggests that lamentation 'is an anthropological universal, to be found in practically all cultures in the world, appearing as an expression of situations of travail in connection with events causing existential privation (Welten 1980, 736), such as death, sin, destruction, loss, military defeat, a threatening criminal process and so forth' (2004, 38). With her study of the musical practices of Vietnamese refugees, Adelaida Reyes (1999) was one of the first ethnomusicologists to address the particular experiences of loss articulated musically by refugees, a theme that has subsequently been taken up by others (for example, Baily 2005). Mourning and loss are clearly related to memory, postmemory and commemoration in complex ways.[1] These relationships, and their musical articulations, are complicated by histories of conflict, colonialism and diasporic encounter.

Twentieth-century Australia was the site of a range of diasporic encounters, of the continuing effects of colonization and of simultaneous movements towards decolonization. Extensive mid-century immigration schemes, based on the 1901 Immigration Restriction Act (known as the 'White Australia Policy'), were designed to boost the proportion of Northern Europeans in Australia's population. Countries represented included the United Kingdom (the Australian government's preferred source), the Netherlands, Germany, the Baltic states, Italy, Greece, Turkey (initially Turkish Cypriots with British passports) and the then Yugoslavia. The inclusion of Southern European source countries, despite the policy preference for the North, was due in part to the need for labourers in Australia and in part to the postwar pressure in Europe to find destinations for those whose lives had been disrupted by the Second World War. Immigration peaked in 1950, with 153,685 people migrating to Australia, which then had a total population of 7,700,000 (Australian Government 2004).[2] Jewish Holocaust survivors or displaced persons, as they were known then, were among the postwar migrants. After Israel, Australia's population now has the highest proportion of Holocaust survivors in the world (Rutland 2001, 50). These Holocaust survivors joined a population that included Australia's diverse indigenous survivors of colonization. Many indigenous people had been, and continued to be, dispersed from their traditional lands, often working for rations in the pastoral industries. Only in the late 20th century was there sufficient popular interest in Australia for narratives of these displacements to enter such public spheres as mainstream popular music and literature.

While there are clear and significant differences between Jewish and indigenous communities and their respective positions in Australia's history, both communities have been disproportionately afflicted with memories of loss and death. For both, mourning is a most significant practice. This article examines some performances of mourning in Australia's Jewish and indigenous communities. It argues that these communities' practices do not represent cultures of hybridity, as is sometimes claimed. Ethnographic literature contains many variations on the notion of hybridity, some more useful than others. Marcia Langton provides a helpful analysis of mid-20th-century Australian anthropological texts that fail 'to understand present-day [urban] Aboriginal communities' (1981, 17). Langton cites a range of authors (including C. D. Rowley, J. Beckett, H. M. Smith and E. H. Biddle) who, in her view, typically 'consider that Aborigines on the white side of the "rolling frontier" lack culture, have no distinctive culture, have only some truncated version of European culture, or have only a "culture of poverty"' (1981, 17). Similarly, and in the same year as Langton's article, Margaret J. Kartomi (1981) addresses the ways some ethnomusicologists 'have indulged in a romantic zeal to save traditional music everywhere from the contamination that was often supposed to result from musical contact between the West and the non-West' (1982, 227). Kartomi critically discusses terms such as 'cross-fertilized, hybrid, creole, mestizo and mulatto' (1981, 229). She goes on to point out that the 'process of intercultural musical synthesis . . . is not a matter of the addition of single elements of one culture to another' (1981, 232). Rather, it concerns 'setting into motion an essentially creative process, that is, the transformation of complexes of interacting musical and extramusical ideas' (1981, 232–3). Of course, partly through the work of Langton, Kartomi and many others, notions of hybridity no longer have exclusively and explicitly negative connotations. Indeed, in recent decades, the level of scholarly celebration of hybridity, especially in the fields of postcolonial and cultural studies, has led Suvendrini Perera to refer to 'happy hyphenation and happy hybridization' (1996, 393).[3] This article suggests that there are more useful ways to represent postcolonial and diasporic cultural and musical practices than as demonstrations of cultural hybridity. Some Jewish and indigenous Australian performances of mourning may be read as complex transpositions, performed within dynamic cultures of survival. This is evident, for example, in a poetic adaptation of the Kaddish by Lily Brett (1987, 17–34), a child of Holocaust survivors and former rock journalist. In different ways, it is also evident in adaptations of country music by Bundjalung elder and bereaved mother Ruby Langford Ginibi and in adaptations of both Celtic folk and Baarkanji traditions by the late Baarkanji educator Evelyn Crawford.[4]

This article focuses on the published memoirs of Brett, Langford Ginibi and Crawford, but it is informed by my fieldwork in sections of each of the communities remembered in those texts. In Brett's case, these are Melbourne's Jewish communities and the Polish cities of Lodz and Krakow. Brett was born Luba Brajsztajn to Polish

Jewish survivors, in a German displaced persons camp in 1946.[5] She and her parents migrated in 1948 to Melbourne, where most of the postwar Polish Jewish migrants to Australia settled. Brett began her writing career as a rock journalist in 1960s Melbourne. While she decided early against a musical career, her poetry, fiction and essays are now published internationally. Brett moved to New York in 1989 and is now seen as part of an Australian diaspora.[6] Langford Ginibi (Figure 1) was born Ruby Anderson to Bundjalung parents on Box Ridge Mission, northern New South Wales, in 1934. As an amateur singer, especially of country and western songs, Langford Ginibi continues to perform at informal gatherings around Sydney, where she lives with her son in an outer western suburb. Langford Ginibi's life narrative *Don't Take Your Love to Town* was published in 1988. In it she remembers rural northern New South Wales, especially mission life, and the inner-city Sydney suburb of Redfern. Crawford (Figure 2) was born Evelyn Mallyer to a Baarkanji mother and Wankamurrah father on a New South Wales sheep station, where her displaced parents worked, in 1928. Until her death in 2001, Crawford was a sought-after player of button accordion, with her repertoire of popular dance tunes from the early to mid twentieth century, Irish and Scottish folk and Australian and United States country songs. Crawford's transcribed oral history *Over My Tracks* was published in 1993. Like many other Baarkanji people, she worked for decades around central and western New South Wales. In her book she tells of life on pastoral stations and in the education system.[7]

Although Crawford, Langford Ginibi and Brett lived and worked in very different contexts and did not meet, their shared moment of movement into the public sphere,

Figure 1 Ruby Langford Ginibi, at her home in front of a portrait of herself (photo: Gay Breyley 2004).

Figure 2 'Evelyn Crawford of Brewarrina, NSW' (photo: John Meredith 1994), image number: nla.pic-an14320677. By permission of the National Library of Australia.

through the publication of memoirs, is one reason to bring their respective stories into conversation with each other. Another reason is the ongoing debate around ways in which the displacement of migrants to Australia is linked to the displacement of indigenous Australians within the country. As it enters this debate, this article supports the argument that indigenous disadvantage and settler privilege are directly linked and ongoing effects of colonialism. A useful way to explore and clarify this argument is by studying the changing musical practices of diasporic and postcolonial performers. (The application of notions of 'diaspora' has broadened over recent decades, so that the term 'diaspora' is now defined as: '1. a dispersion, as of a people of common national origin or beliefs. 2. the people dispersed' (Macquarie University 1982, 508). In this sense, Langford Ginibi is a member of the Bundjalung diaspora, while Crawford belongs to the Baarkanji diaspora[8]).

Postcolonialism

Recent debate has seen calls to 'rethink the relationship between the Holocaust and the indigenous genocides that preceded it', as historian A. Dirk Moses puts it (2002, 7). Moses links 'the colonial genocides of the "racial century" (1850–1950) and the Holocaust to a single modernization process of accelerating violence related to nation-building that commenced in the European colonial periphery and culminated in the Holocaust' (2002, 7). Several 19th-century massacres in New South Wales are documented.[9] In northern Australia, massacres continued into the 1930s. A decade later, in Europe, Brett's parents lost nearly all their relatives in the Holocaust. However, experiences are different for the descendants of survivors of different massacres. For indigenous women such as Crawford and Langford Ginibi, the experience of displacement differs from that of Brett, a white child migrant to 'White Australia'. Australia's ethnically restrictive immigration policies were in force until 1973. In 20th-century Australia's national system, Crawford and Langford Ginibi, like their respective parents, continued to be identified primarily as indigenous. By contrast, in the eyes of 'the nation', Brett was no longer primarily a Jew, the erstwhile object of European persecution and the identity tattooed on her parents' arms, but a 'new Australian'. These apparent inconsistencies in public memory represent further forms of displacement in Australian culture and history.

Whether, as Stephen Blum suggests, ethnomusicologists 'are concerned with musical interpretations of history and with historical interpretations of music and musical life' (1991, 1) or, as Bruno Nettl (2002), 3) puts it, ethnomusicology is 'the study of the world's musical cultures from a comparative perspective, and the anthropological study of music', postcolonial perspectives may be usefully applied to the study of most twentieth-century music. Homi Bhabha suggests that:

> Postcolonial perspectives ... intervene in those ideological discourses of modernity that attempt to give a hegemonic 'normality' to the uneven development and the differential, often disadvantaged, histories of nations, races, communities, peoples. They formulate their critical revisions around issues of cultural difference, social authority, and political discrimination in order to reveal the antagonistic and ambivalent moments within the 'rationalizations' of modernity. (Bhabha 2004, 245–6)

As well as bringing together the theories of time and space suggested by history and anthropology, postcolonial criticism redefines the range of potential objects of cultural study, as Ashcroft, Griffiths and Tiffin explain: 'We use the term "post-colonial" ... to cover all the culture affected by the imperial process from the moment of colonization to the present day. This is because there is a continuity of preoccupations throughout the historical process initiated by European imperial aggression' (2002, 2). For postcolonial critics, both the act of reading texts or cultural forms and some texts themselves constitute 'writing back' from a decolonizing 'periphery' to an imperial 'centre', thus collapsing binaries of 'centre' and 'margin'. Texts or performances may also be understood as rearrangements of canonical texts or 're-narrations' of imperial or other grand narratives. 'All the culture affected by the imperial process', including music and the study of music, is seen as a dynamic 'construction site' of identity and power relations. These are familiar ideas to many ethnomusicologists, whether or not we work in parts of the world that have been directly affected by (or have perpetrated) forms of colonialism or neocolonialism.

Ethnomusicologists and postcolonial critics share a concern with questions of agency. Both groups are called upon to consider their/our own roles as potential 'colonizers' of other people's compositions.[10] As Julia Watson and Sidonie Smith point out, use of the concept of colonization can be problematic and it is important to bear in mind the term's contingent and multivalent nature:

> if we must constantly probe the reach, contradictory strategies, and contested achievements of *decolonization*, we must also probe the reach of the term *colonization*. So widespread has become the practice of weaving the word *colonization* through various critiques of the subject of Western humanism and the politics of representation that the word now seems to signify a universalized descriptor of subjectivity. (Watson and Smith 1992, xiii-xiv)

However, as defined by Chandra Talpade Mohanty, colonization 'almost invariably implies a relation of structural domination, and a suppression—often violent—of the heterogeneity of the subject(s) in question' (1984, 336). This reminder of the self-evident but often suppressed heterogeneity of subjects is useful to this article's study of the work of three very different 'postcolonial' diasporic Australian women.

Postcolonial musical, literary and other compositions use various combinations of structures derived or appropriated from European, or colonial, and non-European sources, depending on the particular choices and impositions of their histories. In the Australian context, Peter Dunbar-Hall and Chris Gibson argue that 'attempts to define Aboriginal expressions through Western concepts such as "traditional" and "contemporary" are futile' (2005, 16). Rejecting notions of a 'dichotomy . . . between music deriving from the pre-colonial past and the present', Dunbar-Hall and Gibson suggest that 'Aboriginal music is a thread of expression that has always, and is continually changing' (2005, 16). Indigenous Australian musicians live in very diverse contexts and perform in a wide range of styles. For example, musically speaking, there seems to be no logic in placing 'traditional' Northern Territory Wadjiginy songman Bobby Lane and urban rap group Native Ryme Syndicate in the same category. However, there are aspects of a shared indigenous, postcolonial history that do link such artists. Similarly, Crawford and Langford Ginibi are from two very different parts of Australia's eastern state, New South Wales. Crawford's Baarkanji country is in the state's dry south west, while Langford Ginibi's Bundjalung country is in the lush north east (and Langford Ginibi has spent most of her life in Sydney, Australia's largest city). New South Wales was colonized before other parts of Australia, with the result that indigenous languages and musical forms changed more quickly there than in northern, central and western Australia. Crawford was multilingual, with a knowledge of Baarkanji musical traditions, but her work (among other things) required her to move often. She spent most of her life away, though not far, from Baarkanji country, and she was most familiar with English-language folk and country music. As a baby, Langford Ginibi heard her parents speak Bundjalung, but she grew up away from the language and found that she could remember only some words and phrases in adulthood. English-language popular music, especially country, is the form she knows best. The postcolonial experiences of Crawford and Langford Ginibi are clearly different from those of some indigenous musicians in northern Australia, where musical forms have survived with different levels and kinds of disruption and where many indigenous languages are spoken as first languages. However, Crawford and Langford Ginibi identify and represent themselves as primarily indigenous. The ways they perform and use the musical forms they know are inextricably related to other aspects of their lives as indigenous Australian women. In effect, by 'claiming' their respective Baarkanji and Bundjalung identities, as well as their chosen 'Western' musical forms, they bring those musical forms into their indigenous repertoires, thus rendering folk and country music also 'indigenous'.

'Traditional' forms of cultural identification were also disrupted for Brett's displaced family. In her texts, Brett represents her parents as preferring to identify with culture not seen unequivocally as 'Jewish' after their survival of Auschwitz. (She attributes this to, among other things, the fearful effects of memories that associate explicitly 'Jewish' situations, especially gatherings of Polish Orthodox Jews, with persecution and death.) Brett recounts a childhood and youth in which she had minimal contact with Jewish traditional music or Orthodox religious practice. However, as she reconstructs memories in her texts, Brett turns to explicitly Jewish traditions such as the Kaddish and musical forms such as *klezmer*, alongside the popular music of her Australian generation. The music heard in Brett's world is most often Western rock and art music, two forms with implicit links to secular Jewish traditions. Ruptures in cultural practice, including perceived moves from 'religious' to 'secular', do not negate Brett's Jewish identity. Rather, they may be seen as embodying it. Through her writing, Brett identifies herself primarily as a child of Jewish Holocaust survivors; the ways she uses and responds to rock and art music relate to her parents' and her own histories. In effect, she 'writes back' to Europe, the site of her family's devastation, while also performing the role of 'countersubject' in Anglo-Australia. (The musical metaphor of counterpoint is one useful way to analyse postcolonial texts and performances.)[11]

While some forms of cultural change are so gradual as to be barely perceptible, others are sudden, violent and extreme. The changes wrought by colonialism and diasporic movement are often extreme, but they do not erase the histories of surviving colonized/decolonizing and displaced communities. Rather than being silenced, those histories continue to reverberate in different forms, as dynamic cultural practices continue to be renegotiated and reconstructed on their traces. Brett, Langford Ginibi and Crawford all had forms of memoir published in the late 1980s and early 1990s. Until this period, narratives of imperial progress, productive settlement and acquiescent assimilation had enjoyed the highest frequency and volume in 20th-century Australia. The three women's texts may be read as diverting the flow of such narratives, as they interrupt (and sometimes join) supercultural discourses.[12] The period around 1988, when Australia commemorated the bicentenary of the founding of New South Wales as a British penal colony, saw an unprecedented public demand both for stories of indigenous dispossession and for stories of 20th-century immigrants' experiences. As more Australians began to address gaps in previous representations of the nation's postcolonial history, relations with the past were unsettled and renegotiated. In their texts, Langford Ginibi and Crawford recall silences associated with dispossession, separation and loss, and use references to or citations of music to evoke the sites of their memories. Brett uses musical imagery and references to articulate her family's memory traces. Her texts sometimes unsettle notions of Australia as a migrant haven in which 'new Australians' cheerfully bloom and the second generation silently assimilates.

Bhabha's contrapuntal notion of evocation and erasure of the nation's 'totalizing boundaries' (2004, 213) is useful to the reading of Crawford, Langford Ginibi and Brett.[13] However, Bhabha's emphases (2004, 38–9) on the models of hybridity and the 'third space' are arguably less useful. Despite his acknowledgement of heterogeneity within cultures, these models may be understood to imply that only the 'modern' space is 'irredeemably plural'. That is, the hybrid's 'two' disparate 'parents', or the 'first' and 'second' spaces (for example, 'British' and 'Aboriginal' or 'Anglo-Celtic' and 'Jewish'), may be read as somehow 'pure', rather than already heterogeneous. In Australia, the notion of hybridity also brings to mind the colonial history of settler legal authorities' classifications of people according to their ratios of indigenous and non-indigenous forebears. These classifications were discursively represented in terms of 'blood', with such categories as 'full blood', 'half-caste', 'quadroon' and those with 'an admixture' or a 'strain' of 'Aboriginal blood'.[14]

Blum writes that every culture is a 'site of encounters' and that the 'transactions through which individuals and groups reproduce cultural knowledge' (1994, 255) should be examined. Australian culture has been the site of two most significant sets of encounters. The first is the series of encounters between indigenous and non-indigenous people. (Before British colonization in 1788, indigenous people had had contact with other non-indigenous people, including neighbours from what is now Indonesia and Europeans such as Dutch and French explorers.) The second is the series of encounters between people identifying as Anglo/Celtic-Australian and migrants with no British or Irish links.[15] In the late 20th century, non-Anglo-Celtic Australians were sometimes—popularly and officially—categorized collectively as 'multicultural', as multiculturalism emerged as an alternative immigration policy. Ann Curthoys (2001) suggests that discourses around the above two encounters 'have been either entirely separate, or there have been attempts to incorporate the indigenous within the multicultural, to see Indigenous peoples as one amongst many ethnic groups making up the nation, and to see racism against Indigenous peoples and non-British immigrants as basically the same'. Curthoys goes on to argue that 'it might be better to understand the multicultural within the indigenous', that is, to understand migration as 'a process occurring *within*, rather than *after*, a history of colonisation and de-colonisation' (2001). This argument forms a useful framework in which to read the textual and musical performances of Crawford, Langford Ginibi and Brett, as well as their contexts of cultural knowledge. In this framework, colonization and decolonization emerge as ongoing, contrapuntal histories. Migrants to and within Australia reproduce cultural knowledge through transactions involving these histories, whether or not the transactions are explicitly acknowledged.

Commemoration and Performance

In the lives of many indigenous Australians and many descendants of Holocaust survivors, performances of mourning assume more general roles than the practice of grieving after the deaths of specific people. There are days dedicated to collective mourning, such as the National Day of Healing (previously Sorry Day, commemorating the forced removal of children from indigenous families under a government policy of assimilation, which persisted into the late 20th century), Invasion Day (countering Australia Day) and Holocaust Memorial Day. On a more individual level, grief and mourning can interrupt or infuse everyday activities for children of survivors. There is an extensive body of music and literature commemorating collective losses, such as the stolen generations (people removed from their families as children), indigenous deaths in police custody and the loss of land, languages and musical forms.[16] These losses, as an inextricable part of postcolonial Australian life, appear at least marginally in the texts of most ethnomusicologists working on indigenous Australian music. However, such ethnomusicological texts do not tend to focus on the relationships between postcolonial loss and performance. Stephen Wild explains that 'accounting for the sounds of Aboriginal songs' (2006, 348), especially in the form of musical notation and analysis, has been 'a strong and continuous tradition' in Australian ethnomusicology, by contrast with the 'American anthropological tradition' (2006, 348).[17] This emphasis on musical analysis (primarily in texts on 'traditional' music) has sometimes served to marginalize the sociopolitical concerns of postcolonial analysis. On the other hand, sociopolitical concerns are often prominent in studies of popular or 'contemporary' music, such as the work of Dunbar-Hall and Gibson, Breen (1989), Barney (2004) and Magowan (2005).[18] However, here too, few ethnomusicological texts focus directly on collective loss and performance in postcolonial Australia. This article does not provide the kind of musical analysis to which Wild refers. Instead, it analyses the cultural complexities of a range of textual and musical performances of mourning in the remembered lives of three postcolonial women. Before turning to examples of specific performances of mourning, I will consider some more general moments of commemoration in the lives of Crawford, Langford Ginibi and Brett. These take the form of maintaining links with imagined or remembered ancestors and/or reconstructing broken links.

Brett did not receive a traditional Jewish education, though her upbringing as a child of survivors, born displaced, is perhaps a new, post-Holocaust form of Jewish education. As an Australian child, before she was able to travel to Poland and attempt an imaginative reconstruction at the scene of the crime, Brett was mainly aware of paradoxical loud silences and absent presences:

It was hard
to be heard
in our house

a loud chorus
sang
the main score

dead people
with strong
voices

an aria
of saints
and angels

a
scattered
madrigal

a
doomed
dirge

it's
your aunty Fela
your uncle Felix

your cousin Mara
your sister Hannah
your brother

your brother
your mother
your father (Brett 1992, 35)

Like many Holocaust survivors' children, Brett has lived without the physical presence of grandparents: 'My grandmother/two words/I've rarely/ put together' (1986, 95). However, their absence, alongside that of all the other relatives, emerges as a constant historical reminder and an everyday hindrance. Brett represents her Polish- and Yiddish-speaking parents as never quite arriving in the 'sanctuary' of Australia. Voices of those left behind accompany and detain these survivors, however distant the scene of parting and however seemingly tranquil the diasporic haven. The survivors are drowned out in their refuge, both by loud local voices entering the house and by the ghosts of people who were taken away and never given a proper burial. There are moments of arrival, but these are repeatedly intercepted by the call of distant choruses.

By contrast with Brett's memories, Crawford's are often of the absence of an 'our house', but they are also punctuated by the loud silences of separation. As a child, Crawford, her sister Gladys and their parents camped near her paternal grandparents in sand hills near their traditional land. The girls witnessed two accidental fires in their beloved grandparents' camp. Their grandmother died in the first, their grandfather in the second. Later, when the family moved to a mission, they lived with a range of displaced and grieving people.[19] Mission management attempted to cut the mixed group's already damaged links with indigenous traditions, by controlling forms of spiritual practice, music and language. Crawford recalls: 'No one from the Aboriginal Protection Board didn't give one damn for our culture or laws or anything we valued' (1993, 68). However, there were moments when the mission community's various traditions resonated, although their sounds had changed. One such moment was the claypan dance. While most of the instruments, tunes and dance steps had entered the repertoire from Ireland and Britain, through interactions in the pastoral industries, the organization and structures of the evening followed traditional forms. Preparation for the dance involved clearing the claypan, killing a kangaroo or emu and mincing its meat. Each member of the fragmentary but newly extended 'family' had a role to play, as Crawford explains:

> Every kid did something. Some would be out on the claypan, pickin' up stones and bits of stick, some would be waterin' it—others helpin' to put up stools where the people could sit around. That way we was all involved. We were part of it all and enjoyed it, even the work getting' ready. …
>
> For music they had an accordion and a mouth organ. One feller had an old violin with only two strings but he could play a lot of tunes on it. The gum leaf was a favourite instrument, all the boys played gum leaves. Girls weren't supposed to, makin' music was a man's thing. That's why I didn't play the accordion, at least not openly, till I grew up. …
>
> They danced waltzes and barn dances, quicksteps—you should've seen the dust rise when the dancin' got goin'. (Crawford 1993, 73–4)

The dance was a rare moment of escape from surveillance. It enabled the dancers and musicians to imagine the voices of their various ancestors, to gesture to their regulations on such things as gender roles and kinship relations, and to remember the dust rising from other dance floors.

There are various reasons why forms of Celtic folk, played on accordion, violin, gumleaf and mouth organ, may have been chosen over traditional indigenous musical forms.[20] Language group differences may have meant that the group as a whole had a limited range of suitable musical forms that could be shared at that time. More significantly, most of the languages spoken on the mission were not those of the land on which the people danced. This is significant for complex reasons. Although based primarily on research in northern Australia, Trevor A Jones' explanation is useful:

> the basic principle of 'exchange' that permeates many facets of Aboriginal life is significant when considering their music, as are the varying applications of 'mutuality' and 'exclusion' in general. These concepts help to explain matters such as *why* some songs can be sung by certain men only while other songs are traded freely, *how* extended series of songs can cover many places and linguistic groups, and *when* and *where* particular songs may or may not be performed. The concepts also underline the fact that music is considered to be a most highly valued property and a powerful asset in Aboriginal society, and any conclusions we may draw about its structure, considered purely as *sound*, must never lose sight of its immense social and spiritual significance to its custodians. (Jones 1980, 157, emphases in original)

Crawford represents all musical forms as socially and spiritually significant. Whether traditionally indigenous or an indigenous transposition of a (post)colonial form, music recurs in her memories as a means of recreating community and renewing social and spiritual connections.

In her early childhood, at the Yantabulla sand hills, Crawford had participated in 'Aboriginal dances' with her family. These were performed 'only in the camps', never at the school, where the children learnt the Irish jig and reel to the accompaniment of her Uncle Archie's accordion (1993, 22). In the public space of her book, Crawford's narrative also focuses on intercultural, rather than Baarkanji or indigenous, encounters. However, she does elaborate on the education she received from the elders in the bush around Yantabulla, which included dancing: 'All kids learnt some corroboree dancing and it was great. Leaves were tied around your ankles and every time you stamped your foot they rattled. You made a big noise and shook all over. We learnt that there was more to dancing than just jumpin' around' (1993, 36). Baarkanji education was enjoyable and hard work, but primarily a means of survival. As they walked for miles in the bush with an elder, Crawford and other children were expected to demonstrate their knowledge of food sources and catching methods: 'If we didn't, they'd go back and report to our teacher that we knew nothing, and we'd have to concentrate better. Even little kids knew why. For us it was survival, and no one could learn it for us' (1992, 35). Baarkanji children were also expected to identify their own areas of strength or interest: 'We all learnt the basics in all parts of Aboriginal learning, so that we knew enough to make a sensible choice. Then we "specialized" in the thing we were best at, or were really interested in' (1993, 35). Crawford specialized in drawing and painting, until this education was disrupted by the move to the mission.

Later, after escaping from the mission, Crawford completed 'tertiary' Baarkanji education at Mootawingee, an important Baarkanji site. This was co-ordinated by Mootawingee elders, who 'sent the message along that the special ceremonial time for kids of a certain age to be initiated was coming' (1993, 101). Crawford recalls the elders' message being sent 'a long, long time ahead because for lots of people it was a hell of a long way. It took us months, workin' on the way as Dad mostly did' (1993, 101). Large groups of people travelled long distances to take part in this 'big corroboree time', filling Mootawingee Station with camps, where 'people would be sittin' on logs and rocks at their own fires, all laughin' and talkin' at the top of their voice from one camp to another, passin' news on' (1993, 105). Education at Mootawingee was extensive and the corroborees were impressive, lasting from mid-afternoon until late at night. Both lessons and performances were inextricably connected with the land on which they took place. Crawford describes aspects of a corroboree:

> A man would stand on the hill and he'd sing. His voice would go right down the hill and all around. It was so strong it would carry way, way off.
>
> Then you'd see the dancers comin' from way down the end of the creek, all done up in their paint and feathers and leaves. (Crawford 1993, 106)

The sounds of the corroboree depended on the forms of the land, as well as the performers' knowledge. Instruments included the 'emu drum', a piece of timber, cleaned out and waxed in, with one small hole: 'You blew in it and it sounded like a bass drum. You could conjure up emus with it' (1993, 106). 'Clever people' played special boomerangs: 'You'd hear a light sound, then it'd go into a deep tone and out again, just like waves in the water. . . . If you watched the hands of those boomerang fellers they'd be goin' just like they had the shakes, and they could keep it up for hours' (1993, 107). Corroboree clap sticks—'one big flat one and one little round one'—were also specially crafted: 'It was just like runnin' the scales on a piano if they tapped from one end of the flat stick to the other. It was the special wood they used and the way they made 'em' (1993, 107). These sounds, in their ancestral place, remained with Crawford as she moved around, on and off Baarkanji land, throughout her long working life. For her, Baarkanji land retained its special qualities, despite the ruptures and complications of colonialism and displacement. Mootawingee, especially, 'stayed a very special place' to Crawford throughout her life (1993, 114).

For Langford Ginibi, Sydney would become 'home', but the town of Bonalbo remained her 'belongin place' (1988, 239).[21] In 1986 she returned to Bonalbo for her school's 75th anniversary. Langford Ginibi recalls the drive into her ancestral home. As the Richmond Range comes into view, she and her sisters sing along to their tape of Kenny Rogers singing 'Ruby don't take your love to town'. Langford Ginibi humorously applies the song's lyrics to events in her personal history, making 'Ruby' the song's subject and bemoaning her own past decisions: 'I turned on a high black mama voice and patted my chest. "I took my love to town too many times!" and burst out laughing' (1988, 242). This song revives bittersweet memories of Langford Ginibi's loves, won and lost, and the women exchange looks, laugh and fall silent. (In 2004 I sat with Langford Ginibi, who was 70 years of age and unwell, as she sang along to 'Ruby don't take your love to town'. She improvised, responding to Kenny Rogers's lines in the voice of Ruby (who is a silent presence in recorded versions of the song). For example, to the line: 'If I could move I'd get my gun and put her in the ground', Langford Ginibi responded with a low-pitched: 'You just try it' and laughter.)

On the drive to Bonalbo, the sight of Mt Lindsay through the van windows evokes 'Old Uncle Roy', a timber-getting mate of the sisters' father. Uncle Roy used to sing to the children 'in the lingo' about Mt Lindsay and now the remembered sound of his voice interrupts both Kenny Rogers and the sisters' reflective silence (1988, 30). This is the sound of the Bundjalung and Githebul area to which the women belong and return. However, it also evokes the effects of colonialism. To support their families, Uncle Roy and the sisters' father had to cut down trees in their own country, in the Taloome scrub where the 'timber was so very tall' (1988, 242). The sound of 'axes ringing' was as much part of Langford Ginibi's childhood as the sounds of the elders' voices, the cows and horses, the baker's caged crow calling 'There's blackfellers in the shop!' and Richard Tauber singing on the gramophone (1988, 7, 9, 15). On Mt Lindsay Highway in 1986, Langford Ginibi's thoughts are interrupted by the state border crossing and tick-gate, further signs of a colonialism unaware of and indifferent to indigenous boundaries. Then the Woodenbong road brings back different memories. At Woodenbong the 18-year-old Langford Ginibi had saved her first child's infant life, only to see him die when he reached 18 himself. She describes her sense of futility as she passes that place, and her response—to sing loudly, to Peggy Lee's 'I'm a woman', which happens to be on her sister's tape. These moments in the van with her sisters, on the road 'home', trace some of Langford Ginibi's entangled memories. Despite apparent incongruities in remembered and reproduced sounds, in vocalized and silent modes of remembrance, all her memories are interlinked. They all relate to her survival of colonization as a Bundjalung woman and they recognize links between places and lives, despite the relocation of some cultural meanings. Although colonialism led to Langford Ginibi's father cutting timber here, the Taloome scrub and Mt Lindsay live on. While her Bundjalung songs have been broken and Langford Ginibi is better able to sing the words of 20th-century superculture (in Slobin's terms), the voices of some ancestors, such as Uncle Roy, still resonate.

Languages and Transpositions

In the texts of Langford Ginibi, Crawford and Brett, different voices intersect and compete for space. As Langford Ginibi is silenced by the memory of Uncle Roy's voice, so Crawford recalls the 'very, very loud voice' of her fellow horse tailer in 1948, old Jimmy Galton, who had been trained since childhood in corroboree singing (Crawford 1993, 164). Similarly, Brett is 'mesmerized' by the 'big' Rabbi Groner's voice:

> he is speaking
> in Yiddish Hebrew and English
>
> his Yiddish
> envelops the graves

enriches the air
sweetens the stones

he sways in prayer
this big man . . .

and
then he sings
Kaddish . . .

and
walks away

as immense
as he arrived (Brett 1990, 67–9)

Like the rising dust on the mission claypan, the rabbi's presence is a momentary reminder of sites of escape from the sense of impotence imposed by other authorities. His powerful voice refuses to grant English the excessive airspace it usually demands. Likewise, Crawford's Wankamurrah-speaking Granny learnt all her in-laws' languages and spoke English only to white people. Her voice was 'big' and everyone 'listened when she talked' (Crawford 1993, 2, 15). The sound of the Hebrew mourner's prayer inspires hope in the midst of grief, as the smoke of the Baarkanji mourner's fire comforts and protects.

For Langford Ginibi too, her parents' language, the Bundjalung 'lingo', is a source of reassurance, excitement and hope. On hearing Bundjalung spoken again after around 26 years, Langford Ginibi describes 'the strangest feeling' (1988, 135)—an evocation of long-forgotten smells, images and sensations. One string of images and sounds recalled by Langford Ginibi relates to the role of Bundjalung in Uncle Ernie's healing of a sick Mrs Breckenridge at Box Ridge:

> I watched him go to his tin trunk and take out an old tobacco tin where he kept the hair of his dead father. He warmed it on the fire-bucket by rubbing his hands together . . . I saw him put his hand with the hair on it, to her forehead. He sang and chanted in the lingo and stayed there for about an hour. When he came out he told us to be quiet, she was sleeping. She slept for a few hours and then she got up and set about doing her work. (Langford Ginibi 1988, 8)

Much later, in the 1960s in Sydney, the sound of Bundjalung reconnects Langford Ginibi to her drowned-out memories, to people, places and her history. It is National Aborigines' Day and, with the Police Band sitting behind her, Langford Ginibi is surprised to hear and see her Uncle Jim Morgan singing in Bundjalung on the dais—'an eerie feeling in amongst the skyscrapers' (1988, 117). Langford Ginibi and Uncle Jim are pleased to see each other, having not met since she was at school; it was 'like meeting someone from your own town in another country' (1988, 117). This was to be their last meeting, but even after his death Uncle Jim's voice continues to educate and reassure Langford Ginibi, as she is able to listen to oral history recordings he made.

Like musical forms, languages change constantly, and at quicker tempos when displacement and the entry of speakers of other languages contribute to their transmutations. The English language is distantly related to Yiddish, even more distantly to Polish, and, until interactions since colonization, unrelated to Baarkanji and Bundjalung.[22] However, English as used by Crawford, Langford Ginibi, Brett and their families carries traces of those 'distant' languages. These traces take many forms, including the vocabulary-searching strategies of a mediating child. The presence of such traces does not render these language communities any less cohesive, emplaced or effective than the monolingual Australian superculture that some political authorities imagine and promote. Australian English, like most languages, clearly bears innumerable, diverse ancestral strains, but it is sometimes used, as Ian Anderson points out, to imply that its non-Anglo speakers represent 'unfortunate "hybrids"' who 'belong nowhere and have no history' (1994, 14). In contrast with such views, the texts and performances of Crawford, Langford Ginibi and Brett represent (Australian English) language communities—rural indigenous, urban indigenous and urban Jewish—that improvise and expand possibilities for meaning. Suvendrini Perera writes that Langford Ginibi's texts 'represent an active process of negotiating with and surviving in a dominant culture that persistently devalues, degrades and disappears her history' (1998, 22). The communities depicted, suggests Perera, represent 'a resourceful, energetic and vital culture that creates and copes, makes do, improvises and gets by, that incorporates the pain and injustice of living and responds with laughter, anger, art and play; that maintains itself, resists and does not let go: *survival culture*' (1998, 22).

In Sydney's indigenous communities, English becomes a dynamic, adapted 'lingo'. Langford Ginibi's community around Redfern was made up of people from many different language groups, some, like Langford Ginibi, fluent only in English, others more fluent in their first languages. Indigenous music in 20th-century Sydney was created and performed by similarly diverse artists, most singing in English. In the 1960s and 1970s, Langford Ginibi often attended events at the Foundation for Aboriginal Affairs cultural centre. Her daughter Dianne's wedding reception was held at the Foundation in 1970, with Mac Silver and Black Lace playing. Silver died in 1989, shortly after the first recordings of his own work. As well as creating significant moments in Langford Ginibi's memoir soundtrack, Silver exemplified inner Sydney's diasporic indigenous adaptations of language. Silver moved to the Redfern area from rural NSW in the 1960s. He took over the Foundation house band, naming it the Silver Linings (in reference to the saying 'every dark cloud has a silver lining') at a time when indigenous Australians were colloquially referred to as 'dark' or 'darkies', among other things. By the 1970s, the band was renamed Black Lace, 'not only after the chains once clamped around Aboriginal men's necks [as witnessed by Crawford in 1949], but also after the sprawling social network from which the band drew its shifting members' (Walker 2000, 258). Black Lace's sound has been described as 'country-rock with a Latin tinge . . . a joyous, freeing sound' (Walker 2000, 258). Like Langford Ginibi and the rest of her urban community, Black Lace adapted a range of sounds to tell diasporic stories. These stories articulated humour, love and forms of unity, while lamenting separation and loss.

Inner Sydney is replete with references to central sites of the British Empire. Langford Ginibi's first Sydney address was Great Buckingham Street, she worked in Elizabeth Street, saw films at the Empire Picture Theatre and danced in George Street. Whatever the empresses and emperors had imagined might be constructed in their names, the Empress Hotel or 'Big E' in Redfern was to become 'the main meeting place for city Kooris [indigenous people of south-eastern Australia]' in the 1960s (Langford Ginibi 1988, 118). Langford Ginibi recalls: 'For the Kooris coming to the city it was a place where you could find out where all your relatives lived. It was also where you could find out things you weren't supposed to know' (1988, 118). In her case, she learnt of her partner Lance's infidelity there. It was a site of gossip, laughter, dancing, affairs, fights, commiseration and comfort. After the death of Alfie, son of Langford Ginibi's friend Neddy, Langford Ginibi and Neddy escaped to the Empress to still their grief. That night, Langford Ginibi's old friend Gerty turned up, and met some of her relations there. Langford Ginibi remembers the effects of hearing Bundjalung, which she had last heard at the age of 6, spoken at the Empress: 'I could smell the smoke from the open fire in our place at Stoney Gully Mission, I saw Mum pick me up and put me down again, I felt her strong arms, she was giving old man Ord his tea and saying, "Here, nyathung." I saw her grinning at Dad when he came in the door with some eggs our chooks had laid in the long bladegrass under the railway culvert' (1988, 135). She reflects on the loss of fluency in one generation: 'Mum and Dad were the last generation to speak Bundjalung in our family' (1988, 135). Despite this loss, 'Empress English' articulates much that 'the Queen's English' might not, including damaged ancestral links and the complex effects of colonization. It is a site of cultural exchange, a diasporic meeting place.

A related, more mobile site of cultural exchange was the pastoral industry in Eastern Australia. In the 1960s, Langford Ginibi's friend James Golden was working in woolsheds in Sydney, but he had been a drover and 'was a well-travelled man' (1988, 139). James came from Tipperina Mission in north-western New South Wales. He often sang his ancestral song *Do wana nanarabi* when he visited Langford Ginibi and her family; her children learnt it and passed it on. James's droving work, alongside various dispersed people, meant that he also knew tribal songs from different places and languages. For many people in the Sydney community, links with traditional land and culture had been broken, but quiet voices like James's could invoke almost-forgotten sounds at crucial moments. These interacted with sounds linked to colonizing culture, which Langford Ginibi and her friends often appropriated and comically adapted to their own lives. Aspects of Hollywood culture presented at the Empire Picture Theatre were a pleasurable example of sounds ripe for appropriation: 'we spread a blanket on the floor in the kitchen and put the smokes and beer in the middle and in a while we were calling ourselves after movie stars. James was James Cagney (Little Big Man) . . . Neddy was Connie Frances because she sang tear-jerking songs; and I was Shirley Bassey because I could out-drown everyone. I always sang too much when I was drunk' (1988, 146). However, in their crowded home in the suburb of Waterloo, these performers' weary hearts eventually sought comfort in other sounds: 'When we got tired of country-and-western late in the night, James played drums on the empty beer carton and sang quietly *Do wana nanarabi* and we joined in, *nanarabi widingay*' (1988, 146). The English-inscribed beer carton effectively accompanied one of James' other languages, as it told the story of an emu resisting a kangaroo's advances, explaining 'I am not of your meat' (1988, 139). Traditional knowledge was thus maintained, as its transmission was improvised.

Religious Practices

Jewish religious practice provides for resolution of grief, with especially significant mourning rituals for children of the dead. Brett was raised with little knowledge of religious practice, but she refers to elements of it in her texts, as it was a significant part of her ancestors' lives. It is an aspect of Jewish identity with which her parents were familiar and which took on various, altered significances for Holocaust survivors. (Survivor testimonies contain examples of a range of responses. Some survivors began to fear Orthodox practice, associating it with persecution; some lost their faith, while others found or renewed theirs, or turned to a different faith.)[23] Traditional mourning practice involves periods of abstinence from pleasurable activities, such as listening to music. A child of a deceased parent avoids concerts, theatre and celebrations for 12 months after the parent's burial. For the first 11 months, the 'mourner's Kaddish' is recited every day by the son of the deceased. The notion of Kaddish is one of the few rituals adopted and adapted by many secular Jewish artists on the death of a parent. However, in keeping with another Jewish tradition, of bending religious rules, literary Kaddish texts bear little resemblance to the conventional mourner's Kaddish, which is a prayer of praise and affirmation of faith in God.[24] Fay Zwicky, an Australian poet raised at an even greater distance from Jewish religious practice than Brett, speaks of her composition for her father:

> against all the rules, I took it upon myself to make amends . . . by writing my own 'Kaddish' . . . trying to find a way into what his death meant through the rituals of a religious tradition of which I was an attenuated product, lacking both knowledge and allegiance. . . . Drawing upon threads of the rediscovered wisdom of a tradition, the poem is haunted by layers of ghostly presences, earlier generations of those whose lives went to make a family, with all that such a fallibly heroic enterprise entails. ('Kaddish' in Zwicky 1982, 1–8)

> I didn't know that what the prayer can tell you about familial love, obligation, guilt, and grief is supposed to be spoken only by men. . . . So what about the man unlucky enough to have three daughters and no sons? (Zwicky 1999)

Zwicky 'felt freer to finish' her poem after reading Allen Ginsberg's (1961) 'Kaddish' for his mother. While Ginsberg did not break the gender rule, he did break many others. Brett followed in the tradition of Ginsberg and Zwicky when she wrote her Kaddish for her mother.

Brett's Kaddish was composed within the traditional mourning period of 12 months after her mother's burial. Melody and rhythm are important aspects of Jewish prayer. In her three-part, 16-blessing poem, Brett uses rhythm to evoke changes of pace in and between the sections and their settings. Each 'blessing' represents a scene in which the daughter recalls a moment shared with her mother, either physically in Melbourne or in imagination in Lodz and elsewhere. 'Kaddish for My Mother' opens with Mario Lanza singing 'Because you're mine' in the Melbourne house of Brett's childhood and closes with the narrator's confession of her fear, at 40, of both her identification with and her enforced separation (by death) from her mother. Brett does not depict her mother's life before migration to Australia. Rather, her poem recounts Brett's own memories, forming a life narrative in which her mother is a secondary, though constant, presence, simultaneously 'blended' with the narrator and separate, untouchable. In 'Part One' she laments her persistent detachment from her mother, even as death nears:

> I thought I would hold
> you
>
> breathe
> your exotic scent
>
> feel your hands
> for the first time
>
> I thought I would touch
> you
>
> and
> be touched by you
>
> smile
> at your crooked English
>
> mixed
> with Polish and Yiddish
>
> I thought I would listen
> to you . . .
>
> when
> I knew
>
> you
> were dying.

In 'Part Three', the mourning daughter claims:

Mother I have never known
where you ended

I have worn us blended
for forty years

I have walked though Melbourne
as though it were Warsaw

on guard for the Gestapo
in fear of informers

alert
to any menace in the air . . .

Each of the sixteen scenes evokes sounds, scents, gestures, colours and shapes around the mother (and, consequently, the daughter), as remembered by the narrator. Brett knew her mother only in Melbourne, but each scene is infused with the memory (and postmemory) of the damaged Polish Jewish identity that is 'exotic', like her mother's scent, to the Australian daughter, while also an ineradicable part of herself. Brett's 'Kaddish' is psychoanalytical in mode. Here, rather than the faith affirmed in the mourner's Kaddish recited by believing sons, a confession of doubts and fears enables the continuation of life. Despite its regrets, Brett's poem, like the mourner's Kaddish, is finally something of a prayer of praise – for her mother's beauty and tenderness, which a believer would see as God's creation – and a hesitant avowal of faith in a kind of continuity, as she considers her inherited qualities. The mourner's Kaddish concludes with a call for life and peace. In her 'Kaddish', Brett too summons life and peace in the face of the permanent absence of her mother, the object of her complex, lived love in ways her unknown ancestors could not be. Like Langford Ginibi and Crawford, Brett adapts ancestral or traditional forms, as they become part of her 'Australian' modes of remembrance.

Like orthodox Jewish practice, traditional Baarkanji laws around mourning are strict. Crawford remembers learning rules around sound, silence and timing, especially when her grandparents died in the 1930s. Immediately after her Granny's death, all the adults left their camps to meet at another site. Older children looked after Crawford and her sister Gladys for two days and a night. Crawford recalls the scene at sunset on the second day:

> We seen all the mums and dads comin' along then. We could hear them cryin' comin' along the creek. We didn't go back home straight away—I suppose we were scared with all the cryin' . . . everything that moved, we thought it was Granny—terrified of ghosts we were. Nobody tells you there's a *gurrnki*—it's just built in you. Although we knew Granny wouldn't harm us, we were still afraid of seein' her because we knew she was dead. (Crawford 1993, 42)

Grandfather responded to his wife's death with silence around other adults. Crawford remembers him saying later, 'I wish you little fellers would've come over and talked to me when Granny died. I 'ad no one to talk to, only me dogs' (1993, 43). However, Crawford and Gladys were not sure whether it was right to speak to their grandfather at that time, as they were already aware of the strictness of their law.

Less than a year later, Grandfather himself died in a night fire. This loss intensified the lingering grief for Granny, in the camps and at the school, where Crawford's grandparents had befriended and helped the young Miss Cook. The sadness in the schoolroom compounded the grief at home, where the girls' father seemed to be losing his strength. Gladys already knew enough to suggest to her father, 'You ought go down the *gulpa* [deep gully] and sit there and smoke yourself, stay there all day' (1993, 44). Crawford recalls him taking his small daughter's advice and disappearing with some other men 'for a couple of days'. He then went away working, fixing fences, for about nine days. Crawford remembers the family's relief on his return: 'he rode up singin' out, "Hello! . . . g'day, Ev! . . . how're you goin', Glad?" and there was our father again! . . . the father that we'd lost all those months while all these bad things were happenin' to him. His voice was Dad's again . . . That night out came Dad's old accordion and he sat at the fire and played' (1993, 44). In Crawford's family, a return to communal, pleasurable music making marked the close of a mourning period, in somewhat similar fashion to the resumption of the enjoyment of music that closes an orthodox Jewish period of mourning.

When Crawford herself died in 2001, a large church funeral was held for her in rural NSW. People travelled from all over the state to attend. Hymns were sung, as is customary at many indigenous funerals, especially of older people, around NSW. However, the particular hymns most loved in indigenous communities tend to differ from those favoured in non-indigenous communities. 'The Old Rugged Cross' (George Bennard, 1913), sung at Crawford's funeral, is especially popular, along with 'The Sweet By-and-By' (words by Sanford F. Bennett, music by Joseph P. Webster, 1868). The lyrics of these hymns speak of relief from sorrow, while the melodies lend themselves to the gently gliding pitch and slow vocal variations that feature more richly in eastern Australian indigenous communal singing than in most non-indigenous singing. Both the above hymns were composed in the United States and arguably bear traces of Celtic folk and African-American singing techniques, like the country music loved and performed by many indigenous Australians. Here too, the notion of hybridity fails to describe indigenous performances effectively. The musical practices remembered by Crawford and performed in honour of her memory are part of a dynamic culture that is, like other cultures, a 'site of encounters', in Blum's words. The body of hymns introduced (and meanwhile largely abandoned) by colonialists contained items with sounds and sentiments ripe for transposition by Australia's colonized and dispersed people. Indigenous Australians' adoption of imposed musical forms was, of course, partly a result of the silence ensuing from the banning of indigenous cultural practice (although bans were rarely fully effective, as communities generally found ways to continue forbidden practices in secret).

Langford Ginibi's mission memories suggest that compliance and the desire of some people to please the missionary who held Sunday services were initially the result of white surveillance, but that, later, her people would adapt colonial forms to articulate their own (largely Christian) beliefs.

In *Don't take your love to town*, Langford Ginibi recounts the deaths of her grandfather, father and children Pearl, Bill and David, among others. Dispersal of the family and the demands of children and work meant that Langford Ginibi did not hear about the deaths of her grandfather and father until it was too late for her to take part in any formal mourning ceremony. She read of her grandfather's death, at 79 in a drover's shack, in a local newspaper. (A drover is 'one who [usually on horseback] drives [herds of] cattle, sheep, etc., to market, usu. over long distances' (Macquarie University 1982, 557).) Langford Ginibi was 18, with two small children, one sick with meningitis. She was staying on Mulli Mulli mission in Bundjalung country while her boyfriend Sam faced a maintenance charge for his child with another woman in Sydney. As a schoolgirl, Langford Ginibi had sometimes found her grandfather waiting for her in the park in the town of Casino, between his droving jobs. He would greet her with 'Hello goodfulla' and ask her to write a letter to her father for him (Langford Ginibi 1988, 27). After reading of his death, she recalls: 'sometimes when I was walking with the kids in the bush I heard a voice saying, "Goodfulla, come on goodfulla." Later I would find out that Grandfather was a great cricketer and a man to be proud of, but at the time I had no idea what people really meant when I was introduced and they said, "Oh, you're an Anderson"' (1988, 67). However, Langford Ginibi does have clear memories of her tall grandfather's graceful movements with the cricket ball and his humour when playing his slightly less gifted three sons: 'He stood there ... calling, "Come on goodfullas, come and play your Dad cricket." ... I remember him, a tall thin figure, the way he said those words and his voice calling and drifting across the sand. There was a grin on his face and the sun falling behind him like a giant ball in slow motion' (1988, 34) She also remembers his gentle comfort the last time she saw him, when he put his arms around her and rocked her, as she feared for the life of her sick child Bill (1988, 66).

In 1960, Langford Ginibi had not long left hospital with her baby Ellen and gone home to the camping area at St George in Queensland when she was woken one night by a spirit trying to take Ellen from her arms. The next day, a truck arrived from NSW and Langford Ginibi was told her father had died two months earlier. Telegrams and police messages had been sent, but Langford Ginibi had been away working on a station. She describes her response to the news of this most significant of deaths, the one she should have been able to mourn in timely and proper fashion:

> I collapsed onto a chair. Now I knew who the spirit was, trying to take the baby out of my arms last night. No wonder I couldn't sleep. I gave way to great sobs and Peter and Sam stood by helplessly watching me. They both knew how Dad had been mother and father to me, and he'd *always* been there when I needed him, and now there was no more always, no Dad. It was very hard for me to believe. (Langford Ginibi 1988, 101)

In her colonized world, where survival meant the impermanence of too many relationships, homes, languages and songs, Langford Ginibi's father had been the one figure who represented '*always*', security and continuity. To ensure her own continued life and peace, Langford Ginibi could have done with a traditional practice like Brett's Kaddish or Crawford's *gulpa* smoking, at the right moment. What she still could and did do was return to Sydney and mourn with her father's widow, Mum Joyce. Of course, this coming together and mutual comfort was a 'traditional' practice. Mum Joyce gave Langford Ginibi her father's cricket cap and trophy. The next time his spirit visited her at night, it was a comforting presence (1988, 103).

Of her time in the bush in Queensland, before hearing about her father's death, Langford Ginibi reflected: 'I felt like I was living tribal but with no tribe around me, no close-knit family. The food-gathering, the laws and songs were broken up, and my generation at this time wandered around as if we were tribal but in fact living worse than the poorest of poor whites' (1988, 96). The breaking up of Langford Ginibi's Bundjalung world necessitated inventive, dynamic ways of reconstructing laws and songs. In Sydney, while much was broken, Langford Ginibi had access to people, to family members who could help her, despite the brokenness of their own lives. After the death of Bill, at 18, Langford Ginibi lost her hearing for several days. The only voice she could hear was that of her mother, who advised her to talk to Bill, at his grave. Langford Ginibi's mother taught her the Bundjalung words she needed to tell Bill to leave her to live in peace (1988, 160). This ancestral intervention assisted Langford Ginibi as she dealt with the effects of her own grief and that of her surviving children.

Mourning involves various forms of performance of a mourner's links with the dead and lost. Those mourned may be individuals known and loved by the mourner, or they may belong to the mourner's postmemory. In either case, the performance or act of mourning demonstrates the continuation of certain links with the dead, despite the physical separation caused by death. In his work on the music of Yolngu people in Australia's Northeast Arnhem Land, Peter G. Toner observes that any:

> particular ritual context, such as a funeral or a *dhapi* circumcision ceremony, involves the activation of a social network with an individual (the deceased or the initiate) as its focal point. Individuals choose to be active participants based on their own personal relationships, as well as on sociocentric relations between patrifilial groups. (Toner 2005, 5)

Of course, Toner refers to the practices of a specific indigenous group in a different postcolonial context from those of Crawford, Langford Ginibi and Brett. However, his observations of the significance of ritual in 'the activation of a social network' and the roles of individuals are useful when considering the rites or performances of the three women. Their respective social networks may not be as clearly defined as those of their ancestors. However, through their musical and textual performances of collective and individual mourning, they not only activate their immediate social networks. They also address the strangers who respond to their texts and thus potentially activate new social networks.

As members of postcolonial diasporas, Crawford, Langford Ginibi and Brett metaphorically transpose/d the structures of their various ancestors' performances of mourning. A structure is defined as 'a set of interconnecting parts of any complex thing; a framework' (Moore 2004, 1417). Because of the ruptures of colonialism and dispersion, the particular structures transposed by each of the women are not musical forms that may be identified or notated in musicological ways. Of the three women, only Crawford had an intimate knowledge of her parents' language and, through her childhood practices and education, of her people's 'traditional' musical structures (although, on a different level, the Kaddish and other Jewish religious structures remain available to Brett). However, Crawford's Baarkanji world was as deeply affected by colonialism and dispersion as the Bundjalung and Jewish worlds of Langford Ginibi and Brett. In ways that are both highly individual and strongly collective, each performs—by contributing to community knowledge and activities through texts and/or music—as part of her dynamic culture of survival. The transpositions of Crawford, Langford Ginibi and Brett may be read as a kind of 'vocalese', which Kurt Elling defines as 'the writing and performing of a lyric which has been tailored to fit the lines of an instrumental solo from someone else's record' (2004). Their respective texts 'fit the lines' of English-speaking Australia, in that they constitute narratives that are published and circulated. In other ways, they also 'fit the lines' of the respective ancestral cultures with which each identifies. They do this by 'performing' the significance of their ancestors' lives, the mysteries of the forces of life and death, and the desire for loved ones to be remembered in ways that are accurate, as well as individually and collectively appropriate. Sol Foster, following Jon Hendricks, defines vocalese as 'the setting of lyrics to established jazz orchestral instrumentals' or 'singing [new] words to a pre-arranged tune. ... Two predominant threads in vocalese lyrics are storytelling and tributes ... frequently lyrics are a tribute to the musician who originally recorded the tune in question' (2004). For Crawford, Langford Ginibi and Brett, the metaphorical 'tune in question' is that of commemoration of ancestors' lives and of links with the dead. Their 'new words', in the forms of Australian English, the modernist diasporic Kaddish, Celtic folk and/or country music, are set to the 'pre-arranged tunes' of respect for ancestral lives. These complex, entangled transpositions are part of the 'transactions through which individuals and groups reproduce cultural knowledge', in Blum's words (1994, 255). In this sense, the performances of Crawford, Langford Ginibi and Brett contribute much to the dynamic structures of cultural knowledge reproduction in postcolonial and diasporic contexts.

Acknowledgements

Many thanks to Dr Ruby Langford Ginibi for her generosity and support. I am grateful to the anonymous readers and Tina K. Ramnarine for their helpful comments and to the Faculty of Arts at the University of Wollongong and the

Faculty of Arts at Monash University for financial assistance. For permission to publish Figure 2, I thank the National Library of Australia.

Notes

[1] Marianne Hirsch defines postmemory as 'the response of the second generation to the trauma of the first. . . . Postmemory most specifically describes the relationship of children of survivors of cultural or collective trauma to the experiences of their parents, experiences that they "remember" only as the narratives and images with which they grew up, but that are so powerful, so monumental, as to constitute memories in their own right' (2001, 8, 9). For an ethnomusicological application of this concept, see Kabir (2004).

[2] During the 20th century, this annual figure was exceeded only twice: in 1919, as troops returned from the Second World War, and in 1988, when 172,794 people immigrated (Australian Government 2004).

[3] In her words, Perera examines 'the positioning of the indigenous body within two related discourses that I term "multiculturalism" and "hybridity", or the discourses of happy hyphenation and happy hybridization, respectively. These discourses, I want to suggest, raise specific problems in an Australian historical context, where the effects of scientific racism are being confronted by indigenous peoples in relation to land rights claims and, more generally, the dominant culture's demands for an "authentic", visible and unproblematic Aboriginality that can be both clearly marked and contained' (1996). For a different, musicological approach, see van der Meer (2004).

[4] In Crawford's book, *Over my tracks*, the spelling of some indigenous language group names differs from standard spelling (for example, 'Baarkanji' is usually spelt 'Barkindji' or 'Paakantji'). I follow Crawford's spelling.

[5] In her texts, Brett refers to her father's family name as 'Brajsztajn', but my research in Lodz would suggest the family name there was 'Brajtsztajn' (corresponding with the German 'Breitstein'). Similarly, Brett's mother's family name, 'Spindler' in Brett's texts, was spelt 'Szpindler' in Poland (reflecting Polish spelling of the Yiddish pronunciation).

[6] Brett and her husband David Rankin were featured as members of 'the Australian diaspora' in the Australian Broadcasting Corporation's television documentary *Another Sun*: 'At any given time there are about a million Australians who are living or working abroad. That's a hefty five per cent of the population. We're now leaving the country in greater numbers than ever before in a phenomenon called the Australian diaspora' (<http://www.abc.net.au/foreign/anothersun/>).

[7] For a more extensive analysis of related aspects of the texts of Crawford and Brett, see my chapter in Huff (2005) (Breyley 2005a).

[8] As I have suggested elsewhere (2003), one way of considering these different forms of diaspora is writer Arnold Zable's adaptation of the Yiddish term *Luftmensh*—literally 'air person'—to apply to the displaced person in Australia (Zable, pers. comm., 2001). In the Yiddish world, a *Luftmensh* was a dispossessed but shrewd survivor, a wheeler and dealer, who moved about making something out of nothing. The process of 'becoming Australian' or of failing to become Australian, in its many different forms, can involve time as a *Luftmensh*, finding no homeland where 'Australian' discourse suggests there should be one or being dispossessed of that which was a homeland. Zable, whose family was left bereft by the Holocaust, points out that an indigenous person could be expected to be the *Luftmensh*'s opposite—indigenous people have strong links to place and know their homelands intimately. However, Zable speaks of a shock of recognition when he encounters the 'hovering' indigenous narrator of Kim Scott's novel *Benang* (1999): all it takes is a generation of dispossession to render even the indigenous person a *Luftmensh*. Zable's adaptation of the

term removes the derogatory connotation it had in Eastern Europe. Historian Mark Raphael Baker considers his Ukrainian-born mother's more traditional use: '"*Luftmenshn*," she likes to characterise those in my profession, idlers living off air' (1997, 138). See also Paul Celan, '*Hüttenfenste*'/'Tabernacle window': 'the wander-/East, the/Hovering Ones, the/Humans-and-Jews,/the Cloud Crowd [*Volk-vom-Gewölk*: literally "people-of-clouds"]' (2001, 197). Much of Celan's Holocaust-derived imagery of clouds, air, earth and smoke, as in his '*Todesfuge*'/'Deathfugue' (2001, 30–3), also evokes both the mourning and the denial (as in *terra nullius*) of indigenous Australian life. While the indigenous *Luftmensh* may leave tracks on local, familiar soil, dispossession repeatedly changes the course of those tracks and with it the languages and musical forms that may be used.

[9] Massacres in New South Wales include one at Bathurst in 1824, which left around 100 indigenous people dead, the 1838 massacres of 28 people at Myall Creek and an unknown number of Camilleroi (Crawford's husband's people) at Waterloo Creek, and the 1864 massacre of around 100 people at Richmond River in Langford Ginibi's Bundjalung country (Commonwealth of Australia/Wilson 1997, available at <http://www.hreoc.gov.au/bth/text_versions/timeline/index.html>; Milliss 1992; Reynolds 1998, 4–6, 20, 40–1, 65–9, 120). See also Rose (2001). On the question of genocide, Larissa Behrendt writes: 'For Indigenous plaintiffs, it doesn't matter whether the crime of genocide was committed as it was defined by international law and it doesn't matter whether there was intention or not. What seems to be more important from the Indigenous perspectives are the *effects* of the actions of the government—these actions have amounted to damage to Indigenous people, families and communities and they choose to use the word "genocide" to describe it. This moves the discussion outside of the words of the statute to the side-effects and legacies of those sanctioned actions' (2001, 142, emphasis in original).

[10] On a different level, an example of this concern was the theme of the 2006 Society for Ethnomusicology (SEM) 51st annual conference: 'Decolonizing Ethnomusicology'.

[11] Alan Belkin defines the countersubject's role as that of 'a recurring counterpoint to the theme, often (but not always) adding its own motives. When present ... [the countersubject] enhances and sharpens the profile of the theme through contrast, filling in rhythmic gaps, enriching the harmony through suspensions' (2004). Through contrast with popular and/or national themes, countersubjects' discourses amplify discrepancies in those themes. Countersubjects enrich popular harmonies with suspension, 'a form of discord arising from the holding over of a note in one chord as a momentary (discordant) part of the combination which follows, it being then resolved by falling a degree to a note which forms a real part of the second chord' (Kennedy and Bourne 1996). When countersubjects maintain 'notes' from their 'first' or parental cultural knowledges into their respective 'second' sites of learning, those imposed on children by 'White Australia', they create dissonance. A general example of this in Brett's work is her preoccupation (deriving from the persistence of her parents' memories) with the ostensibly resolved story of the Holocaust. Brett suspends tones of inherited anguish in chords (her relations with fellow Australians) expected to be free of discord. As children and as adult authors, Crawford and Langford Ginibi enriched Australian harmonies by holding on to languages and practices that white authorities had planned to remove from their repertoires. These suspension techniques constituted interventions in dominant cultural practice. Their dissonance effected change and sometimes resolution in future encounters, as their 'notes' became audibly 'real parts' of 'major' cultural forms. Conversation with and between such 'countersubjects' thus enriches, diverts and alters popular themes.

[12] Mark Slobin explains 'superculture' as an 'overarching structure', encompassing 'the statistically lopsided, the commercially successful, the statutory, the regulated, the most visible'. A superculture includes an industry, the 'state and its institutionalized rules and

venues' and 'more insidious strands of hegemony' that 'define the everyday, and circumscribe the expressive' (1992, 15–18).

[13] 'Counter-narratives of the nation that continually evoke and erase its totalizing boundaries—both actual and conceptual—disturb those ideological manoeuvres through which "imagined communities" are given essentialist identities. For the political unity of the nation consists in a continual displacement of the anxiety of its irredeemably plural modern space' (Bhabha 2004, 213). Edward W Said explains his theory of 'contrapuntal reading' as 'reading a text with an understanding of what is involved when an author shows, for instance, that a colonial sugar plantation is seen as important to the process of maintaining a particular style of life in England. . . . contrapuntal reading must take account of both processes, that of imperialism and that of resistance to it, which can be done by extending our reading of the texts to include what was once forcibly excluded—in *L'Etranger*, for example, the whole previous history of France's colonialism and its destruction of the Algerian state, and the later emergence of an independent Algeria (which Camus opposed). . . . Each text has its own particular genius, as does each geographical region of the world, with its own overlapping experiences and interdependent histories of conflict. . . . In addition, one must connect the structures of a narrative to the ideas, concepts, experiences from which it draws support' (1993, 66–7).

[14] These terms are used, respectively, in The Liquor (Amendment) Act 1905 (NSW) s 8(4), The Aboriginals Protection and Restriction of the Sale of Opium Act 1897 (Qld) s 4, Aborigines Act Amendment Act 1936 (WA) s 2, The Liquor (Amendment) Act 1905 (NSW) s 8(4) and the Queensland Aboriginal Protection Acts. See De Plevitz and Croft (2003). While early to mid 20th-century 'White Australia' made its idiosyncratic distinctions between different categories of European, for example, between 'Brit' and 'Balt' and between 'Australian' and 'Englishman', it remained largely ignorant of the diversity of the indigenous groups who lived in an area larger than Europe. At the time of colonization, it is estimated that more than 500 dialects were spoken, making up about 250 distinct languages (AIATSIS 1994, 279). However, settler authorities saw only 'full-bloods', who were expected to die out, and varieties of 'mixed-bloods', some of whom, like the chosen immigrants, were required to assimilate.

[15] I use the term 'Anglo-Celtic' to refer to the 'major' part of Australia's population that is descended primarily from the first European (willing and unwilling) colonizers, although this term elides the significant differences between and within Anglo-Saxon and Celtic identities. This elision reflects that intended in such policies as 'White Australia'. Various policies and cultural change have contributed to an increasing forgetfulness of certain differences, as successive 'non-Anglo-Saxon/Celtic' groups have been assigned the role of 'other', effectively pushing 'Anglos' and 'Celts' together as 'central' and bringing the term 'Anglo-Celtic' into common usage in Australia.

[16] 'Stolen generations' songs in English include Bob Randall's 'Brown skin baby' (EMI 1987) and Archie Roach's 'Took the children away' (Festival 1990). Songs around deaths in custody include Richard Frankland's 'Malcolm Smith' (Polygram 1993), Paul Kelly's 'Bicentennial' (Chaos Music, 1987) and Mac Silver's 'Malabar mansion', referring to Sydney's Long Bay Jail in the beachside suburb of Malabar (Enrec 1988). Stolen land songs include Kev Carmody's 'Thou shalt not steal' (Larrikin 1990), Jimmy Chi's 'Nothing I would rather be (than to be an Aborigine)' (Polygram 1994), Kev Carmody and Paul Kelly's 'From little things big things grow' (Larrikin, Universal and Song Cycles, 1992) and Midnight Oil's 'Beds are burning' (Columbia/Sony, 1988). Official documents include *Bringing Them Home* (Commonwealth of Australia 1997) (see also 'Bringing Them Home Inquiry', Human Rights and Equal Opportunity Commission, available at <http://www.hreoc.gov.au/social_justice/stolen_children/index.html>) and Australian Institute of Criminology (1992–6). Political responses include *Apology Australia*, 'Paul Keating's Redfern Speech [1992]', available at: <http://

apology.west.net.au/redfern.html>, and *Barunga Statement* [1988], available at <http://www.austlii.edu.au/au/orgs/car/docrec/policy/brief/attach.htm>.

[17] Wild (2006, 348) refers to the 'pioneers of Australian ethnomusicology', Trevor A. Jones, Catherine Ellis and Alice Moyle, as well as the 'second generation', Margaret J. Kartomi, Richard Moyle, Jill Stubington, Allan Marett, Linda Barwick and Wild himself.

[18] All these texts contain references to notions of hybridity. Magowan's article addresses political and cultural aspects of the commodification of 'traditional' music.

[19] See *Royal Commission into Aboriginal Deaths in Custody*, Regional Report of Inquiry in NSW, Victoria and Tasmania, chapter 15: 'The historical background, NSW' 23, 'The policy of concentration': 'Enforced concentration began in 1934 and continued until 1939, but it was implemented only unevenly across the State. Most dramatically affected were Aboriginals living where the rural economy appeared to be undergoing the greatest restructuring, in the western and north coast pastoral industry areas where the largest properties were again being broken up. Whole communities of Aboriginals were moved hundreds of miles by cattle truck and dumped on Protection Board stations at Menindee, Brewarrina, Toomelah and Burnt Bridge. Aboriginals protested bitterly but they had been made even more vulnerable by the legislative changes of 1936, which they called the "Dog Act", because it allowed them to be carted around and penned up like animals. In reality they had few choices, particularly if they had young children. Nevertheless, many were transported only at gunpoint, like the Murries moved from Angledool to Brewarrina in 1936. Others stayed in the new "concentration" stations only so long as economic conditions forced them into dependence on Board rations, like the Wangkumarra [Crawford's father's Wankamurrah people] of the Comer Country, who were forced to Brewarrina in 1938 but left in 1940, 80 strong despite the deaths of many of their old people, to walk the 190 miles back to their country.'

[20] For a useful analysis of gumleaf music, see Ryan (2003).

[21] I present a similar but more extensive analysis of music in *Don't take your love to town* in my article (2005b).

[22] English, Yiddish and Polish all belong to the Indo-European language tree. English and Yiddish stem from the Germanic branch, while Polish stems from the Slavic branch.

[23] There is a large body of memoir written and recorded by survivors in Australia. For a sample, see *Australian memories of the Holocaust*, NSW Jewish Board of Deputies, available at: < http://www.holocaust.com.au/memories.htm >; Jewish Holocaust Museum and Research Centre, Melbourne, available at: <http://www.arts.monash.edu.au/affiliates/hlc/publications. html >; Australian Holocaust memoirs collection, Australian Centre for Jewish Civilisation, Monash University, and *Survivors of the Shoah Visual History Foundation* (Steven Spielberg's project, which includes many Australians), available at: <http://www.vhf.org/vhfmain-2.htm >.

[24] Gershom Scholem reflects on 'the Hebrew prose and poetry of medieval Jewry—the language of the great halakhists and of the "mosaic style," the poetic prose in which linguistic scraps of sacred texts are whirled around kaleidoscopelike and are journalistically, polemically, descriptively, and even erotically profaned' (2003, 131).

References

Anderson, Ian. 1994. Reclaiming Tru-ger-nan-ner: Decolonising the symbol. *Art Monthly* 66: 10–14.

Ashcroft, Bill, Gareth Griffiths and Helen Tiffin. 2002. *The empire writes back: Theory and practice in post-colonial literatures*. London and New York: Routledge.

Australian Government. 2004. Immigration to Australia during the 20th century: Historical impacts on immigration intake, population size and population composition. Department of

Immigration and Multicultural and Indigenous Affairs. Available at: <http://www.immi.gov.au/ >.

Australian Institute of Aboriginal and Torres Strait Islander Studies (AIATSIS). 1994. *Encyclopedia of Aboriginal Australia.* Canberra: Aboriginal Studies Press.

Australian Institute of Criminology. 1992–6. *Deaths in Custody Australia.*

Baily, John. 2005. So near, so far: Kabul's music in exile. *Ethnomusicology Forum* 14 (2): 213–33.

Baker, Mark Raphael. 1997. *The fiftieth gate.* Sydney: HarperCollins.

Barney, Katelyn. 2004. "Where is their costume, where is their paint?" Exploring how indigenous Australian women construct and negotiate their indigeneity through contemporary music. *Perfect Beat* 7 (1): 42–59.

Behrendt, Larissa. 2001. Genocide: The distance between law and life. *Aboriginal History* 25.

Belkin, Alan. 2004. *Principles of Counterpoint.* Available at: <http://www.musique.umontreal.ca/personnel/Belkin/bk.C/5.html >.

Bhabha, Homi K. 2004. *The location of culture.* London and New York: Routledge.

Blum, Stephen. 1991. Prologue. In *Ethnomusicologists and Modern Music History,* edited by Stephen Blum, Philip V. Bohlman and Daniel M. Neuman. Urbana, IL: University of Illinois Press.

———. 1994. Conclusion: Music in an age of cultural confrontation. In *Music-cultures in contact: Convergences and collisions,* edited by Margaret J. Kartomi and Stephen Blum. Sydney: Currency Press.

Breen, Marcus. 1989. *Our place, our music, Aboriginal music: Australian popular music in perspective,* Vol. 2. Canberra: Aboriginal Studies Press.

Brett, Lily. 1986. *The Auschwitz poems.* Melbourne: Scribe.

———. 1987. Kaddish for my mother. In *Properties of the poet and other poems,* edited by Paul Kavanagh. Newcastle: University of Newcastle Press, pp. 17–34.

———. 1990. *After the war.* Melbourne: Melbourne University Press.

———. 1992. *Unintended consequences.* Sydney: Paper Bark Press.

Breyley, Gay. 2003. "Kissing the noose of Australian democracy": Misplaced faiths and displaced lives converse over Australia's rising fences. *Borderlands* 2 (3). Available at <http:/www.borderlands ejournal.adelaide.edu.au/ >.

———. 2005a. Imagined ancestral communities of displaced Australian daughters: Lily Brett's *Unintended consequences* and Evelyn Crawford's *Over my tracks.* In *Women's life writing and imagined communities,* edited by Cynthia Huff. London and New York: Routledge, pp. 17–42. Also in *Prose Studies* 26 (2003) (1–2): 17–42.)

———. 2005b. Unfolding Australia's fan of memory: Music in Ruby Langford Ginibi's *Don't take your love to town. Journal of Australian Studies* 84: 15–29.

Celan, Paul. 2001. *Selected poems and prose,* translated by John Felstiner. New York: Norton.

Commonwealth of Australia (commissioned by Ronald Wilson). 1997. *Bringing them home: Report of the National Inquiry into the Separation of Aboriginal and Torres Strait Islander Children from their Families.* Sydney: Human Rights and Equal Opportunity Commission.

Crawford, Evelyn. 1993. *Over my tracks.* Melbourne: Penguin.

Curthoys, Ann. 2001. Colonisation and immigration: The two faces of the Australian nation. Paper given at "Constituting a 'people': The legacy of White Australia" conference, University of Western Australia.

De Plevitz, Loretta and Larry Croft. 2003. Aboriginality under the microscope: The biological descent test in Australian law. *Queensland University of Technology Law & Justice Journal* 3 (1).

Dunbar-Hall, Peter and Chris Gibson. 2005. *Deadly sounds, deadly places: Contemporary Aboriginal music in Australia.* Sydney: University of New South Wales Press.

Elling, Kurt. 2004. *Elling study guide.* Available at: <www.quadcityarts.com/ELLING.pdf>.

Foster, Sol. 2004. *What is Vocalese?* Available at: <www.harmonyware.com/JonHendricks/vocalese.html>.

Ginsberg, Allen. 1961. *Kaddish, and other poems, 1958–1960.* San Francisco. CA: City Lights Books.

Hirsch, Marianne. 2001. Surviving images: Holocaust photographs and the work of postmemory. *The Yale Journal of Criticism* 14 (1): 5–37.

Jones, Trevor A. 1980. The traditional music of the Australian Aborigines. In *Musics of many cultures*, edited by Elizabeth May. Berkeley, CA, and London: University of California Press.

Kabir, Ananya Jahanara. 2004. Musical recall: Neo-ethnic postmemory and the Punjabi diaspora. *Alif: Journal of Comparative Poetics* 24: 172–89.

Kartomi, Margaret J. 1981. The processes and results of musical culture contact: A discussion of terminology and concepts. *Ethnomusicology* 25 (2): 227–49.

Kennedy, Michael and Joyce Bourne. 1996. *Concise Oxford dictionary of music*, 4th edn. Oxford: Oxford University Press. Available at: <http://www.classicalarchives.com/dict/harmony.html>.

Langford [Ginibi], Ruby. 1988. *Don't take your love to town.* Melbourne: Penguin (this 1st edn published under the name 'Ruby Langford').

Langton, Marcia. 1981. Urbanizing Aborigines: The social scientists' great deception. *Social Alternatives* 2 (2): 16–22.

Macquarie University. 1982. *The Macquarie Dictionary.* Sydney: Macquarie Library.

Magowan, Fiona. 1994. Melodies of mourning: A study of form and meaning in Yolngu women's music and dance in traditional and Christian contexts. D.Phil. thesis, Oxford University.

———. 2005. Playing with meaning: Perspectives on culture, commodification and contestation around the didjeridu. *Yearbook for Traditional Music*: 80–102.

Milliss, Roger. 1992. *Waterloo Creek.* Melbourne: McPhee Gribble.

Mohanty, Chandra Talpade. 1984. Under Western eyes: Feminist scholarship and colonial discourses. *Boundary* 12 (2).

Moore, Bruce. 2004. *The Australian concise Oxford dictionary.* Melbourne: Oxford University Press.

Moses, A. Dirk. 2002. Conceptual blockages and definitional dilemmas in the "racial century": Genocides of indigenous peoples and the Holocaust. *Patterns of Prejudice* 36 (4).

Muller, Carol A. 2006. The new African diaspora, the built environment and the past in jazz. *Ethnomusicology Forum* 15 (1): 63–86.

Nettl, Bruno. 2002. *Encounters in ethnomusicology: A memoir.* Warren, MI: Harmonie Park Press.

Perera, Suvendrini. 1996. Claiming Truganini: Australian national narratives in the year of indigenous peoples. *Cultural Studies* 10 (3): 393–412.

———. 1998. "You were born to tell these stories": The edu-ma-cations of Doctor Ruby. *Meridian* 17 (1): 15–30.

Randhofer, Regina. 2004. By the rivers of Babylon: Echoes of the Babylonian past in the musical heritage of the Iraqi Jewish diaspora. *Ethnomusicology Forum* 13 (1): 21–45.

Reily, Suzel Ana. 2006. Remembering the baroque era: Historical consciousness, local identity and the Holy Week celebrations in a former mining town in Brazil. *Ethnomusicology Forum* 15 (1): 39–62.

Reyes, Adelaida. 1999. *Songs of the caged, songs of the free: Music and the Vietnamese refugee experience.* Philadelphia, PA: Temple University Press.

Reynolds, Henry. 1998. *This whispering in our hearts.* Sydney: Allen & Unwin.

Rose, Deborah Bird. 2001. Aboriginal life and death in Australian settler nationhood. *Aboriginal History* 25: 148–62.

Rutland, Suzanne. 2001. Subtle exclusions: Postwar Jewish emigration to Australia and the impact of the IRO scheme. *The Journal of Holocaust Education* 10 (1): 50–66.

Ryan, Robin. 2003. Jamming on the gumleaves in the bush "down under": Black tradition, white novelty? *Popular Music and Society* 26 (3): 285–304.

Said, Edward W. 1993. *Culture and imperialism.* New York: Knopf.

Scholem, Gershom. 2003. *Walter Benjamin: The story of a friendship*, translated by Harry Zohn. New York: The New York Review of Books.

Scott, Kim. 1999. *Benang: From the heart.* Fremantle: Fremantle Arts Centre Press.

Shelemay, Kay Kaufman. 2006. Music, memory and history. *Ethnomusicology Forum* 15 (1): 17–37.

Slobin, Mark. 1992. Micromusics of the West: A comparative approach. *Ethnomusicology* 36 (1): 1–87.

Toner, Peter G. 2005. Tropes of longing and belonging: Nostalgia and musical instruments in Northeast Arnhem Land. *Yearbook for Traditional Music* 37: 1–24.

Van der Meer, Wim. 2004. The location of music: Towards a hybrid musicology. University of Amsterdam. Available at: <http://musicology.nl/WM/courses/6_postcolonial/LocationofMusic.pdf>.

Walker, Clinton. 2000. *Buried country: The story of Aboriginal country music.* Sydney: Pluto Press.

Watson, Julia and Sidonie Smith. 1992. De/colonization and the politics of discourse in women's autobiographical practices. In *De/colonizing the subject: The politics of gender in women's autobiography,* edited by Sidonie Smith and Julia Watson. Minneapolis, MN: University of Minnesota Press.

Welten, Peter. 1980. Bestattung, II. Altes Testament. In *Theologische Realenzyklopädie,* Vol. 5. Berlin: de Gruyter, pp. 734–8.

Wild, Stephen. 2006. Ethnomusicology down under: A distinctive voice in the Antipodes? *Ethnomusicology* 50 (2): 345–52.

Zwicky, Fay. 1999. "Border crossings". Talk given at the Annual General Meeting of the Council of Christians and Jews. Available at: <http://www.ccjwa.iinet.net.au/bordercrossings.pdf>.

———. 1982. *Kaddish and other poems.* St Lucia: University of Queensland Press.

Discography

Kenny Rogers. 1969. *Ruby don't take your love to town* (by Mel Tillis). EMI.

The *'Danza de las Cañas'*: Music, Theatre and Afroperuvian Modernity

Javier F. León

For most of the second part of the 20th century, Afroperuvian music making has been largely centred on the activities of professional popular musicians. In previous centuries musical practices associated with people of African descent in Peru were largely associated with community-based musical events whose primary intent was to strengthen familial and social bonds within those communities. The last five decades, however, have placed a more marked emphasis on the professional stage, nightclub performances and recorded albums that are widely consumed by largely non-Afroperuvian audiences, both within Peru and more recently in the American and European world music markets. While this shift in performance context helped greatly in the dissemination, recognition and acceptance of Afroperuvian music, some performers have come to question the degree to which the Afroperuvian professional music circuit has become a golden cage that, over time, has disconnected

---

Javier F. León is an Assistant Professor of Music at the Newcomb Department of Music and the Stone Center for Latin American Studies at Tulane University in New Orleans, Louisiana. He specializes in criollo popular music, Afroperuvian music and the politics of ethnomusicological research, and his work has been published in *Latin American Music Review, Selected Reports of Ethnomusicology* and *Black Music Research Journal.* He is currently working on a book on contemporary Afroperuvian musical practice and modernity in the city of Lima.

professional musicians from the communities to which they belong. This article will focus on the recent attempts by one particular group of Afroperuvian performers, the members of *Grupo Teatro del Milenio* (Theatre of the Millennium Group), to devise new performative strategies that can help both performers and their audiences to develop a more critical engagement with their own identities as Afroperuvians. The overall end of such a discussion is not to validate the strategies advocated by this particular group as being more effective than others in addressing some of the growing concerns in the Afroperuvian musical community. Rather, I am interested in how *Milenio*'s unique blend of Afroperuvian popular music, modern dance, social activism and European experimental theatre techniques can help further our understanding of the cosmopolitan aspects of Afroperuvian identity among professional musicians in Lima.

The Modern Reinterpretation of Afroperuvian Musical Tradition

Most of the music performed by Afroperuvian professional musicians at the turn of the 21st century is closely tied to the legacy of a project of cultural reclamation dating back to the 1950s (Feldman 2006; León 2003; Romero 1994). While Afroperuvians had formed an important cultural and demographic component of the Peruvian coast during the colonial period (Bowser 1974; Estenssoro 1989; Flores Galindo 1991), by the turn of the 20th century most musical practices predominantly associated with the Afroperuvian community were in the process of disappearing.[1] Realizing that many musical traditions had begun to fade from Afroperuvian collective memory, a number of intellectuals, culture bearers and professional performers gathered to reconstruct and reinvent extinct and nearly extinct genres. The result of their efforts was the emergence of a clearly defined canon of songs, genres, choreographies and an accompanying genealogy of their origins which were promoted with the hope that their dissemination would re-instil a sense of pride among members of the Afroperuvian community. For leaders of the revival the issue of identity was a crucial concern. By the middle of the 20th century, most people of African descent did not necessarily see themselves as having distinct cultural practices that differentiated them from the rest of the coastal population. Members of this dominant coastal culture, most of whom were of European descent and who identified themselves as '*criollo*', acknowledged certain African, indigenous and even Asian cultural influences but, at the same time, considered these to be relatively minor contributions to what they saw as a predominantly Spanish set of cultural practices that had acquired a distinct local flavour over centuries of colonial rule. In response, the revival sought to identify musical practices associated predominantly with the Afroperuvian community in order to differentiate these from *criollo* musical practices. At the same time, it also tried to raise awareness regarding the important contributions that Afroperuvians had made to the development of Peruvian coastal culture.

Despite this attempt at differentiation, the music of the revival was well received by Lima's middle and upper classes, which were predominantly *criollo*. Early performances, often featuring musicalized theatrical scenes depicting slaves working in the fields, bickering street vendors using song to promote their wares and maidens washing clothes (Feldman 2006; Roel y Pineda 1964; Romero 1994; Tompkins 1981) not only allowed for the re-creation of an Afroperuvian past previously omitted from official accounts of Peruvian history, but also provided *criollos* with the basis for a nostalgic remembrance of romanticized colonial past (León 1997: 151–62). Given that during the second part of the 20th century the Afroperuvian population has been estimated to be less than 5 per cent of the total coastal population, this *criollo* audience was an important factor in the endurance of the musical practices associated with the revival. In the decades that followed, this music was increasingly promoted through live performances, radio and television broadcasts, commercial recordings and institutions devoted to the preservation and dissemination of various types of Peruvian folklore. In the end, both the success of Afroperuvian music, primarily among *criollo* audiences, and its recognition as regional Peruvian tradition by various institutions helped to establish the idea of the existence of an 'authentic' and nearly timeless Afroperuvian musical tradition that had survived relatively unchanged hidden and preserved in small rural communities in the coastal hinterland.

This idea of an invented, or rather re-invented, Afroperuvian musical tradition, and the politics of identity tied to this reclamation of the past, has been the dominant theme of most ethnomusicological scholarship on this topic. Early studies by William Tompkins (1981), Rosa Elena Vázquez (1982) and Luis Rocca (1985) were concerned with documenting surviving musical traditions in a variety of places on the Peruvian coast as a means of differentiating them, both musically and in terms of performance context, from their reinterpreted and expanded counterparts that had developed in Lima during the second part of the 20th century. More recently, Raúl Romero (1994) and Heidi Feldman (2006) have shifted their attention to musicians and intellectuals in Lima and how their negotiation of the tension between local and diasporic identities has informed the development of Afroperuvian music during the second part of the 20th century. These studies are also important because they begin to place more emphasis on understanding the social and performative space in which most contemporary Afroperuvian music unfolds and on the professional musicians that make this music. After all, for the last five decades, professional musicians in Lima have been very important in disseminating knowledge about, and shaping perceptions of, Afroperuvian culture and the Afroperuvian community. One aspect that remains under-examined, however, is how choices made by these professional musicians have also been informed by a particular worldview that reflects their identity as modern cosmopolitans who wish to be perceived not as mere artisans charged with the preservation of musical traditions handed down to them by earlier generations but as creative artists and innovators.

In some respects, the omission is not surprising; after all, for most of the second part of the 20th century Afroperuvian music practitioners, audiences and institutional supporters have placed an emphasis on the documentation, reclamation and preservation of a pre-modern Afroperuvian musical past. Early figures of the revival movement, particularly Nicomedes Santa Cruz, consulted archival sources, conducted 'salvage ethnography' to collect testimonies, song fragments and choreographic descriptions, researched the work of Peruvian and foreign anthropologists, ethnologists and musicologists, and produced their own scholarly writings in an attempt to reconstruct a lost history of origins and acknowledge the important contributions of Afroperuvians to the development of Peruvian coastal culture. Santa Cruz's research had been informed and inspired by the earlier work of *criollo* intellectuals like Rosa Mercedes Ayarza de Morales, Fernando Romero and José Durand. However, he differed from his non-Afroperuvian counterparts in his desire to use the tools of academic research as a means of developing a diasporic identity project that would challenge the assumption that Afroperuvian traditions were little more than a subset of practices previously subsumed into the dominant *criollo* coastal culture. During the 1960s and early 1970s, Santa Cruz's theories challenged *criollo* claims that most Peruvian coastal genres were primarily the result of a local reinterpretation of European forms and offered more Afrocentric alternatives that effectively drew on archival sources as well as on Latin American, Caribbean, European and North American academic scholarship in the fields of history, anthropology, linguistics and musicology to draw parallels between Peru and Afro-Cuban and Afro-Brazilian case studies.[2] His writings on the origins of Afroperuvian music came to be reprinted numerous times in newspaper articles and record liner notes and became the foundation for a primarily orally transmitted history of Afroperuvian music that most professional musicians have come to internalize as part of their identity. Furthermore, since Santa Cruz, reading, collecting and/or engaging in historical music research has been a way in which professional musicians have been able to bolster their cultural capital, often gaining a more authoritative voice on all matters Afroperuvian, not just music and dance, by virtue of having acquired the type of special knowledge deemed necessary to prevent the further dilution or distortion of Afroperuvian tradition.

In this regard, Paul Gilroy has observed that 'the idea of ready access to and command of tradition—sometimes ancient, always anti-modern—has become essential to the disciplinary mechanisms that today's stern traditionalists seek to exercise over diverse processes of black cultural production' (1993, 191). Although not traditionalist in the strict sense of the term, the leaders of the revival movement did find the invocation of tradition an effective strategy with which to maintain authority over the type of Afroperuvian musical production they were promoting. As Raúl Romero (1994: 324) points out, these individuals seldom shared their philosophies or political intentions with the rank-and-file performers of their companies, and more often resorted to the dogmatic prescription of particular dance steps and accompaniment patterns under the justification that they were the ones who held the knowledge necessary to realize an 'authentic' performance (Baca and Pereira interview 1995; Molina interview 2000). In the years to follow, other performers would develop similar strategies to acquire and monopolize knowledge about the Afroperuvian past and in the process bolster their cultural capital within the musical community as well as with state-sponsored cultural organizations interested in inducting the music that grew out of the Afroperuvian revival into the official pantheon of institutionalized music and dance performance in Peru (León 2003: 48–63). Along the way, the creative and innovative aspects of Afroperuvian performance in the second part of the 20th century were largely downplayed in favour of the idea that what made Afroperuvian performance a legitimate form of artistic expression was its ability to preserve and reproduce music and dance from decades and centuries past.

Ironically, the musical reconstruction of the Afroperuvian repertoire during the 1960s and 1970s was the result of a great deal of experimentation and innovation, something that was obscured by discourses of authenticity surrounding its creation and the eventual reification as official form of Peruvian national folklore. Master musicians like the Vásquez brothers, in collaboration first with José Durand and later with Nicomedes Santa Cruz, helped create new accompaniment patterns for musical genres that had ceased to be performed decades, if not centuries, earlier. Nicomedes' sister Victoria, who developed some of the first professional Afroperuvian dance company choreographies, drew not only from surviving Afroperuvian musical practices but from modern dance techniques that she learned during her studies at the Université du Theatre des Nationes and the École Superieur des Études Choréographiques in Paris. She was also strongly influenced by the work of African-American choreographer and anthropologist Katherine Dunham (Feldman 2006, ch. 2) and pursued the development of short theatrical vignettes depicting Afroperuvian daily life. In his recordings Nicomedes occasionally added musical instruments from other parts of the African diaspora in Latin America even though these were not used in traditional Afroperuvian musical practice. This practice was further expanded in the 1970s, when new groups of performers, most notably among them Perú Negro, began stylistically to 're-Africanize' the revival Afroperuvian repertoire by introducing the use of Afro-Cuban musical instruments like *tumbadoras*, *bongos* and cowbells, as well as musical elements derived from Afro-Cuban genres such as *rumba* and *abakwá*[3] (Feldman 2006, ch. 4; León 2007).

Taking this into account, it is clear that the Afroperuvian revival movement, while largely informed by rural and working-class forms of musical expression, was a modern project squarely situated in a decidedly urban-professional musical environment and promoted by middle-class intellectuals well versed not only in Afroperuvian matters and anthropological and musicological literature dealing with African survivals in the Americas, but also in modern dance and ballet, Peruvian literature, Latin American poetry, Western philosophy, etc. From this vantage point, those involved in the revival movement sought to negotiate local, diasporic and cosmopolitan aspects of their identities by promoting Afroperuvian music and dance as a legitimate form of expression, both in the culturally relativist, anthropological sense of term and, perhaps somewhat paradoxically, in the cosmopolitan sense which implies a universal refinement and sophistication associated with 'being cultured' (see Taylor 2001). Thomas Turino has observed that this is often the case when it comes to projects where those who actively shape the music-making environment (performers, audiences, cultural brokers, etc.) are 'typically cosmopolitans themselves' (Turino 2003b, 176; see also Turino 2003a: 74, 2000: 13). But what exactly are the implications of conceiving of professional Afroperuvian musicians as cosmopolitans? Turino's work on Zimbabwean popular music suggests that this is an aspect that has not been addressed sufficiently by current academic trends. From his perspective, the idea of cosmopolitanism has been overlooked or dismissed in favour of paradigms that seek to account for connections across geographic and cultural boundaries. These paradigms either posit over-generalized models of globalization or default to discussions of diaspora with which cosmopolitan cultural formations share some similarities but are nonetheless separate and distinct (2003a: 60–3; in reference to diasporas see also Turino 2004). For Gilroy, cosmopolitanism is an integral and uneasy part of the ambivalent relationship that descendants of Africans in the diaspora have had with modernity and makes a call towards the further problematization of this relationship in academic scholarship. Keeping in step with Gilroy, Michael Hanchard proposes that the notion of alternative modernities may be useful in understanding what he sees as 'the selective incorporation of technologies, discourses, and institutions of the modern West within the cultural and political practices of African-derived peoples to create a form of relatively autonomous modernity distinct from its counterparts of Western Europe and North America' (2001, 274).

The notion of a distinct Afroperuvian modernity is necessary in order to understand the effect of the legacy of the Afroperuvian revival movement on contemporary performers such as the members of *Grupo Teatro del Milenio.* I would also like to suggest that performative critiques regarding the present state of Afroperuvian musical production, such as the ones discussed in the pages that follow, are closely tied to a changing sense of priorities regarding what music should be able to accomplish for members of the Afroperuvian community. The choices made within this debate are political as well as artistic and are drawn from a repository that, as Ted Gordon suggests, is comprised of '(a) ideas and practices that are the production, past and present, of a group involved in struggles over political power relationship and/or social transformation; and (b) ideas and practices appropriated from other groups as tactical manoeuvres in that group's struggles' (1998, 189). However, despite the cobbling together of some ideas and practices with a particular outcome in mind, the ambiguous and at times contradictory character of these disparate strategies often leads to alternatives in which theory may diverge from practice and where different participants may disagree with one another on the finer points of what they are trying to accomplish. What remains important is not so much whether a consensus can be reached, but rather, as mentioned earlier, to gain a better understanding of how, as Dilip Gaonkar would suggest, these negotiations are an attempt by Afroperuvian musicians and dancers to '"make" themselves modern, as opposed to being "made" modern by alien and impersonal forces' (2001, 18).

Urban Musicians and the Professional Music Circuit

Despite the prominent role that intellectuals like the Santa Cruzes had in the early years of the Afroperuvian revival movement, the eventual success and acceptance of Afroperuvian music by Peruvian society was largely the result of a second generation of performers who, making the most out of changing attitudes towards Afroperuvian music, managed to legitimize Afroperuvian music and dance as a form of regional folklore that needed to be preserved and deserved institutional subsidization. The trailblazer in this arena was Perú Negro, a troupe of young dancers, some defectors from Victoria Santa Cruz's Teatro de Danzas Negras del Perú, that were looking for an environment where they could have more creative control. Perú Negro quickly rose to national and international notoriety a mere eight months after its inception when it won the Hispano-American Festival of Song and Dance in Buenos Aires, Argentina, in 1969, and was named Cultural Ambassador of Peru by the military government of Juan Velasco Alvarado (1968–76). The appointment came with a generous subsidy from the National Institute of Culture (INC), and in Lima the group became a symbol of the type of regional vernacular music and dance traditions that the government was seeking to support as part of its populist agenda (Feldman 2001, ch. 3). The group's popularity as well as increased performing opportunities led to the emergence of a number of other dance troupes, many of whom came to emulate the style of Perú Negro.

In the years that followed, members of Perú Negro as well as members of some of these other groups consolidated their relations with the INC and subsidiary offices like the National School of Folklore. Dancers, percussionists and guitarists began to teach at the National School of Folklore, with university groups and for private dance academies. The arrangement was beneficial for both parties: the musicians bolstered their cultural capital by being able to say that they were good enough to be hired by the INC or similar institution charged with the preservation of folklore, while the institutions could improve their own reputation by pointing towards the number of faculty members that were former or current member of well-known professional groups. This institutional environment, which placed emphasis on the strict reproduction of stylized versions of regional music and dance, also helped to consecrate the musical style and repertoire which was being taught by this second generation of performers as the 'authentic' standard by which all other performances should be judged. For example, for more than 30 years, Perú Negro's choreography of the *festejo*, which differs from earlier stage renditions by Durand and Santa Cruz, and from the early 20th-century freestyle dance by the same name found in some rural communities on the southern coast (Tompkins 1981, 241–53), continues to be taught as the one and only 'traditional' way of performing the dance.

At the same time, these performers also helped create a new space for the mass consumption and dissemination of their music among non-Afroperuvian audiences outside the institutional setting. During the 1970s, the efforts to promote the Afroperuvian repertoire benefited greatly from increased mass media exposure, recording contracts, performance opportunities in live venues and governmental and institutional support thanks to a musician-friendly cultural policy sponsored by the regime of the time. Thanks to quotas enforced by the government's cultural policies, local recording prospered, with Afroperuvian music being the most popular type of music among Limeño audiences. Musicians and record industry executives began to look for formulas that could prove successful in this new market, which eventually led to the development of what many musicians today refer to as the 'classic' Afroperuvian sound, a sound whose blueprint was largely provided by groups like Perú Negro. Consequently, this style of performance and its accompanying repertoire gained a naturalized legitimacy not only because of its ties to public and private institutions devoted to the teaching and promotion of 'authentic' Afroperuvian music and dance practices, but also because of the ubiquitous presence of the same music in the airwaves and various *peñas*,[4] theatres and nightclubs in Lima.

Ironically, the remarkable success experienced by these groups also posed a number of challenges for subsequent generations of performers. Throughout the 1980s and 1990s, many of these performing opportunities began to wane as the above cultural policies were relaxed and audiences began to turn their attention to rock, salsa and Latin American pop.[5] The increased violence and the political and economic instability that characterized the late 1980s and early 1990s were also fairly detrimental to the performance of live music in Lima. At the same time, decades of migration from the Andean region to Lima had changed the city's ethnic and cultural make-up, and *criollos* started to become an economic and demographic minority. Lacking subsidies from cultural organizations and with a shrinking demand for their type of music, teaching at dance academies and performing in the relatively small nightclub circuit became one of the few arenas in which professional musicians could make a living for themselves. The environment was fairly competitive and the more established performers of the 1970s in many cases fared a bit better thanks to the cultural capital that they had managed to accrue with audiences, arts and culture organizations and various folklore schools and dance academies in years past. At the same time, much of the economic viability and success of these artists in the nightclub circuit began to depend in their ability to satisfy the expectations of nightclub owners and audiences made up mainly of tourists and upper-middle class *criollos* nostalgic for the 'classic' sound of the 1970s. In the 1990s younger generations of musicians began to enter the professional arena, many of them advocating the need to update the Afroperuvian in order to make it more appealing to younger audiences and to explore its potential for cross-over as part of the world music market. There were a number of attempts at this, but most of them did not outlive their novelty status. Nevertheless, this renewed interest on Afroperuvian music produced a traditionalist backlash on the part of older generations of musicians who were concerned not only with the possibility that these cross-over attempts (for example, fusing Afroperuvian genres with rock, salsa or dancehall reggae) would lead to the dilution of the Afroperuvian repertoire, but also with the prospect that, if successful, this would undermine the older generation's ability to remain competitive in the professional music circuit.

In their capacity as senior members of the musical community, many of these elders became gatekeepers who publicly criticized and summarily dismissed attempts at innovation by declaring that younger musicians' lack of an intimate familiarity with Afroperuvian musical traditions led to their distortion. In some cases the criticism was valid; some of these young musicians had not grown within professional families of musicians and were not always clear on the formal musical features associated with particular Afroperuvian genres. At the same time however, these gatekeepers did not make it easy for these younger musicians to acquire access to that knowledge. Since the time of the revival, most professional groups specializing in Afroperuvian music and dance have been able to enforce a continued adherence to a particular style of performance by enlisting new members from within their own families and closely overseeing their instruction from a very young age (Chinchilla interview 2000; Villanueva interview 2000). The practice of keeping membership recruitment 'in the family' also helped regulate the induction of other performers who were not a part of these lineages. Musicians lacking the appropriate family credentials could, from time to time, gain entry into one of these groups, but this usually involved a rigorous process of apprenticeship that generally discouraged individuality and that was mainly designed for these 'outsiders' to prove themselves in the eyes of the leadership. The situation was similar at folklore academies where most of the faculty members belonged to these professional groups and enforced similar standards.

Today, these continue to be the main avenues through which younger Afroperuvian musicians can gain entry into the professional music environment. Understandably some of them have found both of these avenues alienating. In the mid-1990s, it became common for these musicians to argue that traditionalist stances left little room for individual creativity, new compositions and stylistic innovation (Baca and Pereira interview 1995; González interview 1995; R. Santa Cruz interview 1995). Furthermore, the policing of the professional environment by these gatekeepers came to be perceived as a strategy by those individuals to corner the Afroperuvian music-making market and thus protect their waning cultural capital. Despite the strong feelings that these performers may have with the traditionalist camp, most of them still find the musical legacy of the Afroperuvian revival an important aspect of their identity. Consequently, alternatives proposed by younger generations of musicians do not seek to dismiss the repertoire and musical practices associated with the revival so much as to recontextualize its significance in such a way as to move away from static conceptualizations of notions such as authenticity or tradition. Over the years, there have been a number of alternatives proposed, but relatively few have made a lasting impact in a professional musical environment where traditionalist views continue to be the norm. One such exception is the *Grupo Teatro del Milenio* whose members advocate a return to the type of experimentation with modern dance and theatrical expression that they feel was first pioneered by Victoria Santa Cruz but that was largely obscured by the more traditionalist aspects of the movement.

Grupo Teatro del Milenio

Grupo Teatro del Milenio, or *Milenio* for short, came into existence in 1996 when three Afroperuvian performers with quite different backgrounds, actor and dancer Luis Sandoval, guitarist Roberto Arguedas and choreographer Oscar Villanueva, decided to join forces and begin to explore the possibility of combining Afroperuvian music and dance with theatrical techniques in order to create pieces that would constitute a form of social commentary about the present-day condition of descendants of Africans in Peru. The membership of the group, which has a core of six to eight members (some of them go on leave from time to time due to other professional obligations, such as going on tour outside Lima, or to pursue other projects) and approximately three to six individuals who act as support personnel for larger projects, is an eclectic mix of actors, dancers and musicians. Some of the members have risen through the ranks of professional dance troupes, some got their start at dance academies and neighbourhood theatre groups, and others have a great deal of professional experience performing in the nightclub circuit but not with groups that specialized exclusively in Afroperuvian music and/or the revival repertoire. In many ways, the diversity of the group was part of the attraction since it offered participants the opportunity to work and learn from performers with a variety of backgrounds both within and outside the realm of Afroperuvian music-making. At the same time, this is should not imply that all members of the group were of one mind, hoped to reap the same benefits if the group became successful or shared consistent views regarding the present state of Afroperuvian musical production. However, they all found enough in common with each other to choose to join the project proposed by Sandoval, Arguedas, and Villanueva.

The basis for *Milenio*'s theatrical philosophy comes from Luis Sandoval, the group's artistic director. Sandoval grew up in the district of Comas, one of the first squatter settlements that began to form in Lima's northern cone in the early 1960s. He was raised in a working-class family and, unlike his co-founders who grew up surrounded by professional musicians, his parents and relatives, although great lovers of and listeners of all types of music, had little familiarity with the music associated with the Afroperuvian revival movement. His first contact with this music was in the 1970s when, as a young teenager, he saw and heard performances by Perú Negro and Nicomedes Santa Cruz in the radio and on television (Sandoval interview 2000). Not having a musical outlet, he turned to acting with local community theatre. In 1982 he co-founded Raíces, a theatre group whose membership was intended to reflect the ethnic, cultural and social diversity of Peru. Like many other community theatre groups in Peru at that time, Raíces had a socialist philosophy and felt that theatre should be brought to the masses in a manner that was accessible and that it could spark a dialogue regarding the community's social needs and its identity. The group specialized in open space performances and organized presentations in schools, empty lots and street corners in underprivileged communities in Lima, other parts of Peru and in some neighbouring countries (Villegas 1991). Rather than extensive dialogue, the performers emphasized the use of the body and music to relate to their audience and for Sandoval this led to a renewed interest on his Afroperuvian heritage and the music and dance that was associated with it. Lacking the necessary kinship connections, he had difficulties finding a professional group willing to take him as an apprentice and eventually learned by attending folklore workshops and seeking private instruction with retired prominent musicians (Sandoval interview 2000).

Despite these obstacles, Sandoval became skilled enough to earn a position as a theatre and dance instructor at the Pontificia Universidad Católica del Perú where he met Roberto Arguedas, who would become *Milenio*'s music director. Like Sandoval, Arguedas had a background that began outside the professional Afroperuvian music-making arena. As a young man in the 1960s, Arguedas grew up listening and playing a variety of local music (*valses, polkas, marineras*) as well as Mexican boleros, Cuban son, jazz, blues and rock. One of his first groups was called El Sexto Poder (The Fifth Power), a Cuban son band whose name was inspired by the Black Power movement and the fact that all six members were of African descent, and which included childhood friend and future guitarist and composer Félix Casaverde. Despite his broad musical interests, Arguedas began his professional career in the 1970s and early 1980s as a studio musician and accompanist for a number of *criollo* and Afroperuvian artists who appeared on live radio singing all the hits of the 1950s, 1960s and 1970s. Although reluctant at first, Arguedas eventually left this job and accepted an invitation to join forces with a promising but not very well-known singer: Susana Baca. During his eight-year tenure as her music director Arguedas was introduced to an artistic environment. Under Baca's artistic direction, Arguedas helped develop musical settings of contemporary poems by Peruvian and Latin American writers that were inspired by, but not strictly bound to, stylistic conventions and rhythmic accompaniments associated with Peruvian coastal genres. He also had the opportunity to tour through Latin America, Western Europe and the former Soviet Union and met a wide variety of musicians.[6] Eventually, due to artistic and personal differences, Arguedas left Baca's group in order to pursue a career as a composer and performer in his own right. Unfortunately, in the increasingly traditionalist musical environment of the late 1980s and early 1990s, Arguedas did not find a suitable forum for his compositions until Luis Sandoval approached him with the idea of forming *Milenio* and showcasing Arguedas' music as part of the project (Arguedas interview 2000).

Sandoval and Arguedas also enlisted the help of Oscar Villanueva, a dancer and choreographer who also taught workshops at the university. He differed from his colleagues in that he did rise through the ranks of a professional company specializing in Afroperuvian music and dance: Perú Negro. Villanueva, a nephew of two of Perú

Negro's founding members, Ronaldo Campos and Carlos 'Caitro' Soto, started dancing at the age of 10 with Perú Negrito, a children's group created in order to begin training future members of the company. He danced with the Perú Negro until early his twenties when he decided to leave the group in order to pursue his interest in modern dance. Despite the pride that he had in having grown up at the heart of the Perú Negro family and the importance that he attributed to his older relatives for reconstructing and maintaining alive an oral tradition that might have otherwise completely disappeared, his experience with modern dance left him with the desire to expand his own horizons. The opportunity to do exactly that presented itself when he was approached by Sandoval and Arguedas. He was particularly interested in Sandoval's emphasis on theatrical performance, something that he had always felt had been an important contribution by Victoria Santa Cruz back in the 1960s, but that never received the attention that he felt it deserved.

Over the years, the founders of the group have filled *Milenio*'s ranks with an equally eclectic membership. Villanueva brought in former students and dance partners, most notably among them Clara Chávez, a dance academy graduate with a master's degree in dance pedagogy (Chávez interview 2000), and Percy Chinchilla and William Nicasio, two young and current members of Perú Negro (Chinchilla interview 2000). For his part Arguedas brought in musicians with whom he had worked in the past, including Rosario 'Charo' Goyeneche, a former singer with Perú Negro (Goyeneche pers. comm. 2005), Juan Medrano Cotito, who also is one of Susan Baca's percussionists, and Juri Juárez, a guitarist and bass player with formal classical and flamenco training. From the theatre realm, Sandoval recruited actor Jaime Zevallos and mask maker Paul Colinó, both of whom were attracted to *Milenio* because it gave them the opportunity to learn about musical traditions with which they were not intimately familiar (Colinó interview 2000; Zevallos interview 2000). Most recently, the group's core percussion section has been led by sisters Petronila and Catalina Robles, who are nieces of one of Perú Negro's founding members. They learned percussion by observing relatives perform in after-hours family gatherings but, before *Milenio*, had found little opportunity to play professionally as most professional groups tend to relegate the instrumental music-making to men (Robles pers. comm. 2005). While each individual had a different reason for joining the group, in general these performers found *Milenio* attractive because of the ways in which it differed from other professional groups specializing in Afroperuvian music and dance. For those who were brought up within this professional environment, it offered the possibility of creating and performing new material that was partially based on the musical traditions with which they already were intimately familiar, rather than reproducing that which had been developed by earlier generations of performers. It also offered the possibility of a more egalitarian work environment where the group's philosophy was openly discussed and performers were encouraged to contribute their own insights into the creative process. In most professional Afroperuvian music and dance groups the norm has been a hierarchical system where the leadership expects all members to follow their directions without question and rarely shares any insights behind the choices that they make or seek to enforce. For those with music and dance backgrounds outside Afroperuvian performance, *Milenio* offered the opportunity to work side by side with specialists and to learn more about these practices but within an environment that lacked the type of dogmatic insistence on 'authenticity' that many of them found alienating. Many of the members also saw the chance to develop their acting skills. Others found the opportunity to try their hand at musical composition and, with Arguedas' help or on their own, eventually contributed to the group's growing repertoire of original songs. The group's departure from traditionally gendered roles was something that female performers also found attractive since it gave them the opportunity to hone their skills as percussionists and *zapateadoras*,[7] both activities associated with men.

Since the group's inception, *Milenio*'s approach has been characterized by a shift away from a modernist project of cultural reclamation where historical and ethnographic accuracy are favoured and towards another cosmopolitan alternative that privileges artistic interpretation and individual subjectivity as an alternative means of understanding the Afroperuvian experience. As suggested earlier, for *Milenio*, like other groups proposing alternatives to this more traditionalist perspective, this critique does not involve a disavowal of the legacy of the revival movement. In fact, the group spends a great deal of time making sure that all members of the group, regardless of background, have a thorough command of the repertoire and stylistic musical practices associated with the revival and use this knowledge as an important resource in their artistic creations. Inspired by the type of research and reconstruction work of revival figures like Nicomedes and Victoria Santa Cruz, José Durand and Porfirio Vásquez, the members of *Milenio* have also conducted their own independent research by travelling to rural areas on the coast and trying to organize exchanges with relatives and other local performers. The objection is rather to what the members of *Milenio* feel are the increasingly rigid and dogmatic attitudes that became associated with this repertoire in the years following the revival and how these have been used mainly to protect the economic cultural capital of a privileged few. For Sandoval and Arguedas in particular, this dynamic, and the parallel commodification and institutionalization of the revival repertoire, has led to what they term '*firuletería*'—what they see as the predilection by some professional performers to pander to the expectations of what audiences, institutions and an older generation of performers consider 'authentic' in order to attain celebrity status and remain commercially viable (Arguedas interview 2000; Sandoval interview 2000).

This ambivalence towards the performance of the revival repertoire has led *Milenio* to lead a double life. One side of that existence is devoted to performances in nightclubs, concert halls, public events, etc. *Milenio*'s nightclub and concert hall act, entitled *Noche de negros*, consists of repertoire mostly drawn from the Afroperuvian revival canon and, in some ways, fairly similar to those of other Afroperuvian groups playing the professional circuit in Lima. There are a number of reasons why *Milenio* has chosen to pursue these types of performances, despite some of the reservations that the group has about the professional music circuit. One reason is that these performers are well versed in this repertoire and it forms an important part of their identity as both professional musicians and Afroperuvians. For Sandoval and Arguedas this is crucial since they feel that they must continue to form a part of the very musical environment that they seek to critique. Another is that *Milenio* uses these performances in order to accrue enough cultural capital so that their more experimental work will not be so easily dismissed by those with more traditionalist perspectives. *Noche de negros* has been well received by audiences and critics, so *Milenio* has gained a certain amount of visibility and credibility with both audiences and other performers within the professional circuit. This legitimacy as performers who are well versed in the revival repertoire has allowed them a little leeway occasionally to add a few original compositions and dance pieces into their repertoire. Finally, these professional circuit performances, as well as the occasional dance workshops that they teach for university students, have also been an important way in which *Milenio* has been able to raise money to finance the other half of their double life: the production and performance of collectively written plays that combine Afroperuvian music and dance with various theatre techniques in order to raise some questions regarding the present-day condition of descendants of Africans in Peru.

The content of these experimental plays, the ways in which these performances deviate from the expectations of most audiences in the professional music circuit and the logistics involving their production have made it necessary for the members of *Milenio* to seek an alternative performance environment that is more suitable for these endeavours. Out of the proceeds of the *Noche de negros* performances, each individual member donates a portion of their earnings to a collective fund that is used to finance their plays. In recent years, *Milenio* has also been able to receive some artist subsidies from private investors and theatre organizations. To date, *Milenio* has created three plays which the members have continued to perform on and off for several years. Central to the realization of these experimental performances is Luis Sandoval's engagement with the ideas of Italian theatre theoretician Eugenio Barba (b. 1936) and the European movement known as Third Theatre.

Third Theatre and Afroperuvian Musical Performance

Luis Sandoval, and by extension the other members of *Milenio*, trace their Third Theatre influences through Barba to his mentor, the Polish director Jerzy Grotowski (1933–99), who, along with German playwright Bertolt Brecht (1898–1956), has been influential in the development of popular theatre in many parts of Latin America. As a theoretician, Barba is best known for his comparative study of various primarily Asian theatrical traditions (*kabuki*, *noh*, *kathakali*, *odissi*, Peking opera, Thai and Balinese dances) in order to identify techniques and principles that skilled performers from different cultures and traditions have in common, but have discovered independently from each other, a way of accessing a type of performative intensity that gives an actor his or her commanding stage presence. Barba also finds some of these techniques and principles in certain forms of Western performance (for example, mime, clown theatre, ancient Greek drama, folk storytelling and street performance), but he generally feels that their use is inconsistent or associated with particular individuals because such techniques have generally not been codified as part of the pedagogy associated with that particular tradition. The process by which these techniques and movements are identified is termed 'theatre anthropology', although the term has little to do with the academic discipline with which it shares its name.[8] An underlying assumption of Barba's methodology is that, while the expressive content of each of these performances is rooted in particular cultural beliefs, there are also pre-expressive physiological principles (ways of distributing body weight, projecting the voice, for example) that provide a foundation for the successful performance of that more culturally specific context (Barba and Savarese 1991, 186–204; Watson 1993, 32–40; Watson et al. 2002, 6–12). Through the use of workshops and 'barters', events where Third Theatre practitioners exchange performances with members of the communities they visit, participants learn how to identify and understand these pre-expressive principles and therefore gain access to this intensity, which Barba identifies as an 'extra-daily' use of the body. This type of intercultural collaboration,[9] as Barba and his followers have come to call it, is deemed to be beneficial to everyone because it encourages participants to develop personalized techniques that will supplement those learned within their own traditions. Those belonging to traditions in which movement and expression have not been strictly codified as part of their training can learn how to tap more consistently and effectively into this extra-daily presence. Conversely, those who are brought up in traditions that are highly regimented can learn about the alternative ways in which the principles underlying that regimentation are used, thus keeping their performing traditions from becoming sterile and isolated.

While much of Barba's initial conceptualization of Third Theatre was focused on formal technique and the cultivation of a particular style of theatre that defined itself in marginal opposition to mainstream theatre (i.e. First Theatre) and the avant-garde (i.e. Second Theatre), the influence of his workshops and barters in various parts of the world have prompted the appropriation and reinterpretation of many of Barba's ideas by local performers. In Latin America, the Third Theatre movement has been largely centred in Peru thanks to the influence that the three 'Ayacucho' encounters (1978, 1988 and 1998) organized by Peruvian director Mario Delgado and his group Cuatrotablas had on reshaping the notion of Third Theatre and Barba's role in the Latin American context. In fact, as Ian Watson points out, over the last few decades the creative focus of Third Theatre has decidedly shifted towards Latin America where Third Theatre encounters are more frequent and better attended, and where collectives of performers are more numerous than in Europe, where Barba is still based. Furthermore, the Latin American groups have come to develop their own separate and individual identities so that 'these meetings have become encounters in the true sense of the word as groups demonstrate and discuss their work methods rather than "sit at the feet of the master" who will teach them how to do theatre'

(Watson et al. 2002, 214–15). This recontextualization of Barba's ideas has also led to a decidedly more political take on Third Theatre that is related to the provincialization of Barba's ideas within long-standing local theatrical traditions. As Watson explains:

> in most of Latin America, the social value of theatre far outweighs its economic or aesthetic importance . . . a concern with art for art's sake in societies with fragile democracies, human rights abuses, and precarious economies is, understandably, viewed by many as self-indulgent. For these people, theatre is to be a vehicle for social commentary and a catalyst for civil action. (Watson et al. 2002, 211)

Milenio's connection to Third Theatre falls squarely within this Latin American tradition. In spite of not having received formal academic training as an actor, Sandoval's tenure in Raíces allowed him to become acquainted with a number of theories regarding the use of music and dance in theatrical performance. His first experience with Barba and his theories took place when he, as a member of Raíces, participated in some of the preliminary performances that Barba and his Danish theatre lab, the Odin Teatret, organized in the vicinity of Lima as part of the 1988 Ayacucho encounter. Ten years later, after a recently formed *Milenio* had received good critiques for their first play, *Karibu*, the group was invited to be an integral participant in the 1998 Ayacucho event (Sandoval pers. comm. 2005a). During the intervening decade, Sandoval had begun to ponder the possibility of integrating Third Theatre principles as part of Afroperuvian musical performance. Much as Barba looked at Asian performing traditions for what he perceived as their pre-expressive potential, Sandoval and the other members of *Milenio* have come to regard Afroperuvian music and dance in a similar light. In their case, however, the negotiation of what exactly constitutes the pre-expressive and how it is related to technique can be delicate. After all, one of *Milenio*'s concerns is the lack of reflexivity that they feel has come to characterize most professional performances as a result of the over-codification and commodification of professional Afroperuvian musical practice. In keeping with the spirit of the Latin American reinterpretation of Third Theatre concepts, Sandoval has come to theorize that, while becoming an accomplished practitioner of the Afroperuvian revival repertoire may provide a performer with some of the techniques that are associated with the pre-expressive, such techniques cannot be effectively deployed to gain an extra-daily command of the body unless the performer develops an intimate, personal and reflexive relationship with those movements. It is this last aspect that he and the other members of *Milenio* find lacking in most contemporary Afroperuvian performance and which, in Clara Chávez's opinion, lead to performance 'becoming mechanized, and what is mechanized becomes cold, becomes fake' (Chávez interview 2000).

For the members of *Milenio*, the process of developing personalized methodologies that improve on contemporary Afroperuvian performance practice is closely tied to what they call ancestral memory, a term that they have borrowed from Victoria Santa Cruz and reinterpreted to fit their needs.[10] Generally speaking, using one's ancestral memory refers to how the performers use improvisational exercises as the foundation for the writing of their plays as well as a means to tap into that extra-daily use of the body. When developing a scene for a play, the performers get together in a modest rehearsal space and, after agreeing on a brief outline of the action that is to take place, begin to improvise movements, lines of dialogue and music. At times, Sandoval will step out of the action and ask questions regarding the motivations of the characters that each performer is trying to depict. As the exercise continues, different performers express their satisfaction or dissatisfaction with a particular aspect of the performance and, through a persistent process of negotiation and compromise, a particular moment in the play begins to take shape. Clearly, as artistic director and the individual best versed in theatrical theory, Sandoval exerts a certain amount of influence on what eventually gets presented on stage. However, he and other members of the group are all careful to point out that this is a collective endeavour where the negotiation of different and, at times, contradicting points of view contributes to fostering the type of reflexive environment that they see as lacking in most professional Afroperuvian musical practice.

Because this process places an emphasis on what the individual subjectivity of each performer can bring to the creative process, different members of *Milenio* have different ideas of the role that ancestral memory has in that process. For some, the concept appears to defy explanation. Jaime Zevallos, for example, simply defines ancestral memory as 'an inexplicable thing that simply happens and blossoms' (Zevallos interview 2000). This is a view shared by some of the other members, including Roberto Arguedas for whom the term appears to be synonymous with those aspects of his compositional process that he cannot verbalize (Arguedas interview 2000). As dancers, Oscar Villanueva and Clara Chávez interpret ancestral memory as that which happens in their bodies as they become more intimately acquainted with particular movements during rehearsals and performances. Chávez, positing a diasporically informed version of Barba's notion of the extra-daily presence, suggests that ancestral memory is the ritualized way of using certain movements, something that has always been a part of Afroperuvian, and by extension, African experience, and which allows performers to react to each other's physicality in such a way that it captivates audience and does not let them go (Chávez interview 2000). To Villanueva, ancestral memory refers to the embodied knowledge of many generations of African musicians which he inherited through his relatives in Perú Negro and which he has come to know so intimately that, during a particularly fruitful improvisation session or performance, he can even detect an earthen scent in some of the movements and rhythms that he executes (Villanueva interview 2000). By far the most explicit sense of ancestral memory comes from Sandoval. To him, the concept stands for a creative and artistic process, a means of getting in touch with one's inner self, not through reason, logic or academic research, but through an aesthetic experience.

The '*Danza de las Cañas*'

One of the group's most provocative pieces making use of the concept of ancestral memory is informally known as the '*danza de las cañas*'[11] (Figure 1). In this piece *Milenio* sought to combine their improvisatory exercises with their own imagined memories of what the music and dance of the Africa from which their ancestors originated might have looked and sounded like when the first slaves arrived in Peru. The piece was originally developed in 1996 as part of their play *Karibu*, which aimed to critique the lack of reflexivity that some of the members of *Milenio* found in professional circuit performances. The play begins with a parody of a nightclub act in which the audience in the theatre also doubles as the audience for the staged nightclub performance. The performers not only appear on stage as musicians and dancers but also in the role of waiters and other serving staff, all of whom bear wide, plastic grins and assume the stereotype of the happy and servile Afroperuvian attendant when addressing members of the audience. To make the point that the performers in this environment are trapped and subservient to capitalist interests, the demands of the tourist market and the racialized expectations of mostly *criollo* audiences, the performers borrowed costumes, facial expressions and bodily movement reminiscent of early 20th-century United States minstrel shows. When the ridiculous character of the performance reaches its peak, the nightclub setting

Figure 1 Three members of *Grupo Teatro del Milenio* performing the '*danza de las cañas*' (*left to right*: Percy Chinchilla, Clara Chávez and Luis Sandoval). Larcomar shopping centre, Miraflores, Lima, 14 August 2000. Photograph by the author.

suddenly vanishes and the Afroperuvian musicians and serving staff are magically transported back in time to the Africa of their ancestors, where they once again get in touch with what it means to be proud of their cultural heritage. The '*danza de las cañas*' is a dance that these performers learn while in this magical realm and it serves as a symbol of those traditions that may have existed in Peru among the first African slaves. For Luis Sandoval, the dance symbolizes 'the process of finding, of reacquainting myself with my [inner] African, whose origins I do not know . . . he comes from various places and is everything' (Sandoval interview 2000). Following the success of *Karibu*, the '*danza de las cañas*' has been expanded into a 15- to 20-minute stand-alone piece that the group performs in parks, parades and other public gathering places. Because of what it symbolizes, the piece remains near and dear to the members of *Milenio*, and it is not uncommon for the performers to bring their children, nieces and nephews to these performances and to have follow-up discussions regarding their African ancestry and the need to be proud of that heritage.

Nevertheless, this piece does not constitute an attempt to reclaim a place in what Gilroy would call 'the grand narrative of African advancement' (1993, 190). In fact, at first glance, it is difficult to ignore how seemingly divorced this piece is from African, Afroperuvian or for that matter Peruvian reality. First there is the dancers' appearance: bare feet, brightly coloured single pieces of cloth wrapped about their otherwise naked bodies and Nivea cream doubling as face paint are all used as fairly generic markers of something exotic and tribal. Their bodies continually move in a series of energetic vertical movements like hops, leaps and foot stomping, often accompanied by distorted facial gestures and unintelligible shouts and grunts. The choice of musical instruments, all of them percussion and none of them found in contemporary Peru, suggests something similar. The *djembe* and *balafon*, which the group found during a trip to France, are used as lead instruments during different portions of the piece because of their iconic connection with Africa, but the manner in which they are used is not meant to remain loyal to West African performance practice. The other instruments used have been invented by the performers based on their knowledge of the existence of similar instruments not only in Africa but in other parts of the world. The bamboo poles, or *cañas*, from which the piece derives its informal name bears some resemblance to the Trinidadian *tamboo bamboo*, particularly in those sections when the performers play the *cañas* by alternately stamping them against the ground and hitting them on the side with a smaller bamboo stick (see Blake 1995, 47–50).[12] At the same time they are similar, particularly in terms of length and diameter, to Amazonian stomping poles such as the *waánaba* of the Boras of tropical Peru (see Novati and Ruiz 1984, 14, 19). However, the inspiration for the use of the *cañas* was from a television documentary on the Philippines broadcast in Lima (Sandoval interview 2000). The log drum was also inspired by this documentary but, unlike its Filipino counterpart—most likely the *bantula* which hangs from the performer's neck (see Brandeis 1999 [1993]), this instrument is made out of a single piece of bamboo of wide diameter rather than carved hardwood and it lacks any slits, troughs or tongues; it is also set on top of two bamboo 'Y'-shaped brackets.

To *Milenio*, such disparate borrowings are deemed appropriate given that they are engaged in what they see as an artistic process, not an accurate representation of the Afroperuvian past, a view that is certainly informed by the philosophy of Third Theatre. This is particularly the case in terms of the type of intercultural borrowing from a number of Asian music and dance traditions which are then reinterpreted to fit the needs of the performers doing the borrowing, often placing more emphasis on types of movements than on the socio-historical contexts from which they have been derived. In the case of *Milenio* this appropriative spirit led to the reinterpretation of Filipino musical instruments and dances to create an Afroperuvian reading of an African dance that never existed. Some of the poses, movements and facial expressions used by the performers also show some influence from *kathakali*, *noh* and modern dance, particularly Laban, traditions with which Luis Sandoval is well acquainted as a result of his participation in the Ayacucho encounters and his practical experience in his prior work with Raíces (Sandoval interview 2000, pers. comm. 2005a). At the same time, the members of *Milenio* have come to recontextualize the significance of these borrowings as something that is an integral part of Afroperuvian performative tradition since the time of the revival. After all, as suggested above, the reinvention and reconstruction of the revival repertoire also involved borrowing from musical traditions in other parts of Latin America, Europe and the United States. While these borrowings seemed to have been more explicitly localized within the realm of African diasporic traditions and modern dance, Barba's notions of the intercultural existence of pre-expressive techniques has broadened the palette of choices available to these Afroperuvian performers. Third Theatre techniques, such as encouraging all performers to be able to act, dance and play musical instruments as well as the emphasis on improvisation, are also techniques that are quite compatible with Afroperuvian musical practice where most dancers are also musicians and where competitive poetry, song and dance genres such as the *décima*, *canto de jarana* and the *zapateo* are still actively practised.

At the same time, the '*danza de las cañas*' is not a mere attempt at reproducing Third Theatre techniques using Afroperuvian music and dance as source material. Despite the visual presentation, the use of musical instruments not commonly found in Afroperuvian music and the incorporation of new dance movements and performative techniques, the basic choreographic structure and musical organization of '*danza de las cañas*' is clearly informed by the way in which other Afroperuvian dances are structured. Although very effectively masked by these 'exotic' elements, the piece bears similarity to *Milenio*'s rendition of the traditional dance the *son de los diablos*. In both cases, when the pieces are performed in an outdoor setting, the performance begins some distance away from the stage or central performance space and musicians parade through the crowd as a means of attracting the attention of potential audience members. During this section, the rhythm being played by the

Figure 2 Example of the solo *djembe* and *cañas* parts in the introductory section of '*danza de las cañas*'. Note that the pattern played by the *cañas* is identical to the *cajita* pattern used in the *son de los diablos*. For more information on how the *cajita* is played, see note 13.

cañas is a transposition of the *cajita*[13] pattern in the *son de los diablos*, which in this case accompanies the improvisations of a solo *djembe* (Figure 2). Once the performers reach the stage, two performers lay two of the bamboo poles on the floor in parallel to each other and begin to bang them against the floor and each other as a third performer showcases his skills by dancing in and out of the moving poles (Figure 3). This section of the performance is a reinterpretation of the *tinikling* dance from the Philippines which served as the inspiration for the piece. This is followed by a short series of pre-choreographed sequences that are designed to showcase the versatility and variety of ways in which the instruments can be used. The sequence starts by featuring the log drum, then adding the *cañas* which form a series of different patterns as the dancers who play them move in circle on stage.[14] The last of these sequences immediately segues back to the *son de los diablos* pattern, this time supplemented by melodic ostinatos played by the *balafon*[15] (Figure 4). During this last portion of the dance the performers stand in a circle playing the *cañas* and take turns entering the circle to display their improvisatory dance skills. This section follows closely in format the *festejo* with which the performers usually

Figure 3 Percy Chinchilla (centre) gets ready to dance in between the horizontal bamboo poles that Luis Sandoval (left) and Jaime Zevallos (right) will strike against each other and the floor of the stage. Behind them (from left to right), Roberto Arguedas, Clara Chávez and Charo Goyeneche play the musical and rhythmic accompaniment. Larcomar shopping centre, Miraflores, Lima, 14 August 2000. Photograph by the author.

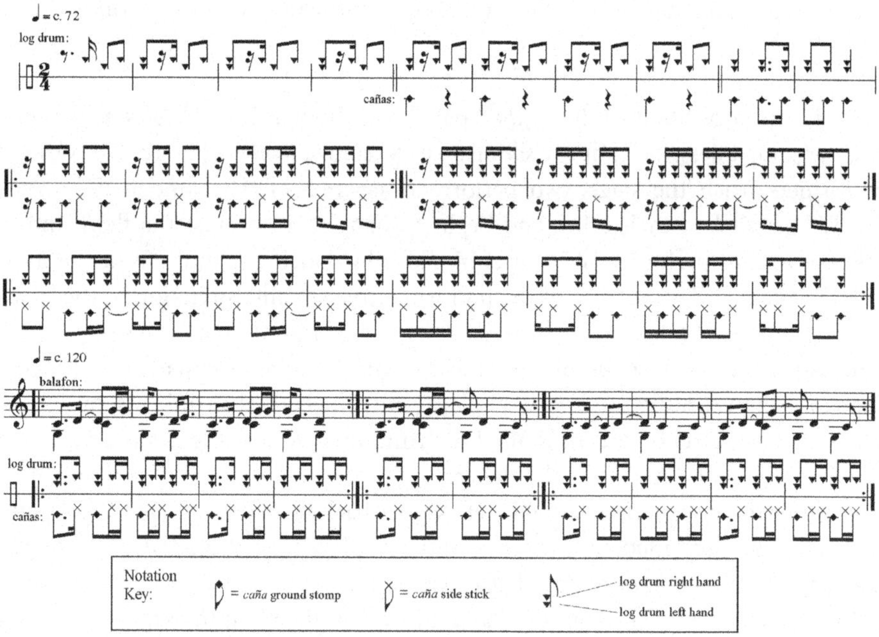

Figure 4 Example of the log drum, *cañas* and *balafon* solo and accompaniment parts used during '*danza de las cañas*'.

close their *Noche de negros* performances and in which the dancers also take turns at the centre of the circle before leaving the stage one by one.

Conclusions

As a piece representative of *Milenio*'s work, '*danza de las cañas*' is unique. However, while it may not be an explicit form of social commentary, as are the group's plays, and the music and choreography strays from the Afroperuvian canon, '*danza de las cañas*' remains an important part of the group's identity and emblematic of what differentiates *Milenio* from other contemporary performing groups. Over the last decade, these differences have become important to some members of the Afroperuvian community, particularly among younger generations, who see in *Milenio* the possibility of doing more than merely reproducing a set of musical practices that was handed down to members of an earlier generation. This is not to say that members of the older generation have not taken notice. Since the group's inception, *Milenio* has made a point of reserving the opening night of one of their performances for family, friends and prominent members of the Afroperuvian community. The by-invitation-only event is free of charge and guests are encouraged to share their opinions on the issues brought up during the performances in a post-presentation discussion forum. Despite the nature of *Milenio*'s criticism, most attendees have been open to discussion and every member of the group has at least one story of a prominent professional musician who, after one of these events, has thanked them for opening up such a discussion. *Milenio* also continues to be one of the few professional groups featuring women performers in principal instrumental roles and dancing genres that are more generally associated with men.[16]

At the same time, *Milenio*'s impact also has to do with changing times. As the years pass, many of the professional dance troupes specializing in Afroperuvian music and dance are beginning to be managed by a second generation that is more open to change. Ironically, this relaxing of traditionalist attitudes to which *Milenio*'s work has contributed has integrated *Milenio* a bit more into professional music establishment, and the group is increasingly being recognized not only for their experimental work but also for some of their contributions to the further reinterpretation and further understanding of the Afroperuvian canon. Perhaps the best example in this area is *Milenio*'s reconstruction of the *son de los diablos* which sought to provide an alternative to the version taught at the National School of Folklore and performed by most professional dance troupes. After extensive archival research, the group recreated the masks depicted on the paintings of the *son de los diablos* by 19th-century artist Pancho Fierro and made changes to the choreography based on their interviews with the last performers to have participated in the dance when it was still practised as part of the carnival celebrations in Lima (Arguedas interview 2000; Colinó interview 2000). In recent years, *Milenio*'s version of the *son de los diablos* has been well received by tough and influential critics from the revival, like Victoria Santa Cruz, and has contributed to set a standard that other groups have come to emulate.

Most recently the noted folkloric dance troupe Perú Negro, one of the groups responsible for popularizing the *son de los diablos* on the professional stage during the 1970s, commissioned *Milenio*'s mask maker, Paul Colinó, to make new masks that were premiered during Perú Negro's 2005 US tour (Goyeneche pers. comm. 2005). Meanwhile, in what can only be characterized as irony upon irony, some teachers at the National School of Folklore have come to recognize the need for their students to have some sort of creative or improvisatory outlet as part of their training so the '*danza de las cañas*' has been adopted as a creative exercise that supplements their folkloric dance training (Sandoval pers. comm. 2005c).

Nevertheless, *Milenio*'s methods, theories and techniques have had their limitations. Despite the importance that many see in the group's commitment to theatrical expression, there are concerns over its outreach potential and the ability that it has to impact on the Afroperuvian community at large, i.e. not just professional musicians. This is because the type of theatrical expression emphasized by *Milenio*, as well as by the architects of the revival movement in the 1950s and 1960s, is one that remains connected to particular cosmopolitan urban contexts in Lima. The members of *Milenio* are aware of this and, in their own way, have tried to rectify this by organizing performance workshops in marginal areas and the aforementioned free premieres for friends and relatives. But, as the members of the group also point out, this is not enough. In the case of the free performances, some people decline the invitations either because they cannot afford to travel into Lima to see a performance, or because they are concerned that they will be looked down upon by *criollo* audiences for not being dressed properly, for not being 'the right class of people'. In the case of the workshops, the target communities often do not have the resources or the time to commit to playing music, organizing parades or doing theatre after the group leaves. Unfortunately, this situation is unlikely to change in the near future since, *Milenio*, like all other professional groups in Lima, has to rely on the demands of the capitalist market that they critique in order to make a living and thus finance their own projects. Consequently, they also lack the time and resources necessary to continue to bring their performances to these more marginal Afroperuvian communities.

This difficulty in having an impact outside a professional urban environment is one of the challenges that professional musicians since the time of the revival have had to face in regard to the role that music and dance have in the making of a distinct Afroperuvian modernity: not only do these performers have to transform traditional practices of other localities and of generations past in order to have them better fit the needs of a modern and cosmopolitan identity project, but, in the process, they end up having a difficult time making those needs relevant to those outside that cosmopolitan environment. Sandoval is keenly aware of this, and is the first to recognize that he does not subscribe to the type of cosmopolitan romanticism that claims that art transcends everything or that artists occupy privileged positions in society that allow them the ability to move in and out of modernity at will. As he is fond of saying, 'music and theatre are not the Revolution, but they can help you think critically about yourself' (Sandoval pers. comm. 2005d). In this spirit, the group continues to be committed to its methods and ideals. Most recently, the group has developed a new music and dance review entitled *Kimba Fa*. Using techniques similar to those used to develop '*danza de las cañas*', the group is interested in exploring the use of bodily movement and rhythm as an alternative form of communication and of exploring the musical potential of everyday objects. The setting is urban contemporary Lima and the instruments are fashioned out of items used by Afroperuvian street vendors, such as *anticucho*[17] grilling racks transformed into thumb pianos, *emoliente*[18] bottles turned into xylophones and bread carts used for percussion (Sandoval pers. comm. 2005b). Perhaps more than their earlier work, even '*danza de las cañas*', *Kimba Fa* lacks an explicit social commentary regarding issues of ethnic identity and a critique of the Afroperuvian musical environment. However, it continues to feature what is perhaps *Milenio*'s most important contribution to the ongoing debate regarding the contemporary role of music in the Afroperuvian community: the notion that performance should be seen as an interpretative form of expression that repositions the notion of that which is deemed authentic as residing in the performer as much as in the songs, choreographies and genres that have become codified as part of 'the tradition'.

Notes

[1] There are a number of reasons for this disappearance, the most salient one being a process of cultural assimilation and miscegenation that greatly reduced the Afroperuvian population during the late colonial period and into the 19th century (Tompkins 1981). In Lima this meant that different cultural musical influences quickly blended into a variety of styles associated with Lima's working classes rather than with any one cultural or ethnic group (León 1997; Lloréns 1983). This *criollo* music, as it became known, appears to have displaced the performance of many genres predominantly associated with Afroperuvians in Lima. While these ceased to be performed in a daily-life context, they continued to be taught and performed within families of musicians (Feldman 2001; Romero 1994; Tompkins 1981). Tompkins' (1981) and Vásquez's (1982) work also suggests that the relative isolation of some rural Afroperuvian communities in the early decades of the 20th century also allowed for the maintenance of local musical traditions into the second part of the same century. These surviving contexts of Afroperuvian musical expression provide an important foundation for the revival movement that followed.

[2] Santa Cruz's theories have been both well disseminated and controversial. For a more detailed discussion regarding the merits of and problems with his theories as well as how they relate to those proposed by *criollo* intellectuals like José Durand and Fernando Romero, see Tompkins (1981, 224–9, 288–98; Romero 1994, 316–18; Feldman 2001, ch. 3, 2005).

[3] Both Santa Cruz and Perú Negro greatly benefited from the input and experience of Afro-Cuban percussionist Gillermo Nicasio Regeira who permanently relocated to live in Lima in the 1950s. A detailed discussion of Regeira's contributions during his collaboration with Perú Negro can be found in Feldman (2001, 281, 307–8, 312–18).

[4] Generally speaking, *peñas* are gatherings of various artists, poets and musicians, often in informal settings, where all participants are expected to perform for everyone else. In Lima, the term came to be associated with the *criollo* music circuit, where the *peña* came to replace the type of neighbourhood gatherings or *jaranas* that were common during the early part of the 20th century. In the 1970s, many *peñas* also became more formal affairs – some

catering to a paying public and others organizing themselves as a social clubs requiring membership of the participants. During the second part of the 20th century, the increase in migrants from the Andean region also led to the emergence of *peñas* featuring music from this region.

[5] This time period also marks the emergence of *chicha*, a popular music genre associated with the children of Andean migrants to the city of Lima. However, despite *chicha*'s incredible popularity among youth of Andean descent, the historical rivalry between highland and coastal populations as well as marked cultural and social differences between these two groups led to the relegation of *chicha* to an informal economic market that was largely ignored by *criollo* and Afroperuvian audiences. Something similar can be said of most forms of Andean popular music in Lima which, up to the turn of the 21st century, have received relatively little exposure in the *criollo*-dominated mainstream mass media.

[6] At the time, most audiences did not consider Baca to be a particularly 'mainstream' Afroperuvian performer and she spent most of her time cultivating her reputation overseas by appearing at a variety of international music festivals. While today Baca has become synonymous with Afroperuvian music, this association took root in Peru only in the wake of her 'discovery' by David Byrne and success in the United States and Europe in the late 1990s. Part of this has to do with Baca's predilection for setting poetry to music and performing songs that are not part of the Afroperuvian or *criollo* repertoires, both practices that were not commercially viable and considered 'too experimental' at a time when most Peruvian listeners are interested mainly in the repertoire of decades past.

[7] The *zapateo* is a form of competitive tap dance that is a favourite of most professional Afroperuvian dance groups.

[8] As Barba explains it, 'Theatre Anthropology is not concerned with those levels of organization which make possible the application of the paradigms of cultural anthropology to theatre and dance. It is not the study of performative phenomena in those cultures which are traditionally studied by anthropologists. Nor should Theatre Anthropology be confused with the anthropology of performance. Again: Theatre Anthropology is the study of the behaviour of the human being when it uses its physical and mental presence in an organized performance situation and according to principles which are different from those used in daily life' (Barba and Savarese 1991, 5).

[9] Barba uses the term intercultural as a means of noting that theatre anthropology should not be taken to be an assertion of the aesthetic universality of art. As he explains, 'The first task of theatre anthropology is to trace these recurring principles. They are not proof of the existence of a "science of the theatre" nor of a few universal laws. They are nothing more than particularly good "bits of advice": information useful for scenic practice' (Barba and Savarese 1991, 8).

[10] To Santa Cruz, the concept is a complex, poetic and highly individualized meta-theory that draws liberally from Eastern concepts of duality, transcendentalism, French existentialist philosophy, dialectical analysis, performance and embodiment theory and Kantian criticism in order to propose potential paths towards the betterment of all human beings through the cultivation of what she calls inner rhythm (V. Santa Cruz 2000). According to Santa Cruz, ancestral memory cannot be formally taught or put in writing; it can only be experienced, and only those who have experienced it, like herself, are able to understand its nature. A good discussion of the role that ancestral memory has on Santa Cruz's creative process can be found in Feldman (2001, 117–30).

[11] There is no formal name for the piece as it grew out of a portion of a scene from a play. Over time the performers have come to identify it as '*cañas*' or '*danza las cañas*' (the dance of the bamboo poles/sticks) due to the predominant use of bamboo instruments in this performance.

[12] The instruments are not exactly the same, however. Based on Blake's descriptions and photographs, the *tamboo* bamboo is shorter in length (even for the longest instruments) and wider in diameter. Also, the sick used to strike the instruments is made from hardwood rather than bamboo.

[13] A *cajita* is an idiophone in the shape of a wooden box with a lid that hangs from the neck. The performer plays the instrument by alternately slamming the lid of the box with one hand (the equivalent of stomping the bamboo pole against the ground in '*cañas*') and hitting the side of the box with a wooden stick or clapper (the equivalent of hitting the side of the '*caña*' with a stick).

[14] In *Milenio*'s rendition of the *son de los diablos*, there is a similar set of sequences in which the performers showcase different patterns that can be played by the *cajitas* and *quijadas de burro* (donkey's jawbones).

[15] The *balafon* used by *Milenio*, which one of the members obtained during a trip to France (Arguedas pers. comm. 2005), is tuned approximately to an A pentatonic scale (A, C, D, E, G). The music played by the *balafon* was invented by Roberto Arguedas and, because it tries to retain the major mode character associated with the *son de los diablos* and the *festejo*, he uses the C as the tonic of the scale.

[16] There are a few exceptions, most notably among them *criollo cajonera* María del Carmen Dongo who is not only a noted percussionist but also a solo recording artist, promoter and producer. Over the last ten years she has done a great deal to attract other young women to the instrument. However, there remain few within the professional Afroperuvian music circuit.

[17] A traditional dish made of marinated beef heart served on wooden or metal skewers.

[18] A hot brew made out different blends of barley, cornhusks, herbs, spices and fruit.

References

Barba, Eugenio and Nicola Savarese. 1991. *A dictionary of theatre anthropology: The secret art of the performer*, translated by Richard Fowler. London: Routledge.

Blake, Felix I. R. 1995. *The Trinidad and Tobago steel pan: History and evolution.* Spain: Grafiques, p. 85.

Bowser, Frederick P. 1974. *The African slave in colonial Peru, 1524–1650.* Stanford, CA: Stanford University Press.

Brandeis, Hans. 1999 [1993]. Music and dance of the Bukidnons of Mindanao: A short introduction. Available from: <aedv.cs.tu-berlin.de/ ~brandeis/bukid_music.html; INTER NET> (accessed 15 July 2005).

Estenssoro, Juan Carlos. 1989. *Música y sociedad coloniales, Lima 1680–1830.* Lima: Colmillo Blanco.

Feldman, Heidi. 2001. Black rhythms of Peru: Staging cultural memory through music and dance, 1956–2000. PhD dissertation, University of California, Los Angeles.

———. 2005. The black Pacific: Cuban and Brazilian echoes in the Afro-Peruvian revival. *Ethnomusicology* 49 (2): 206–31.

———. 2006. *Black rhythms of Peru: Reviving African musical heritage in the Black Pacific.* Middletown, CT: Wesleyan University Press.

Flores Galindo, Alberto. 1991. *La ciudad sumergida: Aristocracia y plebe en Lima, 1760–1830.* Lima: Editorial Horizonte.

Gaonkar, Dilip Parameshwar. 2001. On alternative modernities. In *Alternative modernities*, edited by Dilip Parameshwar Gaonkar. Durham, NC: Duke University Press.

Gilroy, Paul. 1993. *The black Atlantic: Modernity and double consciousness.* Cambridge, MA: Harvard University Press.

Gordon, Edmund T. 1998. *Disparate diasporas: Identity and politics in an African-Nicaraguan community.* Austin, TX: University of Texas Press.

Hanchard, Michael. 2001. Afro-modernity: Temporality, politics, and the African diaspora. In *Alternative modernities*, edited by Dilip Parameshwar Gaonkar. Durham, NC: Duke University Press.

León, Javier F. 1997. El que no tiene de inga, tiene de mandinga: Negotiating tradition and ethnicity in Peruvian criollo popular music. Master's report, The University of Texas at Austin.

———. 2003. The aestheticization of tradition: Professional Afroperuvian musicians, cultural reclamation, and artistic interpretation. PhD dissertation, University of Texas at Austin.

———. 2007. Mass culture, commodification, and the consolidation of the Afroperuvian festejo. *Black Music Research Journal* 27(1): 121–153.

Lloréns Amico, José Antonio. 1983. *Música popular en Lima: Criollos y andinos.* Lima: Instituto de Estudios Peruanos (IEP).

Novati, Jorge and Irma Ruiz. 1984. *Mekamunaa: Estudio etnomusicológico sobre los Bora de la amazonía peruana.* Buenos Aires: Instituto Nacional de Musicología "Carlos Vega".

Rocca Torres, Luis. 1985. *La otra historia: Memoria colectiva y canto del pueblo de Zaña.* Lima: Instituto de Apoyo Agrario.

Roel y Pineda, Josafat. 1964. *Antología de música afroperuana.* Archival audio recording. C/86/23/150. Lima: Centre for Andean Ethnomusicology.

Romero, Raúl. 1994. Black music and identity in Peru: Reconstruction and revival of Afro-Peruvian musical traditions. In *Music and Black ethnicity: The Caribbean and South America*, edited by Gerard Béhague. New Brunswick, NJ: Transaction Publishers.

Santa Cruz Gamarra, Victoria. 2000. El importante rol que cumple el obstáculo. In *El Perú en los albores del siglo XXXI–4: Ciclo de conferencias 1999–2000.* Lima: Fondo Editorial del Congreso del Perú.

Taylor, Charles. 2001. Two theories of modernity. In *Alternative modernities*, edited by Dilip Parameshwar Gaonkar. Durham, NC: Duke University Press.

Tompkins, William David. 1981. The musical traditions of the blacks of coastal Peru. PhD dissertation, University of California, Los Angeles.

Turino, Thomas. 2000. *Nationalists, cosmopolitans, and popular music in Zimbabwe.* Chicago, IL: University of Chicago Press.

———. 2003a. Are we global yet? Globalist discourse, cultural formations and the study of Zimbabwean popular music. *British Journal of Ethnomusicology* 12 (2): 51–79.

———. 2003b. Nationalism and Latin American music: Selected case studies and theoretical considerations. *Latin American Music Review* 24 (2): 169–209.

———. 2004. Introduction: Identity and the arts in diaspora communities. In *Identity and the arts in diaspora communities*, edited by Thomas Turino and James Lea. Warren, MI: Harmonie Press.

Vázquez Rodríguez, Rosa Elena. 1982. *La práctica musical de la población negra en el Perú.* La Habana: Casa de las Américas.

Villegas, Juan. 1991. Desde las poblaciones a UCI: *Raíces*, grupo de teatro popular del Perú. Gestos 6 (11): 199–204.

Watson, Ian. 1993. *Towards a third theatre: Eugenio Barba and the Odin teatret.* London: Routledge.

——— et al. 2002. *Negotiating cultures: Eugenio Barba and the intercultural debate.* New York: Palgrave.

Interviews

Arguedas, Roberto. 2000. Interview by the author. Audio cassette recording. San Isidro, Lima, 10 August.

———. 2005. Personal communication with the author. Written notes. New Orleans, 17 June.

Baca Susana and Ricardo Pereira. 1995. Interview by the author. Audio cassette recording. Miraflores, Lima. 27 March.

Chávez, Clara. 2000. Interview by the author. Audio cassette recording. San Miguel, Lima. 14 August.

Chinchilla, Percy. 2000. Interview by the author. Audio cassette recording. San Miguel, Lima. 10 August.

Colinó, Paul. 2000. Interview by the author. Audio cassette recording. San Miguel, Lima. 10 August.

González, Miguel "Miki". 1995. Interview by the author. Audio cassette recording. Miraflores, Lima. 30 March.

Goyeneche, Rosario. Personal communication with the author. Written notes. New Orleans. 17 June.

Molina, María. 2000. Interview with the author. Audio cassette recording. Surquillo, Lima. 14 August.

Robles, María Catalina. 2005. Personal communication with the author. Written notes. New Orleans. 20 June.

Sandoval, Luis. 2000. Interview with the author. Audio cassette recording. Miraflores, Lima. 15 August.

———. 2005a. Personal communication with the author. E-mail. 7 June.

———. 2005b. Personal communication with the author. Written notes. New Orleans. 15 June.

———. 2005c. Personal communication with the author. Written notes. New Orleans. 17 June.

———. 2005d. Personal communication with the author. Written notes. New Orleans. 20 June.

Santa Cruz, Rafael. 1995. Interview by the author. Audio cassette recording. Miraflores, Lima. 1 April.

Villanueva, Oscar. 2000. Interview with the author. Audio cassette recording. San Miguel, Lima. 14 August.

Zevallos, Jaime. 2000. Interview with the author. Audio cassette recording. San Miguel, Lima. August 14.

Index

Made in the USA
Las Vegas, NV
09 January 2026

39045037R00096